ACCA

Advanced Performance Management (APM)

Pocket Notes

British library cataloguing-in-publication data

A catalogue record for this book is available from the British Library.

Published by:
Kaplan Publishing UK
Unit 2 The Business Centre
Molly Millars Lane
Wokingham
Berkshire
RG41 2QZ

ISBN 978-1-83996-179-3

Printed and bound in Great Britain.

Acknowledgments:

This product contains material that is ©Financial Reporting Council Ltd (FRC). Adapted and reproduced with the kind permission of the Financial Reporting Council. For further information, please visit www.frc.org.uk or call +44 (0)20 7492 2300.

Contents

Introduction to the syllabus

The aim of this paper is to apply relevant knowledge and skills and to exercise professional judgement in selecting and applying strategic management accounting techniques in different business contexts, to contribute to the planning, control and evaluation of the performance of an organisation and its strategic and operational development.

Strong underpinning knowledge is required from Performance Measurement (PM). APM is a step up from PM and focuses on interpretation and application of the topics.

APM builds on knowledge gained in Performance Management (PM). It develops key aspects introduced at the PM level with a greater focus on linking the syllabus topics together and evaluation of the key topics and techniques.

APM also includes knowledge contained in the Strategic Business Leader (SBL) exam but it is not a problem if you are yet to study for this exam. It is important to draw a distinction between the two exams. You need to approach the common topics from an APM perspective, i.e. how do they influence performance management and measurement.

Assumed knowledge from PM	Common topics from SBL
• Risk	• Strategy
• Environmental management accounting (EMA)	• CSFs and KPIs
• Alternative budgeting methods	• Benchmarking
• Absorption costing and activity-based costing (ABC)	• SWOT analysis

• Beyond budgeting • Standard costing and variances • Forecasting • Information and data • Big data • Data analysis • Management information systems (MIS) • Hopwood's management styles • Financial performance measures • Divisional performance measures • Transfer pricing • Not-for-profit organisations • Non-financial performance indicators • Balanced scorecard • Building Block model	• BCG matrix • Porter's generic strategies • PESTEL analysis • 5 forces analysis • Risk • Stakeholders • Sustainability • Integrated reporting • Organisational structure • The value chain • Big data • Investment appraisal

Main capabilities

On successful completion of this exam, candidates should be able to:

A Use **stategic planning and control models** to plan and monitor organisational performance

B Identify and evaluate the design features of effective **performance management information** and monitoring **systems and** recognise the impact of **developments in technology** on performance measurement and management systems

C Apply appropriate **strategic performance measurement** techniques in evaluating and improving organisational performance

D Advise clients and senior management on strategic business **performance evaluation**

E Apply a range of **professional skills** in adressing requirements within the Advanced Performance Management exam, and in preparation for, or to support, current work experience

F **Employability and technology skills**

The examination

Format of the exam	Number of marks
Section A – one compulsory question	50
Section B – two compulsory questions worth 25 marks each	50
Total	100

- The exam is a 3 hour 15 minutes computer based examination (CBE).
- The pass mark is 50%.
- Technical syllabus sections A, B and C (not D) are examinable in Section A.
- In Section B, one question will include technical marks mainly from syllabus section D. The other question will include technical marks from any other technical syllabus section(s).
- There will be 10 professional marks available in Section A and 5 professional marks available in each Section B question.

Professional skills

The inclusion of this syllabus area reflects ACCA's continued focus on ensuring that the professional accountants of the future have the right blend of **technical and professional skills**, coupled with an **ethical mindset**.

The APM exam will expect candidates to demonstrate the following Professional Skills:

<table>
<tr><th>Professional Skill</th><th>Section A (10 marks)</th><th>Section B (5 marks/question)</th></tr>
<tr><td>Communication</td><td rowspan="4">All four Professional Skills will be examined.</td><td>Not examined</td></tr>
<tr><td>Analysis and Evaluation</td><td rowspan="3">Each question will contain a minimum of two professional skills from Analysis and Evaluation, Scepticism and Commercial Acumen.</td></tr>
<tr><td>Scepticism</td></tr>
<tr><td>Commercial Acumen</td></tr>
</table>

- Each of the four professional skills has a number of **leadership capabilities** associated and these will be used to **allocate marks** in each exam question as appropriate.
- **Professional skills marks are earned as you work through the technical marks** by providing a comprehensive and relevant response to the technical requirements. Therefore, **time should be allocated based on the technical marks** available.

Employability and technology skills

By studying for ACCA exams, candidates will be equipped with not only technical syllabus knowledge and professional skills, but also practical, applied software skills. The employability and technology skills syllabus area is included within the syllabus to acknowledge this acquired skillset.

The CBE software will **replicate the work that is performed by accountants in a typical workplace**. It will be used across the syllabus to support a candidate's answer by providing suitable response options for different types of answers. These response options will be most suitable in the following instances:

- For **discursive answers**: it is best to use the **word processing** option
- For **calculations**: it is best to use the **spreadsheet** option.

ACCA candidates can access the **ACCA's Exam Practice Platform** to practice attempting questions using the CBE software. It is imperative that candidates are familiar with the software before attempting the exam.

Key study tips

Ensure you review prior knowledge from PM and understand that topics common to both APM and SBL will focus on the use of models for performance management and measurement.

Revise the course as you work through it and leave sufficient time before the exam for final revision.

Cover the whole syllabus and pay attention to areas where your knowledge is weak.

Practice exam standard questions under timed conditions. Attempt all the different styles of questions you may be asked and practice answering questions using the CBE Practice Platform.

Read the APM articles on the ACCA website and read good newspapers and professional journals.

Key reasons for failure in APM

Poor exam technique	Technical weaknesses
• Repeating learned facts only. • No relation to scenario. • Not answering the question. • Not applying knowledge to the scenario. • Lack of practice.	• Inability to do fundamental calculations. • Poor use of models. • No focus on performance management and measurement. • Poor interpretation of data. • Not understanding differences between key principles.

Quality and accuracy are of the utmost importance to us so if you spot an error in any of our products, please send an email to mykaplanreporting@kaplan.com with full details, or follow the link to the feedback form in MyKaplan.

Our Quality Co-ordinator will work with our technical team to verify the error and take action to ensure it is corrected in future editions.

chapter

1

Introduction to strategic management accounting

In this chapter

- Planning and control.
- Strategic planning.
- The role of performance measures.
- Strategic objectives, critical success factors and key performance indicators.
- Benchmarking.
- Models used in the performance management process.
- Risk.

Exam focus

This chapter sets the scene to Part A of the syllabus, **'strategic planning and control'**.

It looks at the strategic role of the management accountant as a discipline for planning and controlling performance so that the strategic objectives can be set, monitored and controlled. We will consider the difference between these two roles and look at the **different levels of planning and control** within an organisation as well as the **importance of performance measures** in checking towards the achievement of the plans set. A central part of this process is to understand how the **objectives** of the organisation link to the **critical success factors** (CSFs) and **key performance indicators** (KPIs).

Next, we will move onto benchmarking. An important aspect of strategic planning is to understand how to **benchmark** performance so that areas for performance improvement can be identified.

The next part of the chapter will look at some models (**SWOT, PEST, Porter's 5 Forces, Boston Consulting Group** (BCG) and **Porter's generic strategies**) used to assist in the performance management process.

In the final part of the chapter, we discuss the **risk and uncertainty** that exists in the environment and how these risks/ uncertainties can be measured and managed, including the impact of **different risk appetites of stakeholders**.

Planning and control

Planning and control are **fundamental aspects of performance management.**

Planning	Control
The organisation sets its objectives and decides how best to achieve them.	The organisation monitors achievement of objectives and suggests any necessary corrective action.

The performance hierarchy is concerned with planning and control at different levels of the organisation:

A **mission statement** outlines the broad direction of an organisation, its reasons for existing and its values.'

Differences between strategic and operational planning and control

Strategic planning and control	Operational planning and control
Undertaken by senior managers.	Undertaken by operational managers.
Long-term, considering the whole organisation (and its divisions/departments) and all stakeholders.	Ensures objectives set at tactical level are achieved.
Information has an external focus and is commonly qualitative.	Information is detailed, task specific, mainly internal and largely quantitative.
Focus on planning not control.	Focus on control not planning to achieve short-term objectives.

Strategic planning is a **long-term**, top-down process and decisions may conflict with **short-term** localised **operational** decisions.

Strategic planning

Strategic analysis

- External analysis to identify opportunities and threats.
- Internal analysis to identify strengths and weaknesses.
- Stakeholder analysis to identify key objectives and to assess power and interest of different groups.
- Gap analysis to identify the difference between desired and expected performance.

Strategic choice

- Strategies are required to 'close the gap'.
- Competitive strategy – for each business unit.
- Directions for growth – which markets/products should be invested in.
- Whether expansion should be achieved by organic growth, acquisition or some form of joint arrangement.

Strategic implementation

- Formulation of detailed plans and budgets.
- Target setting for KPIs.
- Monitoring and control.

The role of performance measures

An organisation needs to establish SMART objectives and then key factors and processes will be identified that will enable it to achieve its objectives.

It is not enough merely to make plans and implement them.
The results of the plans have to be **measured**.

'What gets measured, gets done'
– i.e. the things that are measured get done much more often than the things that are not measured.

- Once measured, the results should be **compared** to the stated objectives.
- **Action** can then be taken to remedy any shortfalls in performance.

Strategic objectives, critical success factors and key performance indicators

The mission will be translated into a set of SMART, strategic objectives. Achievement of these objectives should ultimately help the organisation to achieve its mission.

Definition

Critical success factors (CSFs) are the vital areas 'where things must go right' for the organisation in order for them to achieve their strategic objectives.

CSFs can be **classified** as **monitoring or building** and also as **internal or external**.

There are different **sources** of CSFs. **For example industry or environmental factors** may drive the CSFs for an organisation.

Definition

Key performance indicators (KPIs) are the measures which indicate whether or not the CSFs are being achieved. Targets will be set for each KPI.

Benchmarking

Definition

Benchmarking aims to understand and evaluate the current position of the organisation in relation to **best practice** (products, services or processes) and to identify areas and means of performance improvement.

1 Determine areas to benchmark and set objectives

2 Identify KPIs

3 Select partners to benchmark against

4 Measure performance of partners using KPIs chosen

5 Measure own performance and identify gap

6 Decide on actions to close gap

7 Implement and monitor actions

Benchmarking evaluation

Advantages	Disadvantages
• Helps to assess current strategic position. • Identifies gaps in performance and sets challenging but achievable targets. • A method of learning from the success of others and applying best practice. • Minimises complacency and provides an early warning sign of competitive disadvantage. • Encourages continuous improvement. • Can help in assessing generic strategy.	• Identifying best practice difficult. • Not forward looking. • Differences between areas benchmarked. • Potential for lack of staff/ management commitment. • Too much focus on areas benchmarked to the detriment of overall performance. • Time and cost.

Types of benchmarking

Type	Advantages	Disadvantages
Internal benchmarking is where another function or division of the organisation is used as the benchmark.	• Share best practice • Obtain detailed operational data • Integrates different parts of organisation	• May not be innovative • No external focus • Often involves non-financial data and this may be less robust
Competitor benchmarking uses a direct competitor in the same industry with the same or similar processes as the benchmark.	• Identify where other organisations have competitive advantage • Identify areas for improvement with a similar business	• Competitor may be reluctant to share information or may want something in return • May not identify how to gain competitive advantage
Process/activity benchmarking focuses on a similar process/ activity in another organisation, which is not a direct competitor.	• Easier to obtain information from non-competitor • Solutions can still be innovative • Easier to translate lessons if done for generic activities	• May be difficult to translate lessons learned • Connecting organisations in different industries more difficult and different information systems may limit sharing

Models used in the performance management process

SWOT analysis

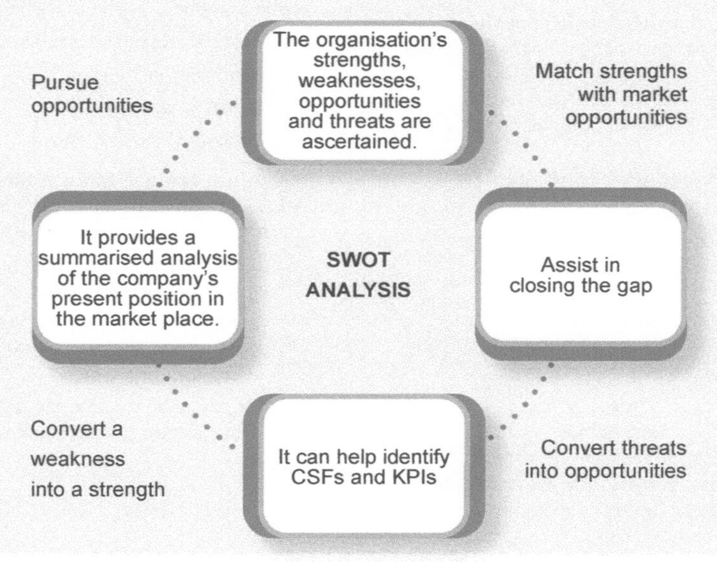

Tools for external analysis

(a) Porter's 5 forces

Industry level analysis looking at the pressures that determine how attractive the sector is.

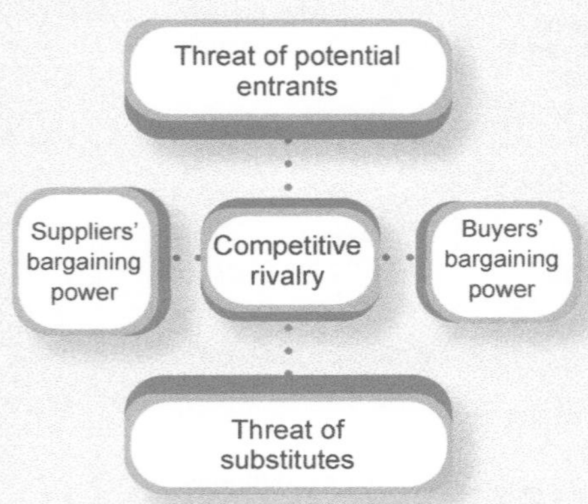

It is important to **measure**, **manage** and **monitor** the forces using suitable performance indicators.

(b) PEST analysis

Approach to analysing the **macro-environment**:

- **P**olitical influences and events
- **E**conomic influences
- **S**ocial influences
- **T**echnological influences

As well as being used for strategic analysis, PEST can be used to **identify key performance management issues** such as:

- identification and exploitation of opportunities in the external environment
- identification and monitoring of threats, risk and uncertainty so that necessary action can be taken
- identification and monitoring of CSFs and KPIs relating to opportunities and risks.

Boston Consulting Group (BCG) matrix

- The matrix shows whether the firm has a balanced portfolio.
- Consider **how to manage different categories to optimise performance, what performance indicators are needed for each category** (and the **alignment of these indicators with the overall mission and objectives**).

Market growth	Relative market share: High	Relative market share: Low
High	**Star** • Is the high reinvestment being spent effectively? • Is market share being gained, held or eroded? • Is customer perception improving? • Are customer CSFs changing as the market grows? • Could measure profit or return on investment. • Is the star becoming a cash cow?	**Problem child** **Investment strategy** • Is market share being gained? • Effectiveness of promotional spend. **Divestment strategy** • Monitor contribution to see whether to exit quickly or divest slowly.
Low	**Cash cow** • Cash generator. Strategy is minimal investment to keep product going. • Is market share being eroded – could the cash cow be moving towards becoming a dog? • Measure net cash flow.	**Dog** • Monitor contribution to see whether to exit quickly or divest slowly. • Monitor market growth as an increase in the growth rate could justify retaining the product.

Advantages	Disadvantages
• Ensures a balanced portfolio. • Used to manage divisions in different ways. • Metrics set in line with analysis. • Looks at portfolio as a whole, rather than assessing the performance of each part separately. • Can be used to assess performance.	• Simplistic; only looks at market growth and relative market share. • Designed for portfolio analysis, not performance management. • Determining what 'high' and 'low' mean is difficult. • Does not consider links between parts of the organisation. • May encourage holding rather than growth strategy for cash cows.

Porter's generic strategies

An important part of strategic choice is deciding on what basis to compete.

	Lower cost	Higher cost
Broad target	Cost leadership	Differentiation
Narrow target	Focus Cost focus	Differentiation focus

The most appropriate strategy should be chosen to help the organisation achieve competitive advantage and to optimise performance.

Risk

All organisations face risk and uncertainty.

Definitions

- **Risk** is the variability of possible returns. There are a number of possible outcomes and the probability of each outcome is **known**.
- **Uncertainty** is also the variability of possible returns. There are a number of possible outcomes and the probability of each outcome is **not known**.
- **Exogenous variables** originate from outside the organisation and are not controllable by it.
- **Endogenous variables** are factors under the control of management.

Four key tools are available for making decisions where there is an element of risk/uncertainty involved.

Risk technique	Suitability	Limitations
Expected values (EVs) – The average return if the decision is repeated again and again.	Organisation has a risk neutral approach to risk.	Not useful for one off decisions, if probabilities and/ or values of outcomes are uncertain/unknown, for non-risk neutral decision makers.
Maximax – Looks at the maximum return for each course of action and chooses the course of action with the highest maximum return.	Organisation is risk seeking and optimistic and can be used for one-off or repeated decisions.	May be considered overly optimistic since risks making a lower profit if the maximum outcome is not delivered.
Maximin – Looks at the minimum return for each course of action and chooses the course of action with the highest minimum return.	Organisation is risk averse and pessimistic and can be used for one-off or repeated decisions.	May be considered overly pessimistic since miss out on the possibility of making a bigger profit.
Mininmax regret - Looks at the maximum regret (opportunity cost) for each course of action and chooses the course of action that minimises the maximum regret.	Organisation does not want to make the wrong decision and miss out. Can be used for one-off or repeated decisions.	Risks making a lower profit.

It is important to consider the **risk appetite of stakeholders** when deciding on the most appropriate tool for decision making under risk/uncertainty.

Shareholders

- Commonly risk seeking. Prepared to take a risk, hold a portfolio of investments to spread risk – **maximax** suitable.
- However, shareholders in a company in financial distress may be more **risk averse or neutral – maximin or EVs** suitable.

Employees and managers

Should act in the best interests of shareholders but:

- may be **risk averse** if an unsuccessful outcome would impact their remuneration or job security – **maximin** preferred.
- may be **risk seeking** if a bonus or reward is offered for a high outcome – **maximax** preferred.

Venture capitalists

- Rational investors seeking **maximum return for minimum risk.**
- Hold a portfolio of investments, monitor progress against targets/to ensure exit strategy can be achieved and place employees on the management team to influence decisions – **maximax** suitable.

Banks

- **Conservative approach** to risk aiming to secure funds/returns – **maximin (or perhaps EVs)** suitable.

Exam focus

Exam sitting	Area examined	Question number
Sept/Dec 2021	Performance hierarchy, CSFs and KPIs	1(iv)
March/Jun 2021	Performance hierarchy, CSFs and KPIs 5 forces and PEST	1(a) 1(b)
Sept/Dec 2020	Performance hierarchy, CSFs and KPIs	1(i)
March 2020	Performance hierarchy, CSFs and KPIs	1(ii)
Sept/Dec 2019	Performance hierarchy, CSFs and KPIs Risk and uncertainty	1(iii) 3(b)(c)
March/Jun 2019	Performance hierarchy, CSFs and KPIs	1(a)

chapter

2

Environmental, social and governance factors

In this chapter

- The impact of stakeholders.
- Environmental, social and governance (ESG) factors.
- The role of the management accountant in sustainability.
- Integrated reporting.
- Environmental management accounting (EMA).

Exam focus

Much of the focus of APM will be on profit seeking organisations and more specifically companies. Companies have the primary objective to maximise shareholder wealth. When considering how best to achieve this objective it can be easy to focus:

- primarily on the shareholders and not the other stakeholders and
- on managing and measuring financial performance (e.g. return on capital employed (ROCE) or gross profit margins) and/or more traditional non-financial areas of performance (e.g. employee and customer satisfaction, or product quality).

Although this focus is important, it is also necessary for organisations to understand how vital it is to consider a range of other issues when managing and measuring performance (such as environmental and social factors) and for an organisation to consider its different stakeholders and not just its shareholders.

The impact of stakeholders

Definition

A **stakeholder** is a group or individual who has an interest in what the organisation does, or an expectation of the organisation. As such, they may attempt to influence its mission, objectives and strategy.

- The primary objective of profit seeking organisations is to maximise shareholder wealth. However, an organisation (whether profit seeking or not-for-profit) must consider the needs of all of its stakeholders.
- There is an increasing recognition amongst stakeholders of the importance of sustainability and the impact of businesses on society and the environment. Stakeholders are interested in how an organisation is performing in these areas.

Definition

Corporate social responsibility (CSR) refers to the idea that a company should be sensitive to the needs of all stakeholders in its business operations and not just shareholders.

Stakeholder mapping (Mendelow's matrix)

Helps analyse the organisation's stakeholders and suggests possible strategies for each one.
Used to manage stakeholders' conflicting demands and to establish priorities.

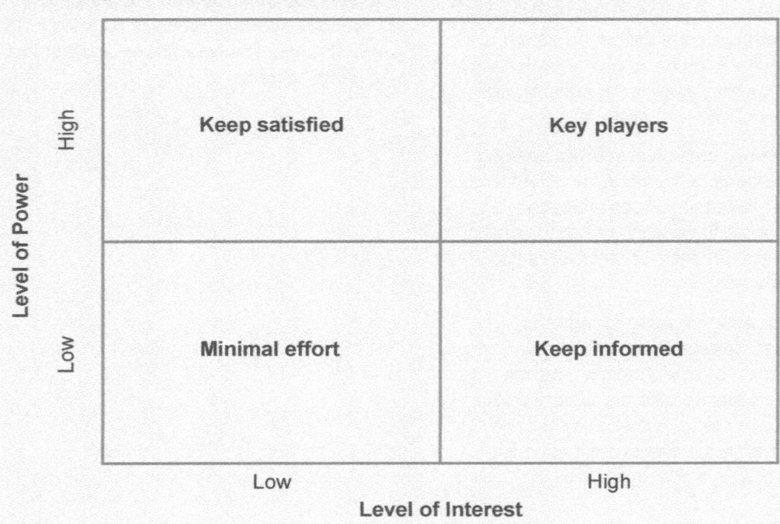

Steps to optimise performance

1. Identify all stakeholders and their needs/objectives.

2. Consider the relative levels of power and interest of the stakeholders and plot these on the matrix.

3. Evaluate, using the matrix, how the different stakeholders should be managed.

4. Establish priorities (for example, prioritise 'key players').

5. Manage conflicting demands

6. Develop the mission and strategic objectives with the stakeholders' needs in mind.

7. Establish CSFs and KPIs that are aligned to the achievement of the mission and strategic objectives.

8. Translate the strategic objectives into tactical and operational objectives and establish performance measures for these.

Environmental, social and governance (ESG) factors

Definitions

ESG refers to the three central factors in measuring the sustainability and societal impact of an organisation and that help to determine the long-term performance of an organisation.

Ethics is a set of moral principles that examines the concept of right and wrong. It relates to behaviour expected by society, but not codified in law.

Business ethics is the application of ethical values to business behaviour. They are a key component of an organisation's ESG strategy.

Corporate governance (the '**G**' in 'ESG') is the set of processes and policies by which a company is directed, administered and controlled. It is concerned with the overall control and direction of a business so that the business's objectives are achieved in an acceptable manner by all stakeholders.

Sustainability is an important aspect of ESG and is a key focus of this chapter. Two possible definitions are:

- Development that meets the needs of the present without compromising the ability of future generations to meet their own needs.
- A need for organisations to focus on economic prosperity, environmental quality and social justice. Sometimes summarised as the **3 P's** of Planet (environmental), People (social) and Profit (economic).

Triple bottom line (TBL) accounting means expanding the traditional company reporting framework to take into account environmental and social performance in addition to economic performance.

ESG and performance management

Arguments for ESG	Arguments against ESG
• Help attract/retain customers. • Help attract a wider and/or higher calibre human resource base. • May reduce costs, fines, lawsuits and allow access to subsidies and government support. • Fulfil the needs of stakeholders who may otherwise join forces and increase power. • Can help attract investors and reduce risk resulting in cheaper finance. The above should improve long-term performance. • In addition to performance improvement, consideration of ESG factors is ethically correct.	• May conflict with a manager's duty to maximise shareholder wealth. • It could be argued that focusing on maximising shareholder wealth can be aligned with consideration of ESG issues. • Potential increased costs. • Lack of knowledge of the benefits, the actions to be taken and how these should be reported and measured. • Lack of skills and resources. • May have to turn away business from customers considered to be unethical. • It could be argued that it is enough to comply with relevant laws and regulations.

Introduction

Management accountants, as trusted advisors, will be at the heart of sustainability action. They will have a significant role in embedding performance measures in the area of sustainability into the core performance measurement process:

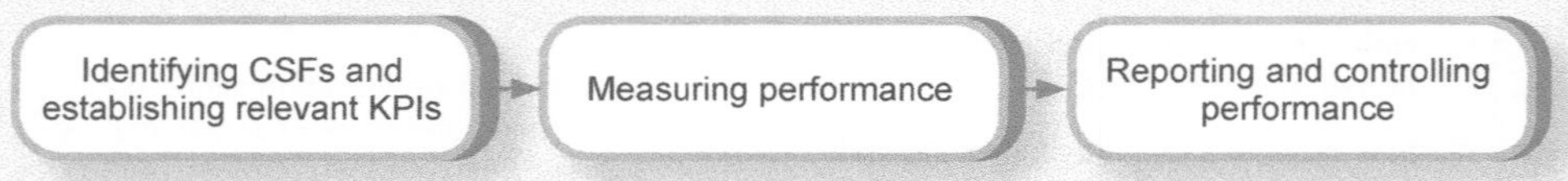

The modern management accountant will need to successfully combine traditional technical accounting skills with business, people, leadership and digital skills (all underpinned by ethics and professionalism) but is well positioned to meet the changing mandate and should view this as an opportunity.

Identifying CSFs and establishing relevant KPIs

The management accountant will work alongside the CEO to embed sustainability issues in the entire performance management process:

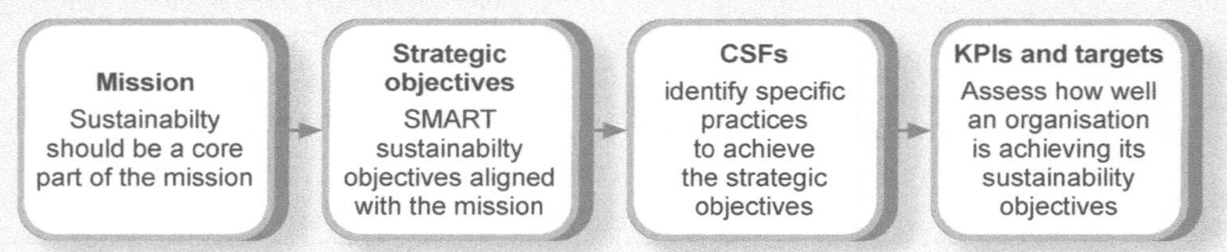

Features of a good KPI for sustainability:

- Actually measure sustainability
- Align with mission, objectives and CSFs
- Recognise interconnectedness between measures
- Balanced picture (good and bad)
- Focus on areas that have greatest potential impact
- Measure over time to identify trends
- Clear and consistent to aid benchmarking

Measuring performance

- Once appropriate KPIs have been established, the management accountant will have a role in collecting KPI data and transforming it into useful information so that sustainability can be measured.
- The management accountant will analyse the information to draw out patterns and insights for those who use the information.
- Information technology (IT) will assist with this

Reporting and controlling performance

The UN climate change conference, COP26, was held in Autumn 2021. The creation of an **International Sustainability Standards Board (ISSB)** was announced at the conference, a major step towards globally aligned ESG reporting. ISSB standards will **provide the foundation for consistent and global ESG reporting standards** that will enable companies to report on ESG factors affecting their business. The standards are still in development but once in place they should act as a transformational event for ESG reporting.

However, at present, there is **no globally accepted framework for reporting** but **two possible frameworks** for sustainability reporting are **The Global Reporting Initiative (GRI) Standards** (best practice for reporting on a range of economic, environmental and social impacts) and **The United Nations' (UN) Sustainable Development Goals (SDGs)**(more detail below).

The United Nations' (UN) Sustainable Development Goals (SDGs)

The UN SDGs encourage countries to embed sustainability measures into their 'core' performance reporting. In 2015, the UN launched 17 SDGs to end poverty, fight inequality and justice and tackle climate change by 2030. Each **goal** has a related set of **targets** (169 in total) and **indicators**.

17 SDGs and 169 related targets is a lot. Organisations need to:

- Prioritise the choice of SDGs and related targets to those where they can make a meaningful contribution and should be ambitious.
- Focus on and pick out the SDGs and targets that are aligned to the mission and objectives (in which sustainability issues should be embedded).

Organisations need to **take steps to measure and monitor performance in order to keep on track of their commitments**. The **management accountant will have an important role** in this.

Integrated reporting

Definition

With Integrated Reporting (IR), instead of having environmental and social issues reported in a separate section of the annual report, or a standalone 'sustainability' report, the idea is that one report should capture the strategic and operational actions of management in its holistic approach to business and stakeholder 'wellbeing'.

There is an increasing recognition that the long-term pursuit of shareholder value is linked to the preservation and enhancement of six different types of capital. These can be broadly related to the three aspects of the TBL:

Aspect of TBL	Type of capital affected
Environmental	**Natural capital** – For example, waste, recycling and emissions.
Social	**Human capital** – Health, skills, motivation of employees. **Social capital** – Relationships, partnerships and co-operation. **Intellectual capital** – Patents, brand value and tacit knowledge.
Economic	**Manufactured capital** – Buildings, equipment and infrastructure. **Financial capital** – Funds available to enable the business to operate. Reflects the value generated from the other types of capital.

The role of the management accountant in IR

The management accountant must produce information that:

- is a balance of quantitative and qualitative information. The IS must be able to capture both financial and non-financial measures
- considers how resources should be allocated
- links past, present and future information. The forward looking nature will require more forecasted information
- considers the impact of relevant laws and regulations and any necessary action
- provides an analysis of opportunities and risks that could impact the future
- Consider how resources should be allocated
- is tailored to the specific situation but remains concise

Environmental management accounting (EMA)

Introduction

Before reporting on environmental matters, e.g. using IR, the organisation needs to identify its existing environmental costs and the effectiveness of its environmental-related activities.

EMA was developed in recognition that traditional management accounting systems were unable to identify or deal adequately with environmental costs resulting in negative environmental and economic impacts.

Definitions

EMA is concerned with the accounting information needs of managers in relation to the organisation's activities that affect the environment as well as environment-related impacts of the organisation. It involves the identification and estimation of the financial and non-financial costs of environmental-related activities with a view to control and reduce these costs.

Categories of environmental cost

Type of environmental cost	Problem
Conventional costs, e.g. energy costs.	Not prioritised since often hidden in overheads.
Contingent costs, e.g. decommissioning costs.	Often ignored due to short-term focus.
Relationship costs, e.g. cost of producing environmental information for reporting.	Ignored by managers who may be unaware of their existence.
Reputational cost, i.e. the cost of failing to address environmental issues.	Ignored by managers who are unaware of the risk of incurring them.

Benefits of EMA

- The focus of EMA is not entirely on financial costs but it also considers the non-financial environmental cost or benefit of any decisions made.
- A clearer understanding of costs should mean that budgets are more realistic and therefore more useful for planning purposes, such as pricing decisions.
- EMA includes environment-related KPIs and targets as part of routine performance monitoring. These will be both financial and non-financial, have an internal and external focus and will relate to both short-term and long-term performance.
- EMA will also often benchmark activities against environmental best practice.

EMA techniques

ABC

- Removes environment-driven costs from overheads and traces them to products or services.
- Should result in the identification of cost drivers and better control of costs.
- Product costs more realistic resulting in better pricing and decision making.

Lifecycle costing

- Considers the costs and revenues of a product over its whole life rather than one accounting period.
- Organisations will have to be financially and environmentally responsible if they have plans to cover these costs.
- In order to reduce lifecycle costs may use techniques such as TQM.

Input-output analysis

- Focuses on waste in processes.
- Records material inflows and balances this with outflows since 'what comes in, must go out'.
- By accounting for outputs in terms of physical quantities and in monetary terms, organisations are forced to focus on environmental costs.

Flow cost accounting

- Aims to reduce the quantity of material, thus reducing costs and having a positive environmental impact.
- Uses not only material flows, but also the organisational structure; looking at material flows and material losses incurred at various stages of the production process.
- Material costs can be divided into different types and the values and cost of each type calculated.

EMA and quality-related costs

In the context of quality, we could consider **environment-related costs as being the costs of ensuring the quality of an organisation's processes or activities in relation to the environment.**

Environment- related cost	Description
Environmental prevention cost	Costs of implementing a quality improvement programme to prevent the negative impact of an organisation's processes or activities in relation to the environment.
Environmental appraisal cost	Costs of quality inspection and testing.
Environmental internal failure cost	Costs arising from a failure to meet quality standards before the product or service reaches the customer.
Environmental external failure cost	Costs arising from a failure to meet quality standards after the product or service reaches the customer.

Exam focus

Exam sitting	Area examined	Question number
Sept/Dec 2021	Stakeholders	2(a)
	ESG factors	2(a)
	EMA	2(b)
Sept/Dec 2020	Stakeholders	3(b)
Sept/Dec 2019	Stakeholders	3(a)

chapter

3

Budgeting and control

In this chapter

- Purposes of budgeting.
- Participation in budget setting.
- Budgeting methods.
- Variances.
- Non-budgetary methods for organisational control.
- Forecasting.

Exam focus

Budgeting will assist with performance management since it is an important tool for **planning** and **control** within an organisation and contributes to performance management by providing benchmarks against which to compare actual results (through **variance analysis**) and develop corrective measures.

It is important that the organisation understands the relative merits of the different budgeting approaches and chooses the approach that is most suitable for them.

In addition, it is important to acknowledge that the business environment has become more complex, dynamic, turbulent and uncertain. Organisations need to be more adaptive to change, rather than be stifled by a need to comply with a fixed plan (budget). As a result, there has been an increased use of non-traditional profit-based performance measures in controlling organisations (e.g. beyond budgeting).

Purposes of budgeting

A **budget** is a quantitative plan prepared for a specific time period.

Budgeting serves a number of purposes:

- **P**lanning
- **R**esponsibility
- **I**ntegration
- **M**otivation
- **E**valuation/control

Participation in budget setting

A **top-down** budget is one that is imposed on the budget holder by senior management.

Advantages:

- Avoids budgetary slack
- Avoids dysfunctional behaviour
- Can be quicker
- Senior managers retain control
- Senior managers understand the needs of the whole organisation

A **bottom-up** budget involves divisonal managers participating in the setting of the budgets.

Advantages:

- More realistic budgets
- Improved motivation
- Increases divisional manager's understanding
- Frees up senior management resources

Budgeting methods

Definition

Fixed budget – when a budget is prepared for a single level of activity.

Definition

Flexible budget – prepared for a number of levels of activity and can be 'flexed' to the actual level of activity for control purposes.

Definition

Incremental budget – starts with previous period's budget or actual results and adds or subtracts an incremental amount to cover inflation and other expected changes. Can be viewed as a traditional approach.

Suitability	Advantages
• Stable business. • Good cost control. • Limited discretionary costs.	• Quick, easy and low cost. • Motivates managers since targets not changing regularly. • Useful if historical figures accurate and the suitability criteria are fulfilled.

Definition

Zero-based budgeting – requires each cost element to be specifically justified, as though the activities to which the budget relates were being undertaken for the first time.

ZBB stages:

1 Managers identify activities that can be individually evaluated.

2 Activities are described in a decision package.

3 Decision package evaluated and ranked using cost benefit analysis.

4 Results used to allocate resources to various packages.

Suitability	Advantages
• Fast moving business • Historic figures inaccurate • High discretionary costs • Public sector organisations	• Inefficient or obsolete operations can be identified and discontinued. • Resources should be allocated economically and efficiently. • ZBB leads to increased staff involvement at all levels, improving motivation and knowledge. • It responds to a change in the business environment, so useful for a dynamic or fast moving organisation and appropriate if the other suitability criteria exist.

Definition

A **rolling budget** is one that is kept continuously up to date by adding another accounting period (for example, a month or quarter) when the earliest accounting period has expired.

Suitability	Advantages
• Fast moving organisation • New business • Any organisation that needs cost control	• Budgeting and control should be more accurate. • Better information to base the manager's appraisal on. • Fixed period budget will always exist. • It forces management to take the budgeting process seriously.

Activity-based budgeting (ABB)

Before we look at ABB, let's begin by recapping our costing knowledge from PM.

Absorption costing (AC)

Aims to calculate the full production cost per unit.

Assumes production overheads are driven by the level of activity.

Activity based costing (ABC)

Aim also to calculate the full production cost per unit.

Recognises the diversity and complexity of modern production meaning that not all production overheads are driven by level of activity.

Steps in ABC

1 Group production overheads into activities **(cost pools)**, according to how they are driven.

2 Identify **cost drivers** for each activity.

3 Calculate an overhead absorption rate **(OAR)** for each activity.

4 **Absorb** activity costs into products.

5 Calculate the **full production cost/unit** and profit/(loss).

Advantages of ABC	Disadvantages of ABC
• Provides a more accurate cost per unit leading to better pricing, cost control and decision making. • Better insight into what drives costs resulting in better control of costs. • Can be applied to all overhead costs and to service costing.	• Cost may exceed benefit. • Limited benefit if overhead minimal or mainly driven by level of production. • Allocating overheads to specific activities and determining cost drivers is difficult. • Assigning responsibility for cost pools is difficult. • Limited benefit if activity costs already well controlled or process is efficient. • Customers may not tolerate changes such as price increases or changes to product specifications.

Definition

Activity based management (ABM) is the use of ABC information for management purposes to improve **operational** and **strategic** decisions. **ABM** applies ABC principles in order to satisfy customer needs using the least amount of resources.

Operational ABM

Helps operational managers make decisions that can **improve operational efficiency** and hence performance:

- Can reduce or eliminate activities that don't add value.
- Find ways to continually improve the value-adding activities.
- May identify design improvements.

Strategic ABM

Uses ABC information to decide which products to develop and sell based on profitability.

- Can assist with customer profitability analysis (CPA).
- May assist in improving relationships with customers and suppliers

BE CAREFUL:

- Some operational activities and strategic decisions will have an implicit value that is not necessarily reflected in the financial value.
- The cost may outweigh the benefit.

Definition

Activity based budgeting (ABB) uses the costs determined in ABC to prepare budgets for each activity.

The cost driver for each activity is identified. A forecast is made of the number of units of the cost driver that will occur in the budget period. Given the estimate of the number of units of the cost driver, the activity cost is estimated.

ABB advantages	ABB disadvantages
• Draws attention to cost of overhead activities, which can be a large proportion of total operating cost. • Recognises that by controlling cost drivers, costs can be better managed and understood. • Can be used to identify CSFs. • Can provide useful information for a TQM environment (links cost and quality).	• Time and effort required. • Staffing issues such as cost of training required and potential resistance to change. • Cost of adapting IS to collect correct information. • Not suited to organisations not using ABC. • Difficult to identify responsibility for activities and hence accountability for achieving budget set. • It could be argued that many overhead costs are not controllable in the short-term.

Variances

Variances are a key element of management control.

1. Targets and standards are set.
2. Actual performance is measured.
3. Actual results compared to flexed standard, using variance analysis.
4. 'Significant' variances investigated and appropriate action taken.

Exam focus

In APM, you may be asked to calculate a variance, although it is likely that calculation marks will account for only the minority of marks available for a question on variances. Do spend a little bit of time reviewing the variances covered in PM to ensure you are comfortable with the calculations and the meaning of each variance. Without being able to do this first, it will be difficult to address the requirements of the APM syllabus area on variances.

Planning and operational variances

The variances calculated can be divided into planning and operational elements if the original budget was inappropriate.

- The **planning variance** is the difference between the original and the revised budget (due to inaccuracies in the original budget, not controllable by operational manager so should not be held accountable for these).
- The **operational variance** is the difference between the revised standard and the actual performance (due to decisions of operational managers and therefore they are controllable by them and can be held accountable to these variances).

Non-budgetary methods for organisational control

The use of traditional budgeting (including methods such as incremental budgeting) is comfortable and predictable and it may still have its place in organisations.

However, there are also many **weaknesses and limitations of traditional approaches to budgeting:**

- Costly and time consuming
- Focus is on short-term results
- Insufficient external focus
- Top-down approach to strategy and decision-making (hierarchy of control and accountability)
- Less suited to modern organisations where change is the new norm and the importance of an empowered and adaptive organisation is paramount.

One example of a non-budgetary approach is **beyond budgeting**.

<table>
<tr><td colspan="4">Beyond budgeting (BB) is the generic term given to the body of practices intended to replace traditional budgeting as a management model.</td></tr>
<tr><td colspan="4">Principles:</td></tr>
<tr><td>Governance and transparency
For example, bound to a common cause by the mission and set of values rather than controlled by a central plan.</td><td>Accountable teams
For example, teams empowered to make decisions and any budgets used are bottom-up.</td><td>Goals, targets and rewards
For example, using a range of relevant financial and non-financial, external and internal, targets linked to shareholder wealth.</td><td>Planning and control
For example, planning is continuous (using rolling budgets) and the focus is on the future.</td></tr>
</table>

Beyond budgeting advantages	Beyond budgeting disadvantages
• Planning continuous and organisation more proactive. • Lower costs due to move away from concept of budget entitlement. • Targets more challenging and with an external focus. • Managers not constrained by traditional budgets and fixed resources. • Creates IS which provide fast and open information.	• Planning, co-ordination, performance evaluation and rewards systems become more complicated. • Effort and motivation low if targets and benchmarks viewed as unachievable. • Goals may be less clear or not communicated. • Staff resistance. • May be difficult to adopt culture of decentralisation. • Costly investment in IS may be needed.

Forecasting

The hi-low method	Analyses, for example, a semi-variable cost into its fixed and variable elements. These elements are then used to forecast the total cost at any level of activity.
Regression analysis	Used to estimate the line of best fit and can be used for forecasting whenever a linear relationship is assumed between two variables.
Time series analysis	Makes assumptions about past patterns in data, such as the general trend, seasonality and cyclical variations, to forecast figures.
The learning curve model	Takes account of the learning curve effect to forecast the average labour time/unit or labour cost/unit.

Exam focus

Exam sitting	Area examined	Question number
Mar/Jun 2019	Budgeting methods	3(a)
	ABB and ABM	2 and 3(a)
	Variances	3(b)

chapter

4

Business structure and performance management

In this chapter

- Organisational forms.
- Complex business structures.
- The needs of services.
- Business integration.
- Business process re-engineering (BPR).

Exam focus

In this chapter we will look at the information and information system requirements of **different business structures**. We will also discuss the implications of a particular structure for performance management.

An important element of structure is **business integration**. Performance management can improve as a result of linkages between people, operations, strategy and technology. This chapter reviews two important frameworks for understanding business integration; Porter's value chain and McKinsey's 7s model.

The chapter also introduces the topic of **business process re-engineering**. This is the fundamental redesign of business processes and, amongst other things, it can result in a change of structure.

Organisational forms

	Functional organisations (centralised)	Divisional organisations (decentralised)
Information needs (the IS should aid these needs)	• Data passed from functional to upper levels. • Data aggregated at the highest level before feedback given.	• Information needs to be available lower down organisation due to the high level of autonomy. • Top management need information to measure and control divisions.
Advantages for performance management	• Better standardisation and control. The IS should aid this communication. • Defined career path and sense of belonging for specialists. • Lower costs since roles are not duplicated.	• Easier to grow/diversify. • Clear responsibility for decisions. • Training of general managers. • Speed and quality of decision making. • Top management can focus on strategy.
Problems for performance management	• Empire building and conflicts between functions. • Slow decision making. • Hard to grow/ diversify.	• Loss of control and co-ordination (goal congruence not achieved). • Determining accountability difficult. • Difficult to appraise divisions due to inter-dependence. • Difficult to re-apportion head office costs. • Cost of duplicated functions.

Responsibility accounting

Definition

Responsibility accounting is a system of accounting based on the identification of individual parts of a business (responsibility centres) which are the responsibility of a single manager. The areas of responsibility may be a cost centre, profit centre or investment centre.

- Each division will be a responsibility centre.
- Divisional managers should only be held accountable for those areas of responsibility they can control.
- The information systems should ensure that costs and revenues can be traced to those responsible.

Network (virtual) organisation	
Information needs	• The organisation needs to establish shared goals and contractual agreements. • Those responsible for regulating performance will need information for decision making. • Each party needs feedback on its performance. The IS will need to be sophisticated with the ability to gather and process the information from all parties.
Advantages for performance management	• Flexibility to meet project needs. • Can exploit market opportunities. • Can compete with larger organisations. • Lower infrastructure costs.
Disadvantages for performance management	• Difficult to agree common goals and measures. • Planning and control difficult. • Monitoring of the workforce difficult. • Information gathering difficult if IS not compatible. • Loss of competitive advantage if partners work for competitors. Many of the problems can be addressed using a service level agreement (SLA).

Complex business structures

Definition

A **joint venture (JV)** is a separate business entity whose shares are owned by two or more business entities

Why form a JV?

- To facilitate development of new products or expansion into new markets.
- Sharing of resources, costs, risks, skills, experience and intellectual property.
- Flexibility since business retains its unique identity and partners are only bound for the pre-agreed period.

Planning difficulties

- Difficult to agree on common goals, measures and targets.
- Difficult to agree how to share, e.g. resources, accountability etc.
- Planning difficult, e.g. due to different locations or IS.
- Difficult to form an effective JV board.

Performance measurement difficulties

- Difficult if no integrated or common IS.
- Measurement and reporting of performance, difficult if partners are unwilling to share information.
- Different opinions on how measures should be calculated or determined.

Control difficulties

- Hard to compare actual performance (performance measurement may be difficult) to target performance (establishing this will be difficult).
- Attributing accountability for performance (good or bad) is difficult.

Strategic alliances

Definition

A **strategic alliance** is similar to a JV but a **separate business entity is not formed**.

Comparison to a JV

The **reasons for forming a strategic alliance** and the **challenges for performance management and measurement** are very **similar to those discussed for a JV**.

A **relative benefit** of a strategic alliance over a JV is greater flexibility since the strategic alliance is not constrained by the reporting and compliance requirements of a separate legal entity.

Additional problems more specific to a strategic alliance are:

- Independence is retained.
- Security of information may be more of a concern.
- Does not have other benefits of a separate legal entity.

Complex supply chains

Definition

A **supply chain** consists of a network of organisations. Together they provide and process the necessary raw materials firstly into work-in-progress and then into finished goods for distribution and sale to the customer. As organisations have grown in size and complexity, **complexity** in the supply chain is becoming **more commonplace**.

Benefits for performance management	Challenges for performance management
• Harnessing of the knowledge and skills of partners. • Builds positive relationships based on the joint quest to, e.g. improve quality. • Partners work together to fulfil customer needs in an optimum way, driving competitive advantage. • Reduces reliance on one or a small number of partners.	• Difficult if the supply chain is more 'complicated' than 'complex'. • Each partner will have their own goals and these will have to be aligned to a common purpose. • Skills required to manage the relationships. • Measuring performance may be difficult, e.g. what to measure, collection of information.

The needs of services

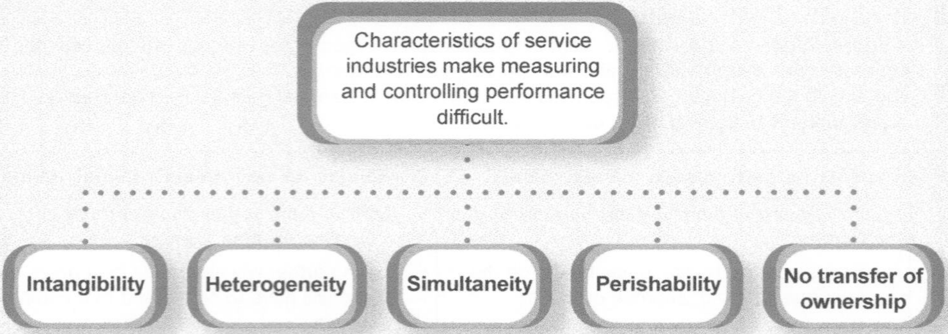

Characteristics of service industries make measuring and controlling performance difficult.

- Intangibility
- Heterogeneity
- Simultaneity
- Perishability
- No transfer of ownership

These differences will result in different objectives and CSFs. Appropriate performance measures should be established.

Business integration

Definition

- Business integration is an important part of business structure. It means that all aspects of the business must be aligned to secure the most efficient use of the organisation's resources so that it can achieve its objectives effectively.
- Rather than focusing on individual parts of the business, the whole process should be considered (two possible frameworks are explored below).

Porter's value chain

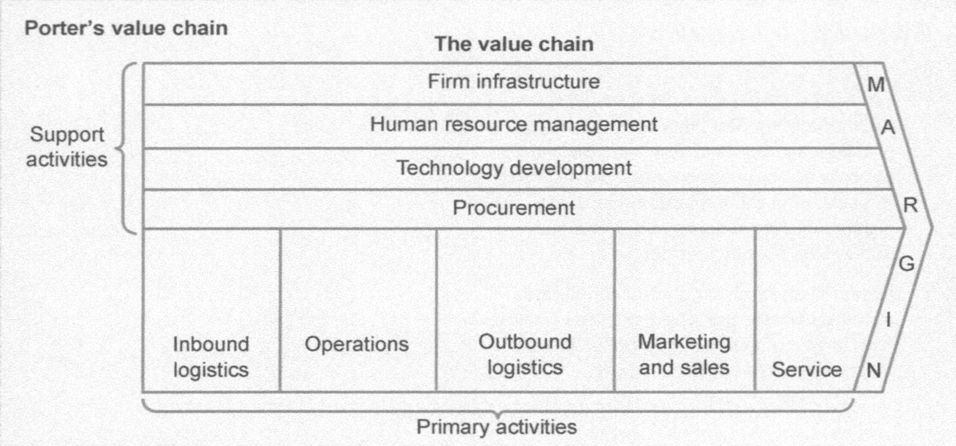

Uses in performance management:

- Used to identify **strengths and weaknesses** as part of strategic analysis.
- Used to identify **CSFs** within each activity and establish appropriate **measures**.
- Shows linkages between activities leading to **common information systems**.
- Considers **support activities** which may have been dismissed as overheads.
- Extend to include the value chain of customers and suppliers (**value system**).

Mckinsey's 7s model

- Describes an organisation as consisting of seven interrelated internal elements which must be aligned to secure success.
- Used to identify elements to realign to improve performance or to maintain alignment and performance during a period of change.
- Three hard elements (systems, strategy and structure) and four soft elements (skills, staff, style and shared values).

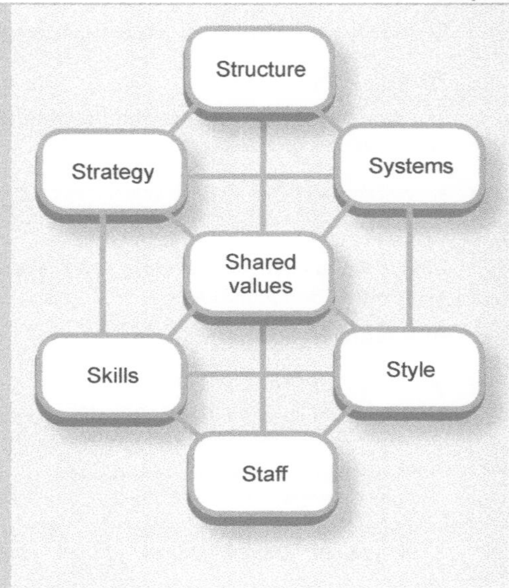

Business process re-engineering (BPR)

What is BPR?

The way in which an organisation's activities (as per the value chain) and interrelate constitute an organisation's processes.

Definition

BPR is the fundamental rethinking and radical redesign of business processes to achieve dramatic improvements in performance.

BPR requirements:

- Investment in systems to adequately monitor and control performance
- Employee training
- Clear communication and leadership
- Rewards aligned to new roles and performance measures
- A change in culture to a process view with process teams
- Greater automation and use of IT

Advantages for performance management	Disadvantages for performance management
• Encourages long-term strategic view. • Revolves around customer's needs. • Allows workers more autonomy. • Can help eliminate unnecessary activities and make a process cheaper.	• Additional costs, for example of new information systems or training. • Staff cuts/cost cutting demoralising. • Staff feel devalued if role changes. • Lost co-ordination if middle managers stripped out. • Often utilises outsourcing which has its own problems. • Processes may be merely automated and not redesigned. • Backward looking.

Exam focus

Exam sitting	Area examined	Question number
Sept/Dec 2021	BPR	3(a)
Sept/Dec 2020	Organisational forms and complex structures	3(a)
	7S model	2(a)
Sept/Dec 2019	Value chain	1(iv)

chapter

5

Information systems and developments in technology

In this chapter

- Management information.
- Developing management accounting information systems.
- IT developments.
- Big data.

Exam focus

Managers need access to good information in order to be able to effectively plan, direct and control the activities that they are responsible for. The first part of this chapter focuses on management information and on the development and importance of an effective management accounting information system.

The chapter then goes on to look at some IT developments and discusses how advancements in technology have enabled organisations to better measure and control performance and to improve performance.

The final part of the chapter discusses the development of big data and data analytics and its impact on the role of the management accountant. It discusses the methods of data analysis and data analytics and some of the ethical issues involved.

Management information

Managers need access to 'good' information for planning, control and decision making. Good information should be 'ACCURATE':

- **A**ccurate
- **C**omplete
- **C**ost < benefit
- **U**nderstandable
- **R**elevant
- **A**daptable (or **A**ccessible)
- **T**imely
- **E**asy to use

Sources of information are internal and external. Internal information is from a known origin, should meet the organisation's needs and should be easier and cheaper to collect but external information should also be used alongside it.

Types of information include financial or non-financial, quantitative or qualitative.

Developing management accounting information systems

Definition

A management information system (**MIS**) converts internal and external data into useful information which is then communicated to managers at all levels and across all functions to enable them to make timely and effective decisions for planning, directing and controlling activities.

There are a number of types of MIS:

Executive information system (EIS)

- Gives senior managers access to internal and external information
- Presented in a user-friendly summarised form
- Option to drill down to a greater level of detail

Decision support system (DSS)

- Aids managers in making decisions
- Predicts the consequences of a number of possible scenarios
- Manager then uses their judgement to make the final decision

Transaction processing system (TPS)

- Records, summarises and reports daily transactions to aid operational managers' decisions.

Expert system

- Hold specialist knowledge
- Allow non-experts to interrogate for information, advice and recommended decisions

Quality MIS

A MIS should produce quality information, consistent with the characteristics of 'good' information.

Definition

A lean approach aims to identify and eliminate waste in the MIS and improve the efficiency and flow of information to users. A **lean MIS** aims to get the right thing to the right place at the right time.

The **5 Ss concept** is often associated with lean principles and aims to create a workplace (or in this case, a MIS) which is in order:

S	Example of application to MIS
Structurise	Structured and ordered IS allowing quick access by those who require it and to fulfil their needs.
Systemise	The IS should improve efficiency and accuracy with items arranged for ease of use and duplication eliminated.
Sanitise	Removal of obsolete or duplicated data. Also, only producing reports for people who need them or are authorised to receive them.
Standardise	Establishing an optimum standard for producing output reports and then applying this consistently.
Self-discipline	Motivating employees to continually perform the above will result in continuous improvement of the IS.

The importance of IS integration

It is important that IS (and the information produced by them) do not exist in isolation but rather the IS in the organisation should be connected and integrated.

Definition

A **data silo** is when data exists in separate areas of the organisation or in separate IS and does not connect up with or integrate with other organisational data or information systems.

Issues of data silos	How to address the issues
• May result in **duplicated information** – this is inefficient and therefore costly and the information may not be 'good'. • The **data may be held in one silo only**, creating a barrier to collaboration and co-ordination since: – information is inaccessible or invisible to other systems or users – different parts of the business start to work independently, perhaps prioritising their own objectives – if users identify a need to access other information and to co-ordinate with other users, this process will be slow, time consuming and costly.	Data silos occur naturally as organisations grow can be overcome through: • the **adoption of new technology**, e.g. cloud or network technology. • by **changing the organisation's culture** and processes to encourage the sharing of information.

The need for continual systems development

Information and accounting systems need to be developed continually to maintain or improve performance.

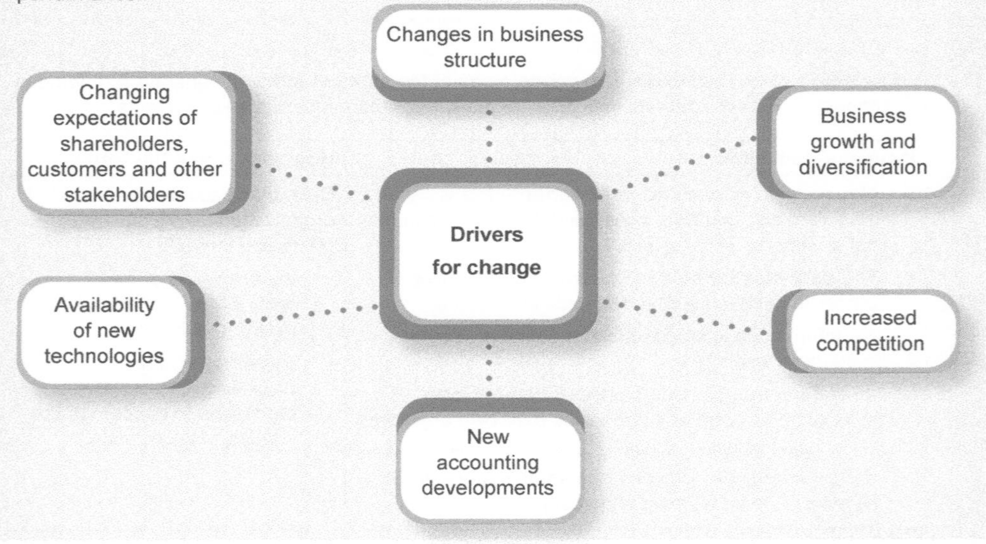

IT developments

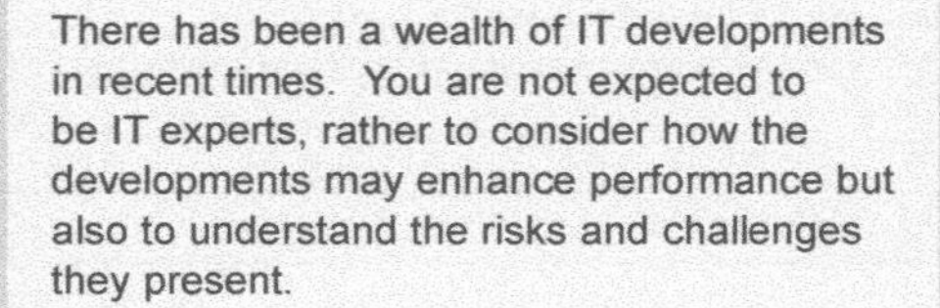

Exam focus

There has been a wealth of IT developments in recent times. You are not expected to be IT experts, rather to consider how the developments may enhance performance but also to understand the risks and challenges they present.

Networks

Facilitate the transfer of information across the organisation.

- Intranets, extranets and the internet all rely on netwok technology.
- All of the IT developments discussed in this chapter reply on networks.

Cloud technology

Definition

Storing and accessing data and programs over the internet instead of on a computer's hard drive.

Benefits	Risks
• Flexibility • Scalability • Lower costs • Improved security • Flexible working • Lower environmental impact	• Organisational change • Contract management • Security threat • Reliance

Data warehouses

Definition

Data is combined from multiple and varied sources into one comprehensive, secure and easily manipulated store. Data can be accessed to suit the user's needs and can be mined to understand patterns and correlations.

Advantages	Disadvantages
• Reduced duplication and storage • Improved integrity • Flexible to user's needs • Aligned across the organisation and can be linked to suppliers' and customers' systems • Instant access to data	• Cost of system and training • Failure/ security breach more catastrophic

Enterprise resource planning system (ERPS)

Definition

An ERPS is an example of a **unified corporate database**. It integrates data from all different parts of the organisation into a single system that allows all users to access the same information, to see an overall picture of performance and helps inform business decisions.

Benefits (Includes the advantages of databases but more specifically the below)	Impact on role of management accountant
• Senior managers have access to data all in one place. • Decision support features aid management decisions. • Improved flow/communication of information across the organisation. • Plans use of resources across the organisation. • Less duplication of data. • Can extend to include customer and supplier software.	• Less routine assembly of information. • More analysing the information to gain insight. • Management accountants will work more alongside others in the organisation.

Knowledge management systems (KMS)

Definition

A KMS is any type of IT that helps to capture, store, retrieve and use knowledge to enhance the knowledge management process.

Examples include:

- groupware
- intranets/extranets
- data warehouses
- decision support systems (DSS).

Management accountants will play an important role in knowledge management.

Customer relationship management (CRM) systems

Definition

Technology needed to gather the information needed to attract and retain customers.

Most systems are based on a database of customer information. The data is analysed so that any gaps in customer related performance can be identified and appropriate strategies and targets can then be set.

Radio frequency identification (RFID)

Definition

Radio receivers are used to tag items and hence keep track of assets.

Benefits include access to better real time information, improved accuracy and control.

Process automation

Definition

The technology enabled transformation of business processes previously carried out by human workers, aimed at implementing consistency, quality and speed whilst delivering cost savings.

- Automation of low value, low skilled, repetitive tasks will free up time for higher value adding activities.
- Technology developments are now enabling automation of more complex processes.

Internet of things

Definition

The network of 'smart' devices with in built software and connectivity to the internet allowing them to constantly monitor and exchange data.

Artificial intelligence (AI)

Definition

AI is an area of computer science that emphasises the creation of intelligent machines that work and react like human beings.

Definition

Machine learning is a subset of AI. Computer code mimics how the human brain works, using data and experiences to improve their function over time in making predictions and recommendations.

Definition

An **algorithm** is a sequence of instructions to perform a computation or solve a problem. The term algorithm includes simpler sets of rules as well as more advanced AI or machine learning code.

Big data

Definition

Big data refers to extremely large collections of data that may be analysed to reveal patterns, trends and associations.

Characteristics include **variety**, **volume**, **velocity**, **veracity** and **value (The 5Vs)**.

Benefits of effective data management	Risks associated with big data
• Fresh insight and understanding • Performance improvement • Market segmentation and customisation • Improved decision making • Innovation • Improved risk management	• Skills required not available • Data security • Time spent measuring relationships that have no value • Poor veracity leading to incorrect conclusions • Cost of analytics hardware and software • Technical difficulties integrating big data system and current system • Keeping abreast of system developments

Big data analytics

Data analytics is used to extract the value from big data.

Definition

Data analytics is the process of collecting, organising and analysing large sets of data to discover patterns and other information that an organisation can use for future decisions.

The volume of data as well as its importance is increasing and therefore it is important to make sense of this data.

Definition

Data visualisation allows large volumes of complex data to be displayed in a visually appealing and accessible way that facilitates the understanding and use of the underlying data.

Data analysis methods

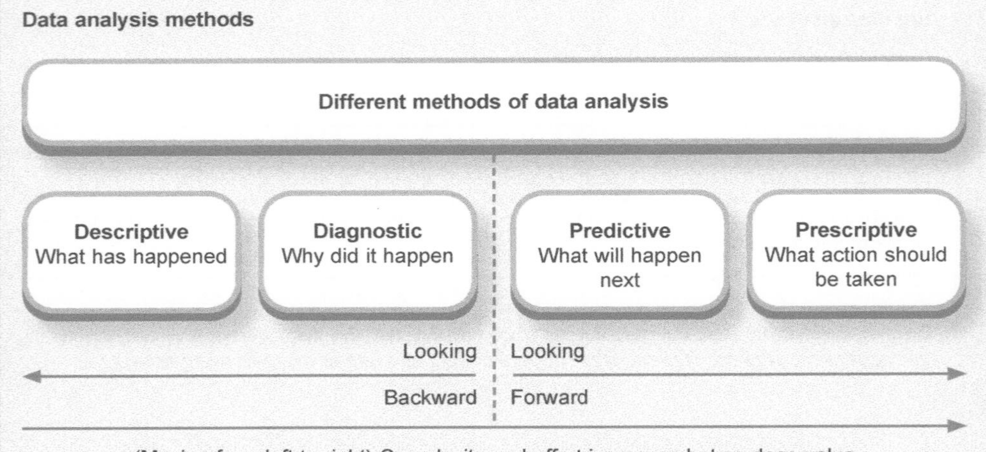

Tools for data analysis

A number of tools can be used for each of the respective methods of data analysis. For example, **descriptive analysis** may use **simple statistical tools** (e.g. percentages) and **visual tools** (e.g. graphs) where as **prescriptive analysis** may use **AI and machine learning algorithms**.

The following tools can be used for **predictive analysis**:

Definition

Linear regression is a statistical technique that attempts to identify factors that are associated with the change in the value of a key variable.

Definition

Regression analysis is a technique for estimating the line of best fit given a series of data.

Definition

A decision tree is a diagrammatic representation of a multi-decision problem, where all possible courses of action are represented, and every possible course of action is shown.

Definition

Sensitivity analysis considers the effect of changing one variable at a time. Simulation improves on this by looking at the impact of many variables changing at the same time.

Alternative methods of data analytics

The data analysis methods above will use data in a variety of structured and unstructured forms:

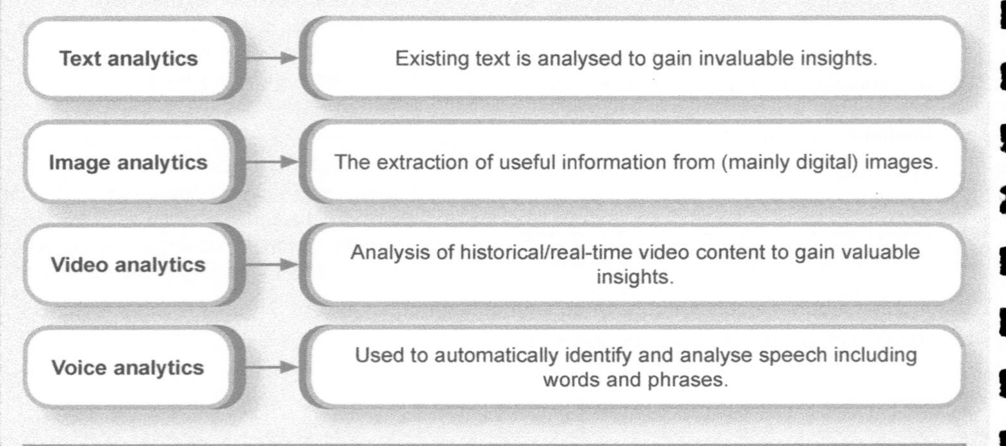

Definition

Sentiment analysis (also known as opinion mining) determines the emotional tone behind a series of written (text) or verbal (voice) words to understand attitudes, opinions and emotions.

Ethical issues associated with information collection and processing

The amount of personal data available to and used by organisations means that the privacy, sensitivity and security of this data are very significant considerations in modern business.

General Data Protection Regulation (GDPR) was introduced to address the growing significance of ethical information collection and processing. The legislation details a number of principles about data (for example, it should be used fairly, lawfully and transparently).

A **voluntary** commitment to corporate digital responsibility may also be used.

Definition

Corporate digital responsibility (CDR) is the application of CSR to the digital world and involves a commitment to protecting both customers and employees and ensuring that new technologies and data are used both productively and wisely.

The ethics of big data, AI and algorithms – Algorithms produce an outcome or answer that organisations and people may rely on for making a decision. However, most algorithms do not explain how they arrived at that answer. These are known as 'black box' algorithms.

Definition

One way to gain public trust is to use **explainable AI**. This generates an audit trail alongside the answer, showing the working of the algorithm and other supporting information, to explain how the answer or conclusion is arrived at. The information is available in a human-readable way, rather than being hidden in code.

The role of the management accountant in big data

Management accountants are well placed to provide organisations with the competencies needed to realise the value in the data.

1. **Data manager** – establishing metrics, working with data scientists to ensure the information is collected and used, reporting back to senior managers.
2. **Data scientist** – help meet the challenges of advanced data analytics. The management accountant will more often partner with data scientists.
3. **Data champion** – the management accountant can help cascade this influence from board level throughout the organisation.
4. **Finance business partner** – partner with business managers, IT professionals and data experts from across the organisation to support performance improvement through harnessing the value of big data.

Exam focus

Exam sitting	Area examined	Question number
Sept/Dec 2020	IT developments	2(b)
March 2020	IT developments	1(iii)

chapter

6

Performance reports for management

In this chapter

- Reports for performance management.
- Presentation techniques.
- Problems dealing with quantitative data.
- Problems dealing with qualitative data.

Exam focus

An important component of this good information will be the performance reports produced for management. The output reports produced from a management information system might include overall performance reports for managers or they may be more specific and tailored to the manager in question. Importantly, the performance reports need to be tailored to suit the needs of the users of those reports. The qualities of a good performance report are discussed in the first part of this chapter.

The chapter then moves on to discuss data visualisation. This was touched upon in Chapter 5 and is also relevant here since it can be used to present the information in the performance report in a user friendly and accessible way.

The final part of the chapter focuses on the types of information, firstly looking at the common mistakes and misconceptions that people make when using numerical data for performance measurement and then secondly the chapter discusses qualitative information. Qualitative information is highly subjective and hard to pin down and is therefore often ignored to the detriment of the quality of the performance report. However, although it is difficult to record and process data of a qualitative nature these factors still need to be considered when making a decision.

Reports for performance management

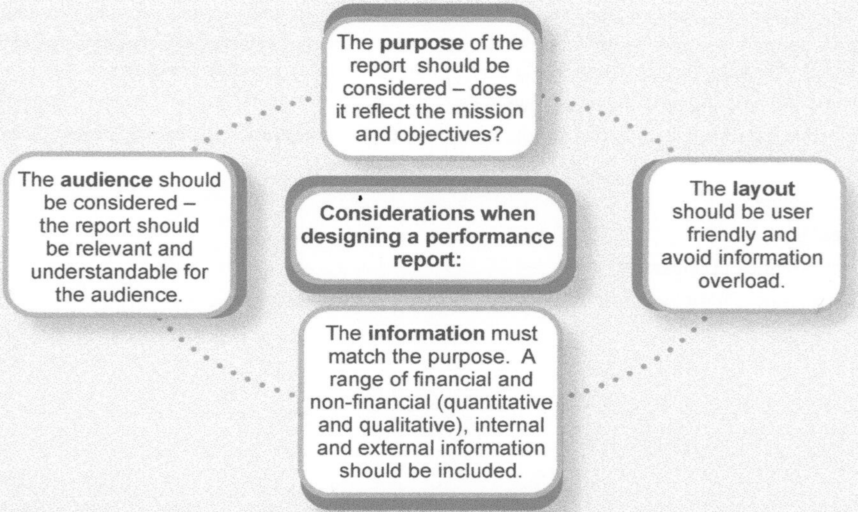

Considerations when designing a performance report:

- The **purpose** of the report should be considered – does it reflect the mission and objectives?
- The **audience** should be considered – the report should be relevant and understandable for the audience.
- The **layout** should be user friendly and avoid information overload.
- The **information** must match the purpose. A range of financial and non-financial (quantitative and qualitative), internal and external information should be included.

Note: Do not be constrained by this list. Ensure your points are relevant to the given scenario.

Presentation techniques

Definition

Data visualisation allows large volumes of complex data to be displayed in a visually appealing and accessible way that facilitates the understanding and use of the underlying data.

For example, a dashboard displaying live KPIs.

An effective data visualisation tool should consider **purpose, audience, information** and **layout.**

Benefits:

- Accessible
- Real time
- Performance optimisation
- Insight and understanding

Problems dealing with quantitative data

There are a number of common mistakes and misconceptions that people make when using numerical data for performance management:

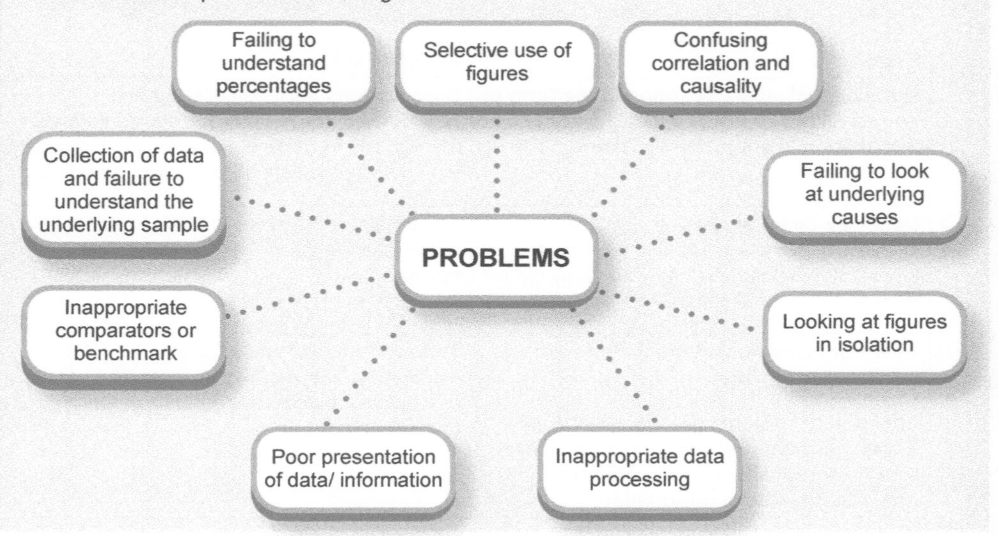

Problems dealing with qualitative data

Definition

Qualitative data is information that cannot normally be expressed in numerical terms.

Potential problem	Potential solution
Qualitative information is **often in the form of opinions**. This presents a problem since the **information is subjective in nature**.	Such opinions must be collected and co-ordinated into meaningful 'good' information, for example by looking at trends, transformation into quantitative data or using data analytics.
Data may be incomplete. Qualitative information gathered will often be from a sample of the population only and may not be representative of all employees' opinions.	The organisation needs to find a way to encourage the individual to provide their opinion.
A **lack of management familiarity** with qualitative information. **Information systems are often set up in a way** that adequately captures quantitative data but **are unable to generate the required qualitative information**.	This problem may be overcome using, for example, employee training, systems upgrades or additional checks and controls of the qualitative data.

Exam focus

Exam sitting	Area examined	Question number
Sept/Dec 2021	Performance reports	1(i)(ii)
	Quantitative and qualitative data	1(i)(ii)
Mar/June 2021	Performance reports	1(a)
March 2020	Performance reports	1(i)
Sept/Dec 2019	Performance reports	1(i)
	Quantitative and qualitative data	2(a)

chapter

7

Human resources aspects of performance management

In this chapter

- Introduction to human resource management (HRM).
- The purpose of reward systems.
- Methods of reward.
- Linking reward schemes to performance measurement.
- Management styles.

Exam focus

This chapter looks at the link between human resource management and performance measurement and considers the impact of the employee reward system on the behaviour of employees and on the performance of the organisation as a whole.

It also discusses the accountability issues that might arise from performance measurement systems.

It concludes by looking at how management style needs to be considered when designing an effective performance measurement system.

Introduction to human resource management (HRM)

Definition

HRM is the strategic and coherent approach to the management of an organisation's most valued assets: the people working there who individually and collectively contribute to the achievement of its objectives for sustainable competitive advantage.

HRM includes the recruitment, selection and induction of employees, the development of policies relating to human resources (e.g. reward systems), the management and development of employees (e.g. through training and development and through performance measurement and the appraisal system) and the termination of employees. In APM, the **focus is on performance measurement and reward practices**.

Today, employees are seen **less as an expensive necessity** and more as a **strategic resource** that may provide the organisation with **competitive advantage** and assist it in **achieving its mission and objectives**.

The purpose of reward systems

Definition

Reward schemes are the monetary, non-monetary and psychological payments an organisation provides for its employees in exchange for the work they perform.

A **key purpose** of reward systems is **to assist in the achievement of strategic objectives**. The reward system offered to employees should ideally include a method that is aligned with and motivates the employee to achieve the organisation's plan, objectives and mission since:

- **what gets measured, gets done**
- **what gets measured and fed back, gets done well and**
- **what gets rewarded, gets repeated.**

Other purposes include:

- To ensure the recruitment and retention of appropriately skilled and experienced staff.
- To provide a fair and consistent basis for rewarding employees.
- To motivate staff and maximise performance.
- To reward performance through promotion or progression.
- To control salary costs.
- To comply with legal requirements and ethical obligations.
- To ensure the employee's attitude to risk is aligned with that of the organisation.

Methods of reward

Method	Advantages	Disadvantages
Basic pay – the minimum amount the employee receives (e.g. per hour or year).	• Easy and cheap to administer. • Helps meet employee's basic needs. • Competitive rate helps attract and retain the best employees.	• No alignment to mission and strategic goals. • Does not motivate employees to improve performance.
Benefits – a wide range of rewards other than wages or pensions, such as company cars or health insurance.	• Can be tailored to the employee. • May be a cheaper method. • Tool to attract and retain the best employees. • Can compensate for lower amounts of other rewards.	• No alignment to mission and strategic goals. • Employees may not want the benefits offered. • May be costly to provide and/or difficult to administer.

Method	Advantages	Disadvantages
Executive share option schemes – gives (normally senior) employees the right to purchase shares at a specified exercise price after a specified time-period in the future.	• Should align management and shareholder interests. • A tool to attract and retain the best employees. • May encourage risk-averse directors to take positive action. • Can compensate for lower amounts of other rewards. • Can be a tax-efficient method.	• Can encourage risk-seeking behaviour. • It may give directors an incentive to manipulate share price. • Costly and time consuming to administer.
Performance-related pay - based on the level of performance achieved. Types include pay that is linked to individual performance, group performance or to profit and also the use of commission.	• Motivates employees to achieve strategy, if aligned to this. • Motivates employees to improve performance. • A tool to attract and retain the best employees. • Can compensate for lower amounts of other rewards.	• Can be subjective and inconsistent. • Can be viewed as unfair if based on team/company performance. • Can be stressful for employee if they rely on this pay for basic needs. • Can be complicated, costly and time consuming to administer.

Linking reward schemes to performance measurement

Part of the employee's reward (e.g. a bonus or pay increase) may be performance-related and linked to the achievement of pre-agreed objectives.

Appropriate **SMART** targets (performance measures) should be set for employees. The targets should be:

- Specific – i.e. not vague.
- Measurable – the achievement should be measurable.
- Attainable – i.e. not too difficult or impossible to achieve.
- Relevant – to the organisation's mission and objectives.
- Time-bound – i.e. should be achieved by a specified date.

In **addition to being SMART**, targets should be:

- controllable by the employee.
- a prioritised, small set.
- rewarded appropriately.

Benefits and problems of linking reward schemes to performance measurement

Benefits	Problems
• Makes it clear to all employees that employee performance creates organisational success. • This will benefit both the employee (motivated by the reward to work towards this success) and the employer (reward is given only if the organisation achieves its goals). • Targets that are SMART, controllable, small in number, prioritised and rewarded will be considered fair and consistent. • Effective schemes also attract and retain the employees valuable to an organisation. • Creates an organisation focused on continuous improvement ('what gets rewarded, gets repeated').	• Targets that are not SMART, are uncontrollable, large in number or not prioritised or rewarded, will be considered unfair and will not motivate employees. • Employees may become highly stressed if a significant proportion of their income is performance related. • Employees may prioritise the achievement of the reward, which can impact their risk appetite. • If the targets are not aligned to the organisation's overall objectives, employees will have an extra incentive towards dysfunctional behaviour. • It may be difficult to decide if targets should be based on individual, team, division or group performance.

Problems of poorly designed performance measurement systems

A poorly designed performance measurement systems can result in wrong signals and dysfunctional behaviour:

- Misrepresentation
- Gaming
- Sub-optimisation
- Misinterpretation
- Myopia
- Measure fixation
- Tunnel vision
- Ossification

Management styles

Hopwood identified three distinct management styles of performance appraisal. The style needs to be considered when designing an effective performance measurement system.

Management style	Advantages	Disadvantages
Budget constrained – manager's reward linked to achievement of short-term financial targets, for example ROCE used as a target.	• Should ensure short-term targets are met. • It may also motivate managers, who find it easier to focus on short-term targets.	• Short-termism. • Stress and difficult working relationships. • Lack of flexibility. • Stifles ingenuity. • Can result in manipulation of data.
Profit-conscious – manager's reward linked to achievement of long-term profitability, for example project NPV used as a target.	• Compared to budget constrained should result in a focus on long-term profitability, greater flexibility, less stress and better working relationships and less manipulation of data. • May motivate and help retain employees if rewards linked to achievement of long-term targets.	• Loss of short-term control could result in, for example, cash flow issues. • May ignore non-financial aspects such as ESG issues.

Non-accounting – Manager's reward linked primarily to achievement of the non-financial aspects that drive long-term performance. For example, employee satisfaction and productivity.	• Focus is on causes (such as customer satisfaction) rather than effects (profitability) which should lead to long-term success. • Compared to budget constrained should result in greater flexibility, less stress and better working relationships and less manipulation of data. • Meaningful targets may motivate and help attract/retain employees.	• Short and long-term financial implications of behaviour may be neglected.

Note: The potential for the **'manipulation'** of data is discussed above and in a number of subsequent chapters. In the exam, exercise caution when including this as part of your answer. Accounting data is not simple to manipulate; there are checks and balances and audit requirements in place. 'Manipulation', if it does exist, would more likely be in the form of the accounting method used or policy changes than fraud.

Exam focus

Exam sitting	Area examined	Question number
Sept/Dec 2021	Reward schemes	1(iv)
	Reward schemes	3(b)

chapter

8

Financial performance measures in the private sector

In this chapter

- Objective of a profit-seeking organisation.
- Financial performance measures.
- Short- and long-term financial performance.

Exam focus

In the exam, you may be required to look at performance measures in a variety of contexts. In this chapter, we focus on the principal measures used by the private sector. The emphasis will be on financial measures (non–financial measures will be reviewed in Chapter 11).

Objective of a profit-seeking organisation

Shareholders are the legal owners of the company.

Main objective of a business is to **maximise shareholder wealth**.

Financial performance measures

Introduction

- Financial performance measures are used to measure the performance of the whole organisation, its divisions (Chapter 9) and key projects.
- Financial performance can be assessed in terms of profitability, liquidity and risk.

Exam focus

- APM is all about a **critical approach**. It is about selecting from the range of indicators that you know from PM and using those that are most appropriate to the scenario.
- Indicators are **meaningless if calculated in isolation** but should be compared to, for example, a previous period or an appropriate benchmark (such as a competitor or to an industry average) or to any targets set.
- In addition to calculating the numbers, the examining team will expect you to give **performance management advice based on what you have calculated**.

Measuring profitability (whole organisation)

Profitability measure	Advantages	Disadvantages
Gross and operating profit (Can calculate as a margin)	• Information readily available. • Easy to compare between companies. • Widely understood. • Ignores uncontrollable figures.	• Poor correlation to shareholder wealth. • Can be distorted by accounting policies. • Operating profit less useful for highlighting product profitability issues.
ROCE (return on capital employed) = operating profit ÷ (capital employed) × 100	• Easy to calculate. • Figures readily available. • Measures how well a firm is utilising resources invested in it. • Often used by external investors/analysts.	• Poor correlation to shareholder wealth. • Differences between companies or accounting policies make comparisons less meaningful. • Possible dysfunctional behaviour.
EPS (earnings per share) = (PAT – preference dividends) ÷ weighted average number of ordinary shares	• Easy to calculate and widely understood. • Calculation precisely defined by accounting standards.	• Poor correlation to shareholder wealth. • Accounting treatment may distort measure.

EBITDA, i.e. earnings before interest, tax, depreciation and amortisation (and write-offs such as goodwill)	• A measure of underlying performance since it is a proxy for cash flow generated from operating profit. • Ignores tax and interest since these are externally generated and therefore not relevant to the underlying success of the business. • Ignores depreciation/ amortisation (a write off over several years. • Easily calculated and understood.	• Poor correlation to shareholder wealth. • Comparison between organisations difficult due to differences in accounting policies and the calculation of an absolute figure. • It can be easily manipulated. • Ignores changes to working capital or amount of non-current asset replacement needed.

Other profitability measures (whole organisation)

Can be used alongside main measures such as ROCE and include the following:

EVA, ROI and RI	Chapter 9
Asset turnover	$\frac{\text{Sales}}{\text{Capital employed}}$
Dividend cover	$\frac{\text{PAT}}{\text{Dividends paid during the year}}$
Dividend yield	$\frac{\text{Dividend per share}}{\text{Current share price}} \times 100\%$
P/E ratio	$\frac{\text{Share price}}{\text{EPS}}$
Earnings yield	$\frac{\text{EPS}}{\text{Share price}} \times 100\%$
Return on equity	$\frac{\text{Net profit after tax}}{\text{Average shareholder's equity}} \times 100\%$

Measuring profitability (key projects)

Profitability measure	Advantages	Disadvantages
NPV • Based on DCF analysis. • Looks at present value of cash inflows less present value of outflows of project. • Any project with a positive NPV is viable.	• Aligned to shareholder wealth. • Considers time value of money. • Can allow for risk. • Cash flows less subject to manipulation than profits. • Considers whole life of project.	• Difficult to calculate/ understand. • Absolute figure makes comparison difficult. • Based on a number of assumptions. • Challenging to use for target-setting (profit based measures still often used).
IRR • Discount rate when NPV = 0. • Accept project if IRR > firm's cost of capital.	• Provides alternative to NPV when cost of capital of project is uncertain. • Percentage aids comparison.	• Possible to get multiple rates of return. • More difficult to calculate and to understand than NPV.
MIRR • Represents the actual return generated by a project.	• Eliminates the problems associated with IRR. • As for IRR.	• More difficult to calculate and to understand than NPV.

Liquidity ratios

There is often a trade-off between liquidity and profitability. Liquidity needs to be considered alongside profitability to ensure the organisation can meet its short-term obligations.

Current ratio	$\frac{\text{Current assets}}{\text{Current liabilities}}$
Acid test (quick ratio)	$\frac{\text{Current assets} - \text{inventories}}{\text{Current liabilities}}$
Inventory period	$\frac{\text{Average value of Inventory}}{\text{Cost of sales}} \times 365$
Receivables period	$\frac{\text{Average receivables}}{\text{Sales revenue}} \times 365$
Payables period	$\frac{\text{Average payables}}{\text{Purchases}} \times 365$

Risk ratios

These ratios measure the ability of the company to meet its liabilities

Financial gearing A higher figure = higher financial risk - If profits fall the organisation is less able to finance its LTD (and pay preference dividends)	$\frac{\text{LTD + Preference share capital}}{\text{Shareholders' funds}} \times 100\%$ or $\frac{\text{LTD + Preference share capital}}{\text{LTD + Preference share capital + Shareholders' funds}} \times 100\%$
Operating gearing A higher figure = higher business risk - A fluctuation in sales volume might lead to falling profits as fixed costs are not covered.	$\frac{\text{Contribution}}{\text{PBIT}}$
Interest cover A low interest cover indicates the company may have difficulty financing its debts if profits fall.	$\frac{\text{PBIT}}{\text{Interest charges}}$

Note: LTD = Long-term debt

Short- and long-term financial performance

Short-term financial performance measures are used for:	BUT a focus on short-term financial performance can damage shareholder wealth, for example:	Therefore, need steps to reduce short-termism, for example:
• control purposes, for example variance analysis • determining rewards • assessing the quality of past decisions and the impact of decisions yet to be made.	• investment in new assets is cut • investment in training and development is cut.	• use a range of financial and non-financial measures • switch from a budget-constrained style • give managers share options or link bonuses to long-term performance • use long-term measures such as NPV and IRR • use VBM • reduced decentralisation.

Exam focus

Exam sitting	Area examined	Question number
Sept/Dec 2021	Assessing financial performance	1(iii)

chapter

9

Divisional performance appraisal and transfer pricing

In this chapter

- Problems associated with divisional structures.
- Structuring divisions as responsibility centres.
- ROI.
- RI.
- EVA.
- Value-based management.
- Transfer pricing.

Exam focus

Business structure (including divisional structures) was covered in Chapter 4. A feature of modern business management is the practice of splitting a business into semi-autonomous units with devolved authority and responsibility. Such units could be described as divisions, subsidiaries or strategic business units (SBUs) but the principles are the same.

This chapter will review some of the methods available for appraising divisional performance. Before looking at these methods, the problems associated with divisional structures, the concept of responsibility accounting and the types of responsibility centre, will be reviewed.

The chapter then covers the value-based management approach to performance management and how this might help to address some of the issues of short-termism already discussed.

The chapter concludes with a discussion of transfer pricing, focusing on why a transfer price may be needed and considerations when setting a transfer price.

Problems associated with divisional structures

Problems:

- **Controllability** - divisional managers should only be held responsible for what they can control **(responsibility accounting)**
- **Co-ordination** of units to achieve overall objectives
- **Dysfunctional behaviour** and **sub-optimal decisions**
- **Interdependence** - the performance of one unit may depend to some extent on others
- Whether/how **head office costs** should be **re-apportioned**
- How **transfer prices should be set**

Structuring divisions as responsibility centres

A manager should only be held accountable and assessed on aspects of performance they control.

Types of responsibility centre

Cost centre

Division incurs costs but has no revenue stream.

Measures:

- Costs, e.g. cost ratios and variances
- Relevant non-financial measures, e.g. for productivity or efficiency.

Profit centre

Division has both costs and revenues but does not have the authority to make investment decisions.

Measures:

- Costs, revenues and profit, e.g. profitability ratios and cost/sales variances
- Relevant non-financial measures, e.g. based on customer satisfaction.

Investment centre

Division has both costs and revenues but in addition has authority to make investment decisions.

Measures:

As profit centre PLUS

- Return on investment (ROI)
- Residual income (RI)
- Economic value added (EVA).

ROI

- Divisional equivalent of ROCE.

ROI = (controllable operating profit ÷ controllable capital employed) × 100

- **Decision rule:** If ROI > target cost of capital then accept divisional project or appraise division as performing favourably.
- The **advantages and disadvantages** are as for ROCE. Two of the disadvantages, i.e. dysfunctional behaviour and a tendency to hold onto old assets are key drivers for one of the alternative measures (RI or EVA) being used.

RI

Residual income (RI)	Advantages	Disadvantages
Controllable operating profit X **less: imputed interest** X **RI** X • Imputed interest = controllable capital employed x cost of capital. • **Decision**: accept the project, if the RI is positive.	• Reduces the problems of ROI, i.e. dysfunctional behaviour and holding on to old assets. • Easy decision rule. • Highlights cost of financing a division. • Different cost of capitals can be applied to different divisions based on their risk profiles.	• It does not always result in decisions that are in the best interests of the company (EVA is a superior measure). • Absolute figure does not facilitate comparison. • Different accounting policies can confuse comparisons. • It is difficult to decide upon an appropriate cost of capital. • May encourage manipulation of profit and capital employed.

EVA

Economic value added (EVA)	Advantages	Disadvantages
NOPAT X **Adjusted value of capital employed at start of year × WACC** (X) **EVA** X • A similar but superior measure to RI. • **Decision:** accept the project if the EVA is positive.	• EVA is consistant with NPV and should create real wealth for shareholders. • The adjustments made avoid distortion by accounting policies and should therefore result in goal congruent decisions. • Emphasises cost of financing to division's manager. • Long-term value-adding expenditure can be capitalised, removing any incentive for managers to take a short-term view. • Easy decision rule.	• Requires numerous adjustments to profit and capital employed figures. • Its complexity may be poorly understood by managers who as a result are less likely to achieve EVA targets. • Some of the adjustments (e.g. economic depreciation) may be difficult to measure. • Many assumptions made when calculating WACC. • Absolute measure (as is RI) so divisional comparisons difficult. • Based on historical data where as shareholders are interested in future performance.

How to calculate EVA

NOPAT

Controllable operating profit	X
Add:	
accounting depreciation	X
increase in provisions	X
non-cash expenses	X
advertising, r&d, employee training	X
Deduct:	
economic depreciation	(X)
decrease in provisions	(X)
amortisation of advertising, r&d and employee training	(X)
tax paid including lost tax relief on interest	(X)
NOPAT	X

Adjusted value of capital employed at the beginning of the year

	$
Capital employed at beginning of year	X
Adjust to reflect replacement cost of assets	X/(X)
Adjust to reflect economic and not accounting depreciation	X/(X)
Add back value of provisions in the year	X
Add back non-cash expenses in the previous year	X
Add NBV of advertising, R&D and employee training at end of previous year	X
Adjusted value of capital employed at beginning of year	X

WACC

WACC = (proportion of equity x cost of equity) + (proportion of debt x post tax cost of debt).

Value-based management (VBM)

Definition

VBM is an approach to management whereby the company's strategy, objectives, culture and processes are aligned to help the company focus on **key drivers of shareholder wealth** and hence maximise this value.

- VBM takes the **interests of its shareholders as its primary focus**.
- It begins with the view that the **value of a company** (and hence shareholder wealth) is the **total value of its discounted cash flows.**
- To measure performance under VBM a **single overall organisational metric** is established, **such as EVA, market value added (MVA)** or **shareholder value added (SVA).**
- Then **value drivers are identified.** These are activities linked to long-term shareholder value that:
  - managers can influence and control
  - cascade throughout all levels of the organisation and across all divisions
  - link to staff/manager objectives
  - cover financial and non-financial areas of performance.

Implementing VBM

1. **Strategy developed** to maximise shareholder value, measured using a single overall organisational metric. Value drivers defined.
2. **Performance targets created** for value drivers.
3. **Operational plans** – targets are assigned to specific employees and specific operational plans are defined.
4. **Performance measures and rewards** (aligned to these targets) are created for all levels of staff.

VBM evaluation

Advantages	Disadvantages
• Focus on value (not profit) and therefore takes the interests of shareholders as its primary focus. • Is long-term and forward-looking. • Value drivers are established and aligned at all levels of the organisation and across all divisions. • Controllable targets created and assigned to specific employees. • Specific plans are created to help the employee achieve these targets. • Performance metrics (financial and non-financial) are created that are compatible with these targets and that motivate employees.	• Requires a cultural shift (and perhaps training). • Shareholders may need to be educated to understand VBM. • Requires a change adept organisational culture plus commitment and leadership from the board. • It may be difficult to identify value drivers. • May need to adapt MIS to take account of new measures. • Can become an exercise in valuing everything and changing nothing.

Note: Since EVA and NPV are two of the key measures used in VBM, the advantages and disadvantages of these will also be relevant here.

Transfer pricing

Definition

The transfer price is the price at which goods and services are transferred from one division to another in the same organisation.

Characteristics of a good transfer price:

- Goal congruence
- Fair for divisions
- Autonomy for divisions
- Assists bookkeeping
- Minimises global tax liability
- Considers spare capacity

General rules for setting transfer prices

Perfect competition in market for intermediate product

- Transfer at market price.
- Include any small adjustments, e.g. savings on delivery.

Surplus capacity

- Minimum price selling division will accept = marginal cost.
- Maximum price the buying division will pay is the lower of the external purchase price (if available) and the net marginal revenue.

Production constraints

- Minimum price selling division will accept = marginal cost + lost contribution from other product.
- Maximum price the buying division will pay is the lower of the external purchase price (if available) and the net marginal revenue.

Note:

- The selling division will want to cover some/all of the **fixed costs** and recognise a **% profit** whereas the buying division will want to pay the minimum amount acceptable to the selling division.
- When using the cost, the **standard cost** should be used rather than the actual cost to aid planning and prevent inefficiencies being passed on to the buying division.

Issue (fairness)

- Selling division wants to use total cost to ensure recover fixed overheads and would prefer to recognise a % profit.
- Buying division will not want to be charged for fixed costs or a % profit.

Solutions

- **Two part tariff** – Transfer price is marginal cost/unit (favoured by buying division) + periodic lump sum to cover fixed costs (thus keeps the selling division happy).
- **Dual pricing** – The buying and selling division recognise two different transfer prices. This will be perceived as fair by both divisions but the problem with this is that a period end adjustment to the accounts will be needed.

International issues

Two issues

Transfer pricing and taxation

- Buying and selling division may be based in different countries.
- They may try to increase profits by adjusting transfer price to take advantage of different tax rates in each country.
- Tax authorities will not allow. They can alter the transfer price and can **treat the transactions as having taken place at a fair arm's length price** and revise profits accordingly.

Remittance controls

A country's government may impose restrictions on the transfer of profits from domestic subsidiaries to foreign multinationals.

Exam focus

Exam sitting	Area examined	Question number
Mar 2020	Divisional performance including ROI, RI and EVA	2(b)
	VBM	2(a)
Sept/Dec 2019	Divisional performance including ROI, RI and EVA	1(ii)

chapter

10

Performance management in not-for-profit organisations

In this chapter

- What is a not-for-profit organisation?
- Problems associated with performance management.
- Measuring public sector performance using value for money (VFM).
- The use of benchmarking (league tables) and targets in the public sector.

Exam focus

You need to be able to discuss the issues which affect not-for-profit organisations and the implications of these for performance management.

What is a not-for-profit organisation?

Not-for-profit (NFP) organisations exist in:

Private sector

For example, charities, sports clubs.

Public sector

For example, healthcare, defence.

- Their **objective is not the maximisation of shareholder wealth**.
- Instead, it is to **maximise the benefit to beneficiaries**.

Problems associated with performance management

Problem	Possible solution
Non-quantifiable costs and benefits (in monetary terms)	• Cost benefit analysis (CBA), i.e. try to quantify in monetary terms all of the costs and benefits associated with a decision. • Assess **value for money (VFM)**.
Assessing the use of funds Many NFP organisations (particularly public sector organisations) do not generate revenue; rather funds are invested in them (by government for public sector organisations). Need to assess if these funds are being put to the best use but this can be difficult.	An assessment of the use of funds can be carried out using a **VFM** framework.

Problem	Possible solution
Potential conflict due to multiple and diverse objectives NFP organisations do not have an objective of maximisation of shareholder wealth. Instead, they are seeking to satisfy the needs of a range of stakeholders. Multiple stakeholders give rise to multiple and diverse objectives and these objectives may conflict.	• **Prioritise** the objectives of the organisation. • Make **compromises** so that the needs of all stakeholders are taken into account to a greater or lesser degree. • Achievement of the established set of objectives can be measured using a **VFM** framework.
Impact of politics Public scrutiny of some sectors, such as health and education, make them a prime target for political interference.	• Difficult – need to encourage politicians to have a long-term focus. • League tables and targets are commonly used in the public sector as a method of managing and measuring performance.

Measuring public sector performance using value for money (VFM)

NFPIs in NFP organisations

A key component in assessing VFM is the use of non-financial performance indicators (NFPIs).

Financial performance measurement remains important to NFP organisations. However, NFPIs are particularly important for measuring performance in NFP organisations due to the following reasons:

- NFP organisations do not have the underlying financial objective to maximise profit in order to maximise shareholder wealth, making financial indicators of performance less relevant.
- Many NFP organisations do not have a revenue stream and it can be difficult to define a cost unit or to quantify the benefits. This makes traditional financial indicators less relevant or easy to use.
- Many NFP organisations have numerous stakeholders with multiple and often diverse objectives. Many of these objectives are non-financial in nature and therefore NFPIs are required to measure performance.
- Financial objectives are less relevant in NFP organisations. NFPIs are more relevant for measuring the achievement of the objectives of NFP organisations and capturing aspects of the organisation's mission that are fundamentally non-financial and subjective.

Assessing value for money using the 3 Es

Economy	Efficiency	Effectiveness
Are the appropriate quantity and quality of resources (inputs) bought at the lowest cost possible?	How well are the inputs (resources used) converted into outputs? This means optimising the process by which inputs are turned into outputs to maximise the output generated from the units of resource used.	How well do these outputs (actual results) help achieve the stated objectives of the organisation?

- Appropriate (financial and non-financial) **performance indicators** should be chosen for each E.
- **Comparison** should be made internally to historic performance and perhaps benchmarked against suitable external organisations.
- The aim of VFM is to achieve an appropriate balance between the 3 Es but this can often be difficult to achieve and **conflict** may arise.
- Sometimes a **fourth 'E', equity**, is included.

The use of benchmarking (league tables) and targets in the public sector

Benchmarking and league tables

Benchmarking is undertaken by many public sector organisations. The **results from a benchmarking** exercise can be used to **rank organisations in a league table**.

Advantages	Disadvantages
• Stimulates competition and the adoption of best practice. • Monitors and ensures accountability. • Performance is transparent. • Allow consumers to make choices. • Many different areas of performance summarised into one weighted average score.	• Dysfunctional behaviour if targets not aligned to mission. • Only measures relative performance. • Differences between organisations make comparisons and accountability difficult. • What areas/weightings to use in the scoring system to arrive at the ranking? • The quality of information output dependent on quality of data input. • Poor ranking impacts employee morale and public trust and can result in worsening future performance. • Can become measuring rather than learning exercise. • Measures chosen may be based on what is practical and not meaningful. • Costly and time consuming. • May encourage creative reporting

Targets

Benefits	Issues
Targets should improve: • efficiency, effectiveness and economy • accountability and transparency • responsiveness to stakeholders and • employee motivation, if linked to reward.	• Central control • Difficulty level • All or nothing • Too many targets • Targets not always appropriate • Cost • Lack of ownership of targets • Gaming • Conflict

Exam focus

Exam sitting	Area examined	Question number
Sept/Dec 2020	Performance management in NFPOs	1(ii)
	Benchmarking (league tables) and targets	1(iii)

chapter

11

Non-financial performance indicators

In this chapter

- Introduction to non-financial performance indicators (NFPIs).
- The balanced scorecard.
- Fitzgerald and Moon's Building Block model.
- The performance pyramid.

Exam focus

In Chapters 8 and 9 we looked at a wide range of financial performance measures. In order to fully appraise the performance of an organisation, and to understand if the best techniques are being used to drive its success, it is useful to use a range of financial performance indicators (FPIs) and non-financial performance indicators (NFPIs).

Introduction to non-financial performance indicators (NFPIs)

Limitations of financial performance indicators

- Short-termism
- Internal focus
- Do not convey the whole picture
- Backward looking
- Manipulation of results

Solution – use NFPIs and FPIs

In order to overcome these issues the following should be used to assess performance:

- **FPIs** (these reveal the results of actions already taken) and
- Non-financial performance indicators (**NFPIs**) (reflect the long-term viability and health of the organisation and will drive future financial performance).

NFPIs and business performance

NFPIs play a key role in a number of areas.

Management of human resources (HR)	Product and service quality	Brand awareness and company profile
• Recruitment and selection – time to fill a position. • Training and development – training feedback. • Motivation – employee satisfaction scores. • Reward systems – adherence to laws and regulations.	• The quality of incoming supplies. • The quality of work completed. • Customer satisfaction.	• Customer awareness. • Customer opinions.

The balanced scorecard

Allows managers to look at the business from four important perspectives.

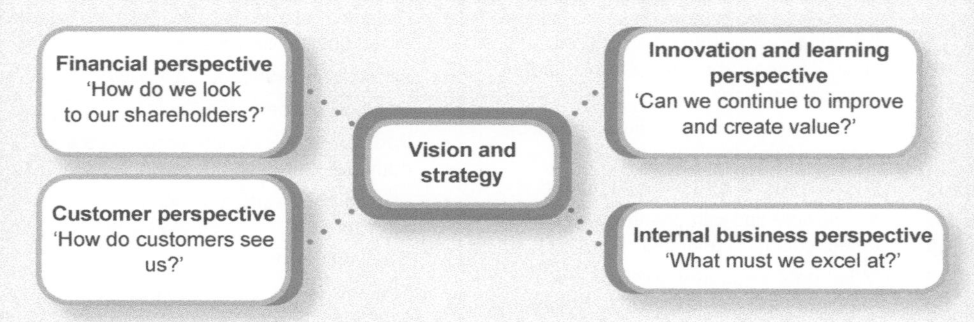

Within each perspective the organisation should **identify a series of goals (CSFs)** and **establish appropriate measures (KPIs)** in line with the overall vision and strategy.

Evaluation of the balanced scorecard as a performance measurement tool

Advantages of balanced scorecard	Disadvantages of balanced scorecard
• Includes financial measures – these reveal the results of actions taken and non-financial measures – these drive future financial performance. • Distorting performance harder if multiple measures used. • Covers internal and external matters. • It is flexible and can change over time to reflect changing priorities. • 'What gets measured gets done' so managers will pay attention to the various aspects of performance that they know they are being appraised on. • Links achievement of long-term and short-term objectives to achievement of strategy and vision.	• Difficult to record and process non-financial (often qualitative) data. • Information overload. • Conflict between measures. • Poor communication to employees and manager threatens success. • Lack of commitment by senior management. • Time/cost involved. • The lack of some key perspectives, for example ESG. • Measures chosen many not align with strategy/vision. • Focuses on strategic level.

Implementing the balanced scorecard

Make the strategy explicit

- Strategy forms the basis of the scorecard.
- May involve strategy mapping.

Choose the measures

- Align measures with strategy.
- Relationships between measures must be clearly understood.

Define and refine

- Put performance measures into place.
- Scorecard becomes the language of the company.

Deal with people

- People and change must be properly managed.
- Rewards aligned to achieve targets.

Fitzgerald and Moon's Building Block model

What is the Building Block model?

A performance measurement system for the service sector based on three building blocks

DIMENSIONS

6 dimensions (CSFs)

Downstream results:

1 Financial performance

2 Competitiveness

Upstream determinants:

3 Quality of service

4 Flexibility

5 Resource utilisation

6 Innovation

Need suitable metrics (**KPIs**).

STANDARDS

These are the targets set for the metrics (KPIs) chosen.

Standards should have three characteristics:

1 **Ownership.**

2 **Achievability.**

3 **Fairness.**

REWARDS

The model makes a link between the achievement of corporate strategy and the management of HR.

To ensure **employees are motivated to meet the standards,** the standards need to be:

1 **Clear** (SMART, prioritised, not too many)

2 Linked to **controllable** factors

and the reward should be desirable.

<table>
<tr><th>Advantages of building block model</th><th>Disadvantages of building block model</th></tr>
<tr><td>The first five advantages discussed for the balanced scorecard are relevant. In addition:
• It differentiates between downstream results and upstream determinants.
• Tailored for service industry.
• Targets are set in such a way to engage and motivate staff, i.e. due to ownership, achievability and fairness.
• Reward system should optimally motivate staff due to it being clear and linked to controllable factors.</td><td>The first seven disadvantages discussed for the balanced scorecard are relevant. In addition:
• It is less suitable for non-service companies.
• Difficult to see how building blocks link to strategic objectives and mission/vision since there is no explicit link to this.</td></tr>
</table>

The performance pyramid

What is the performance pyramid?

- Defines the links between objectives and performance measures at different levels in the organisation.
- Designed to ensure that activities of every department, system and business unit support the overall organisational vision.

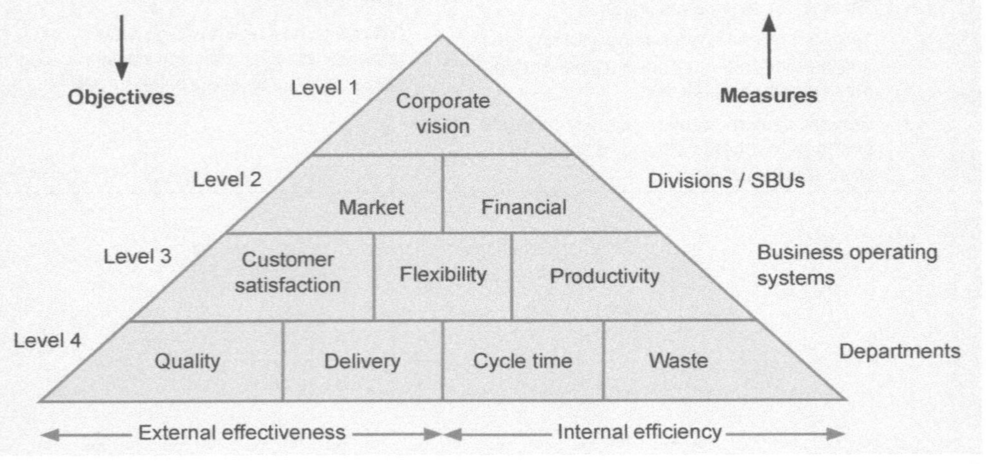

Evaluation of the performance pyramid as a way to link strategy, operations and performance

Advantages of performance pyramid	Disadvantages of performance pyramid
The first five advantages discussed for the balanced scorecard are relevant. In addition: • It is hierarchical requiring senior managers to set objectives and relevant performance measures for each level of the organisation. • It is process focused considering how processes combine to achieve organisational goals. Considers the interaction of measures both horizontally and vertically. • Recognises that financial and non-financial measures can support each other.	The first six disadvantages discussed for the balanced scorecard are relevant. In addition: • The model is quite complicated making the time and resources required significant.

Exam focus

Exam sitting	Area examined	Question number
Sept/Dec 2021	Building Block model	3(b)
Mar/June 2021	Performance pyramid	2
Sept/Dec 2019	Balanced scorecard	2(b)

chapter

12

The role of quality in performance measurement

In this chapter

- What is quality?
- Six sigma.
- Kaizen costing.
- Total quality management (TQM).
- Just-in-time.
- Lean production.

Exam focus

In today's competitive global business environment, quality is one of the key ways in which a business can differentiate its product or service, improve performance and gain competitive advantage. Quality can form a key part of strategy.

What is quality?

Quality is one of the key ways in which a business can differentiate its product or service, improve performance and gain competitive advantage. It can form a key part of strategy and can be defined in a number of ways.

Definition

Quality can be defined in a number of ways:

- Is the product/service free from errors and does it adhere to design specifications?
- Is the product/service fit for use?
- Does the product/service meet customers' needs?

Definition

A **quality management system** is a set of co-ordinated activities to direct and control an organisation. These quality management activities should be aligned to the organisation's quality objectives and complement the organisation's strategy.

Quality-related costs

Monitoring the costs of quality is key to the operation of any quality improvement programme.

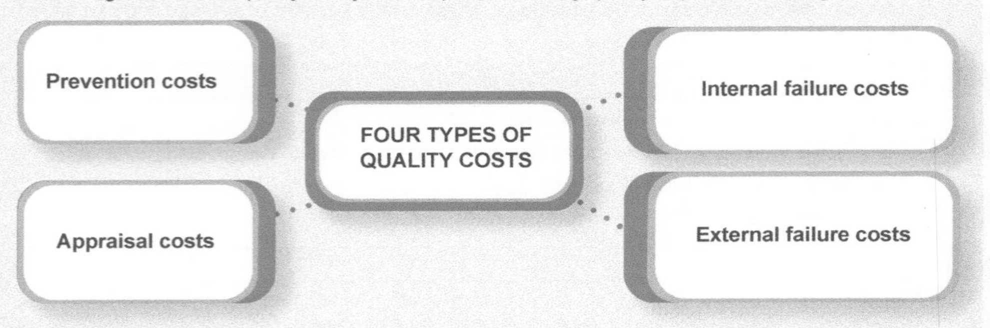

The organisation's costing system should be capable of identifying and collecting these costs.

KPIs should be developed based on the costs of quality and these can be used as a basis for staff rewards.

Six sigma

Aims to reduce the number of faults that go beyond an accepted tolerance level of 3.4 defects per 1 million units produced.

Step 1: **D**efine the process

Step 2: **M**easure existing problems

Step 3: **A**nalyse the process

Step 4: **I**mprove the process

Step 5: **C**ontrol the process

Kaizen costing

Definition

Kaizen costing focuses on producing small, incremental cost reductions throughout the production process through the product's life.

Steps:

1 During the design phase, a target cost is set for each production function.

2 The target costs are totalled to give a baseline target cost for the product's first year of production.

3 As the process improves, cost reductions reduce the baseline cost.

4 Cost reduction targets are set on a regular basis and variance analysis is carried out.

A traditional costing system is inappropriate in a Kaizen environment.

Target costing is an important part of Kaizen costing. It involves setting a target cost by subtracting a desired profit from a competitive market price.

Step 1
A competitive market price is set based on what customers are willing to pay and how much competitors are charging for similar products.

Step 2
The desired profit margin is deducted from this price to arrive at a target cost.

Step 3
The difference between the estimated cost of the product and the target cost is the cost gap.

Step 4
Techniques are used to close the gap. Many of these will be employed at the design stage. The focus should be on features that do not add value (value analysis).

Kaizen costing uses the principles of target costing but it is the process of long-term continuous improvements by small, incremental cost reductions throughout the product's life.

Total quality management (TQM)

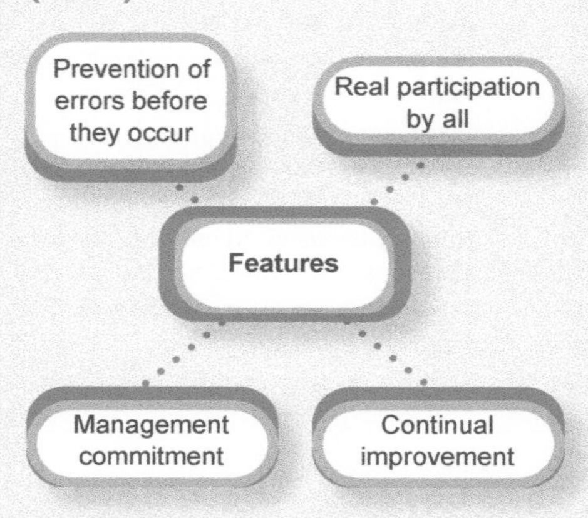

Performance measures should be linked to the programme's CSFs.

Just-in-time

Definition

Just-in-time (JIT) is a system whose objective is to produce or procure products or components as they are required rather than for inventory.

Requirements:

- High quality and reliability.
- Elimination of non-value added activities.
- Speed of throughput to match demand.
- Flexibility.
- Lower costs.

Traditional performance measures such as inventory turnover will be replaced with more appropriate measures, such as total head count and productivity.

Lean production

Definition

Lean production is a philosophy of management based on cutting out waste and unnecessary activities including:

- Over-production
- Inventory
- Waiting
- Defective units
- Motion
- Transportation
- Over-processing

Characteristics of lean production:

- Production in smaller batches leading to quick set up and flexibility.
- HR focuses on empowering staff, giving them a career path and job for life.
- Employees trained in all aspects resulting in flexibility and problem solving.
- Supplier expertise harnessed, fair price agreed and JIT operated.
- Customer flexibility delivered and feedback is valued.

The 5 **Ss** concept is often associated with lean principles and has the aim of creating a workplace which is in order.

5 Ss	Explanation
Structurise	Introduce order where possible.
Systemise	Arrange and identify items for ease of use and systematic approach.
Sanitise	Be tidy, avoid clutter.
Standardise	Find the best approach and then be consistent in using it.
Self-discipline	Do above daily.

Exam focus

Exam sitting	Area examined	Question number
Mar 2020	Costs of quality	3(b)
	Quality practices	3(a)
Mar/June 2019	Costs of quality	1(c)
	Quality practices	1(b)

Index

D

E

F

G

H

I

J

P

Q

R

S

T

U

V

W

Z

MID WALES & SHROPSHIRE

Seiclo yng nghan ol barth Cymru a swydd amwythig

Published by Collins
An imprint of HarperCollins*Publishers*
77–85 Fulham Palace Road
London W6 8JB

www.collins.co.uk
www.bartholomewmaps.com

First published 2002

Routes compiled by the following:
CTC Cymru, CTC Shropshire & Mid Wales DA, Claire Ashton, Martin Beardwell,
Annie Benyon, Chris Buck, Jeff Burton, Bill Dorrell, Helen Gilmour, Dave Hill,
John and Jenny Leese, Graham Mills, Neville and Mary Roberts, Colin Venus.

Design by Creative Matters Design Consultancy, Glasgow.
Typeset by Bob Vickers.

Photographs reproduced by kind permission of the following:
Bill Meadows Picture Library pages 5, 8, 21, 32, 37, 41, 45, 57, 61, 95, 115;
Wales Tourist Board Photo Library pages 11, 19, 26, 53, 65, 68, 70, 75, 78, 83, 85, 88, 90, 109, 111.

The Publishers welcome comments from readers. Please address your letters to:
Collins Cycling Guides, HarperCollins Cartographic, HarperCollins Publishers,
Westerhill Road, Bishopbriggs, Glasgow, G64 2QT or email cycling@harpercollins.co.uk

Printed in Thailand

ISBN 0 00 712392 2
02/1/12

CONTENTS

KEY TO ROUTES

Distances have been rounded up or down to the nearest 0.5km (mile).

Route colour coding

undemanding rides compiled specifically with families in mind
16–32km (10–20 miles)

middle distance rides suitable for all cyclists
32–48km (20–30 miles)

half-day rides for the more experienced and adventurous cyclist
48–64km (30–40 miles)

challenging full-day rides
over 64km (over 40 miles)

grande randonnée – a grand cycling tour
over 100km (60 miles)

Routes marked with this symbol are off-road or have off-road sections
(includes well-surfaced cycleways as well as rougher off-road tracks)

On the Long Mynd

LOCATION MAP

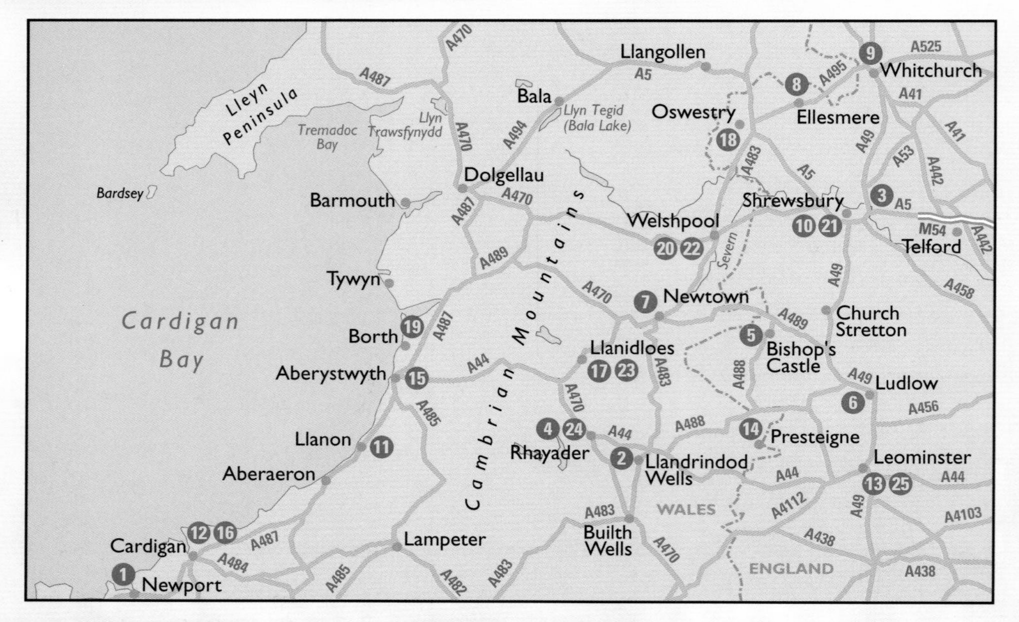

KEY TO ROUTE MAPS

M23 Service area	Motorway		Cycle route / optional route		Telephone
A259	'A' road / Dual carriageway		Start of cycle route		Picnic site
B2130	'B' road / Dual carriageway	12	Route direction		Camping site
	Good minor road	B	Place of interest		Public toilets
	Minor road		Public house		Place of worship
	Track / bridleway		Café / refreshments		Viewpoint
	Railway / station		Restaurant		Golf course
	Canal / river / lake		Convenience store		Tumulus
	Ferry route	i	Tourist Information Centre		Urban area
50	Contour (height in metres)	P	Parking		Woodland

Height above sea level

50	100	150	200	300	400	500	600	700	800	900 metres
165	330	490	655	985	1315	1645	1975	2305	2635	2965 feet

INTRODUCTION

How to use this guide

Collins' *Cycling in Mid Wales & Shropshire* has been devised for those who want trips out on their bicycles along quiet roads and tracks, passing interesting places and convenient refreshment stops without having to devise their own routes. Each of the 25 routes in this book has been compiled and ridden by an experienced cyclist for cyclists of all abilities.

Cycling in Mid Wales & Shropshire is easy to use. Routes range from undemanding rides compiled specifically with families in mind to challenging full-day rides; the type of route is easily identified by colour coding (see page 5). At the start of each route an information box summarises: total distance (in kilometres/miles – distances have been rounded up or down throughout to the nearest 0.5km/mile and are approximate only); grade (easy, moderate or strenuous based on distance and difficulty); terrain; an average time to allow for the route; directions to the start of the route by car and, if appropriate, by train.

Each route is fully mapped and has concise, easy-to-follow directions. Comprehensive information on places of interest and convenient refreshment stops along each route are also given. Accumulated mileages within each route description give an indication of progress, while the profile diagram is a graphic representation of gradients along the route. These should be used as a guide only.

The following abbreviations are used in the route directions:

LHF	left hand fork
RHF	right hand fork
LHS	left hand side
RHS	right hand side
SO	straight on
SP	signpost
TJ	T junction
TL	turn left
TR	turn right
XR	crossroads

Cycling in Mid Wales & Shropshire

The routes are designed to stay away from busy main roads as much as possible, to allow cyclists to discover peaceful back lanes and cycleways, passing all manner of museums, castles and other attractions.

Shropshire, bordered to the south and west by hills and areas of moorland, is the former heart of the Marches of Wales and there are still the remains of many border defences. Herefordshire, to the south, is mainly rural and the orchards make a wonderful sight in spring. The routes also take in Powys and Ceredigion in mid Wales – mountainous terrain and 80.5km (50 miles) of coastline.

Sections of the National Cycle Network are used. This is being developed by the charity Sustrans with the help of a £43.5 million grant from the Millennium Commission. The cycle network runs through towns and cities and links urban areas with the countryside. For information write to Sustrans, 35 King Street, Bristol, BSA 4DZ, telephone (0117) 926 8893, or visit their web site at www.sustrans.org.uk

Some of the routes are hilly with steep and undulating sections to be tackled along the way. However, this is compensated for by the spectacular views – and you can always get off and push your bike!

Preparing for a cycling trip

Basic maintenance

A cycle ride is an immense pleasure, particularly on a warm sunny day. Nothing is better than coasting along a country lane gazing over the countryside. Unfortunately, not every cycling day is as perfect as this, and it is important to make sure that your bike is in good order and that you are taking the necessary clothing and supplies with you.

Before you go out on your bicycle check that everything is in order. Pump the tyres up if needed, and check that the brakes are working properly and that nothing is loose – the brakes are the only means of stopping quickly and safely. If there is a problem and you are not sure that you can fix it, take the bike to a cycle repair shop – they can often deal with small repairs very quickly.

When you go out cycling it is important to take either a puncture repair kit or a spare inner tube – it is often quicker to replace the inner

Eardisland

tube in the event of a puncture, though it may be a good idea to practise first. You also need a pump, and with a slow puncture the pump may be enough to get you home. To remove the tyre you need a set of tyre levers. Other basic tools are an Allen key and a spanner. Some wheels on modern bikes can be removed by quick release levers built into the bike. Take a lock for your bike and if you have to leave it at any time, leave it in public view and locked through the frame and front wheel to something secure.

What to wear and take with you

It is not necessary to buy specialised cycling clothes. If it is not warm enough to wear shorts wear trousers which are easy to move in but fairly close to the leg below the knee – leggings are ideal – as this stops the trousers catching the chain. If you haven't got narrow-legged trousers, bicycle clips will hold them in. Jeans are not a good idea as they are rather tight and difficult to cycle in, and if they get wet they take a long time to dry. If your shorts or trousers are thin you might get a bit sore from being too long on the saddle. This problem can be reduced by using a gel saddle, and by wearing thicker, or extra, pants. Once you are a committed cyclist you can buy cycling shorts; or undershorts which have a protective pad built in and which can be worn under anything. It is a good idea to wear several thin layers of clothes so that you can add or remove layers as necessary. A zip-fronted top gives easy temperature control. Make sure you have something warm and something waterproof.

If you wear shoes with a firm, flat sole you will be able to exert pressure on the pedals easily, and will have less work to do to make the bicycle move. Gloves not only keep your hands warm but protect them in the event that you come off, and cycling mittens which cushion your hands are not expensive. A helmet is not a legal requirement, but it will protect your head if you fall.

In general it is a good idea to wear bright clothing so that you can be easily seen by motorists, and this is particularly important when it is overcast or getting dark. If you might be out in the dark or twilight fit your bicycle with lights – by law your bicycle must have a reflector. You can also buy reflective bands for your ankles, or to wear over your shoulder and back, and these help motorists to see you.

You may be surprised how quickly you use up energy when cycling, and it is important to eat a carbohydrate meal before you set out. When planning a long ride, eat well the night before. You should eat small amounts of food regularly while you are cycling, or you may find that your energy suddenly disappears, particularly if there are hills or if the weather is cold. It is important to always carry something to eat with you – chocolate, bananas, biscuits – so that if you do start fading away you can restore yourself quickly. In warm weather you will sweat and use up fluid, and you always need to carry something to drink – water will do! Many bicycles have a fitment in which to put a water bottle, and if you don't have one a cycle shop should be able to fit one.

It is also a good idea to carry a small first aid kit. This should include elastoplasts or bandages, sunburn cream, and an anti-histamine in case you are stung by a passing insect.

It is a good idea to have a pannier to carry all these items. Some fit on the handlebars, some to the back of the seat and some onto a back rack. For a day's ride you probably won't need a lot of carrying capacity, but it is better to carry items in a pannier rather than in a rucksack on your back. Pack items that you are carrying carefully – loose items can be dangerous.

Getting to the start of the ride

If you are lucky you will be able to cycle to the start of the ride, but often transport is necessary. If you travel there by train, some sprinter services carry two bicycles without prior booking. Other services carry bicycles free in off-peak periods, but check the details with your local station. Alternatively, you could use your car – it may be possible to get a bike in the back of a hatchback if you take out the front wheel. There are inexpensive, easily fitted car racks which carry bicycles safely. Your local cycle store will be able to supply one to suit you.

Cycling on-road

Cycling on back roads is a delight with quiet lanes, interesting villages and good views. The cycle rides in this book are mainly on quiet roads but you sometimes cross busy roads and have stretches on A and B roads, and whatever sort of road you are on it is essential to ride safely. Always be aware of the possibility or existence of other traffic. Glance behind regularly, signal before you turn or change lane, and keep to the left. If there are motorists around, make sure that they have seen you before you cross their path. Cycling can be dangerous if you are competing for space with motor vehicles, many of which seem to have difficulty in seeing cyclists. When drivers are coming out of side roads, catch their eye before you ride in front of them.

You will find that many roads have potholes and uneven edges. They are much more difficult to spot when you are in a group because of the restricted view ahead, and therefore warnings need to be given. It is a good idea to cycle about a metre out into the road, conditions permitting, so that you avoid the worst of the uneven surfaces and to give you room to move in to the left if you are closely overtaken by a motor vehicle.

Other things to be careful of are slippery roads, particularly where there is mud or fallen leaves. Sudden rain after a period of dry weather often makes the roads extremely slippery. Dogs, too, are a hazard because they often move unpredictably, and sometimes like to chase cyclists. If you are not happy, stop or go slowly until the problem has passed.

Pedalling

Many modern bikes have 18 or 21 gears with three rings at the front and six or seven on the back wheel, and for much of the time you will find that the middle gear at the front with the range of gears at the back will be fine. Use your gears to find one that is easy to pedal along in so that your feet move round easily and you do not put too much pressure on your knees. If you are new to the bike and the gears it is a good idea to practise changing the gears on a stretch of flat, quiet road so that when you need to change gears quickly you will be ready to do so.

Cycling in a group

When cycling in a group it is essential to do so in a disciplined manner for your own, and others', safety. Do not ride too close to the bicycle in front of you – keep about a bicycle's length between you so that you will have space to brake or stop. Always keep both hands on the handlebars, except when signalling, etc. It is alright to cycle two abreast on quiet roads, but if it is necessary to change from cycling two abreast to single file this is usually done by the outside rider falling in behind the nearside rider; always cycle in single file where there are double white lines, on busy roads, or on

Poppit Sands

narrow and winding roads where you have a restricted view of the road ahead. Overtake on the right (outside) only; do not overtake on the inside.

It is important to pass information to other members of the group, for example:

car up – a vehicle is coming up behind the group and will be overtaking;

car down – a vehicle is coming towards the group;

single up – get into single file;

stopping – stopping, or

slowing/easy – slowing due to junction, etc., ahead;

on the left – there is an obstacle on the left, e.g. pedestrian, parked car;

pothole – pothole (and point towards it).

Accidents

In case of an accident, stay calm and, if needed, ring the emergency services on 999. It is a good idea to carry a basic first aid kit and perhaps also one of the commercial foil wraps to put around anyone who has an accident to keep them warm. If someone comes off their bicycle move them and the bike off the road if it is safe to do so. Get someone in the party to warn approaching traffic to slow down, and if necessary ring for an ambulance.

Cycling off-road

All the routes in this book take you along legal rights of way – bridleways, byways open to all traffic and roads used as public paths – it is illegal to cycle along footpaths. Generally the off-road sections of the routes will be easy if the weather and ground are dry. If the weather has been wet and the ground is muddy, it is not a good idea to cycle along bridleways unless you do not mind getting dirty and unless you have a mountain bike which will not get blocked up with mud. In dry weather any bicycle will be able to cover the bridleway sections, but you may need to dismount if the path is very uneven.

Off-road cycling is different to cycling on the road. The average speed is lower, you will use more energy, your riding style will be different and there is a different set of rules to obey – the off-road code:

1. Give way to horse riders and pedestrians, and use a bell or call out to warn someone of your presence.
2. Take your rubbish with you.
3. Do not light fires.
4. Close gates behind you.
5. Do not interfere with wildlife, plants or trees.
6. Use only tracks where you have a right of way, or where the landowner has given you permission to ride.
7. Avoid back wheel skids, which can start erosion gulleys and ruin the bridleway.

Some of the off-road rides take you some miles from shelter and civilisation – take waterproofs, plenty of food and drink and basic tools – especially spare inner tubes and tyre repair equipment. Tell someone where you are going and approximately when you are due back. You are more likely to tumble off your bike riding off-road, so you should consider wearing a helmet and mittens with padded palms.

Useful contacts

Cycling organisations
CTC – see page 119

Sustrans – see page 8

Cycling websites
Online resources for cyclists in the UK
www.cyclecafe.com

Internet bicycling hub
www.cyclery.com

Information and support for cyclists in the UK
www.cycleweb.co.uk

Cycling information station
www.cycling.uk.com

Cycle touring in Wales & the Welsh Borders
www.kc3.co.uk/-bicycle/sideways

Local cycle hire
Stuart Barkley Cycles
Salop Road, Oswestry
Telephone (01691) 658705

Cyclemart
Cilcennin
Telephone (01570) 470079

Greenstiles, Auto Palace
Llandrindod Wells
Telephone (01597) 824594

Dave Mellor Cycles
New Street
Frankwell
Shrewsbury
Telephone (01743) 366662

Newport Bike Hire
Llysmeddgy, Newport
Telephone (01239) 820008

Local cycle shops
Butler Cycles
Scotland Street, Ellesmere
Telephone (01691) 622101

Climb on Bikes
21 The Bull Ring, Ludlow
Telephone (01584) 872173

Jack Davies
58 High Street, Wem
Telephone (01939) 235485

Elan Cyclery
Somerset House
East Street, Rhayader
Telephone (01597) 811343

Halfords Unit 10
Meole Brace Retail Park
Shrewsbury
Telephone (01743) 270277

Stan Jones & Sons
Hills Lane, Shrewsbury
Telephone (01743) 343775

Wheelbase
21 Watergate Street
Whitchurch
Tel: (01948) 663323

See also Stuart Barkley Cycles, Cyclemart, Greenstiles and Dave Mellor Cycles above.

Tourist information
Wales Tourist Board
Telephone (029) 2049 9909
www.visitwales.com

Heart of England Tourist Board
Telephone (01905) 763436
www.visitheartofengland.com

Aberystwyth Tourist Information Centre
Telephone (01970) 612125

Bishop's Castle Tourist Information Centre
Telephone (01588) 638467

Cardigan Tourist Information Centre
Telephone (01239) 613230

Ellesmere Tourist Information Centre
Telephone (01691) 622981

Leominster Tourist Information Centre
Telephone (01568 615546

Llandrindod Wells Tourist Information Centre
Telephone (01597) 822600

Ludlow Tourist Information Centre
Telephone (01584) 875053

Newtown Tourist Information Centre
Telephone (01686) 625580

Oswestry Tourist Information Centre
Telephone (01691) 662753

Presteigne Tourist Information Centre
Telephone (01544) 260650

Rhayader Tourist Information Centre
Telephone (01597) 810591

Shrewsbury Tourist Information Centre
Telephone (01743) 281200

Tenbury Wells Tourist Information Centre
Telephone (01584) 810136

Welshpool Tourist Information Centre
Telephone (01938) 552043

Whitchurch Tourist Information Centre
Telephone (01948) 664577

Local councils
Ceredigion Council
Telephone (01545) 570881
www.ceredigion.gov.uk

Hereford Council
Telephone (01432) 260000
www.herefordshire.gov.uk

Powys Council
Llandrindod Wells
Telephone (01597) 826000
www.powys.gov.uk

Shropshire Council
Telephone (01743) 251000
www.shropshire-cc.gov.uk

Travel by rail
National Rail Enquiries
Telephone (08457) 484950

Railtrack
www.railtrack.com

Central Trains
Telephone (0121) 654 1200
www.centraltrains.co.uk

First Great Western
Telephone (08457) 000125
www.great-western-trains.co.uk

The Train Line
www.thetrainline.com

Valley Lines
Telephone (029) 2044 9944
www.valleylines.co.uk

Virgin Trains
Telephone (08457) 222333

Wales & West
Telephone (029) 2043 0090
www.walesandwest.co.uk

Weather forecasts
BBC Weather
www.bbc.co.uk/weather

The Met. Office
Telephone (09003) 406 108
www.met-office.gov.uk

UK Weather Links
www.ukweather.links.co.uk

Youth Hostels Association of England and Wales
Telephone (01727) 855215
www.yha.org.uk

Route 1

NEWPORT SANDS AND HENLLYS

Route information

Distance 22.5km (14 miles)

Grade Moderate

Terrain Mainly lanes with a few short stretches of main road, which can be busy during the summer holidays. The terrain is hilly in places.

Time to allow 2–3 hours.

Getting there by car Newport is 14.5km (9 miles) south west of Cardigan, on the A487 Fishguard/ Cardigan road. There is limited parking in the town, which is particularly busy during weekends in summer, when it may be necessary to park away from the town centre. The route starts from the Parrog car park, at Newport Sands by the sea.

Getting there by train The nearest railway station is at Fishguard (12.5km/ 8miles away), but it is served by only two trains a day. Telephone (08457) 484950 or visit www.nationalrail.co.uk for travel information.

From Newport the route climbs steadily north, with goods views of the coast and the Preseli Mountains. Turning east and then south the route climbs and descends again offering superb views for the return to Newport. There are two optional extensions. The first of 6.5km (4 miles) takes you to Castell Henllys hill fort; the second of 4km (2.5 miles) allows a visit to Pentre Ifan burial chamber. Note that outside of the holiday season (October to April) it is difficult to purchase refreshments along the route and cyclists should carry drink and food with them.

Route description

TL out of Parrog car park.

1 TL onto A487, no SP (1km/0.6 mile). Continue on this road, ignoring first and second TL.

2 Take third TL, SP Moylgrove/Trewyddol, and descend to Newport Bridge (excellent views and, often, heron can be seen from here). Climb steadily past Berry Hill Farm to top of hill for good views of the sea and Preseli Mountains.

3 TR at TJ, no SP (4km/2.5 miles). Continue along this road, ignoring first TR.

4 Take second TR, SP Glandrhyd/Nevern (6.5km/4 miles). Continue along this narrow road, sometimes used by large tractors, ignoring first TR.

5 Take second TR, SP Glanrhyd (9km/ 5.5 miles) and climb to XR.

6 TR at XR, SP Felindre Farchog (10km/ 6 miles). Superb views behind over Dinas Head to Fishguard.

7 SO at XR, SP Henllys Farm Park. Continue along this road. To visit farm, TL and follow SP. After visit TL at TJ and continue to TL to rejoin route.

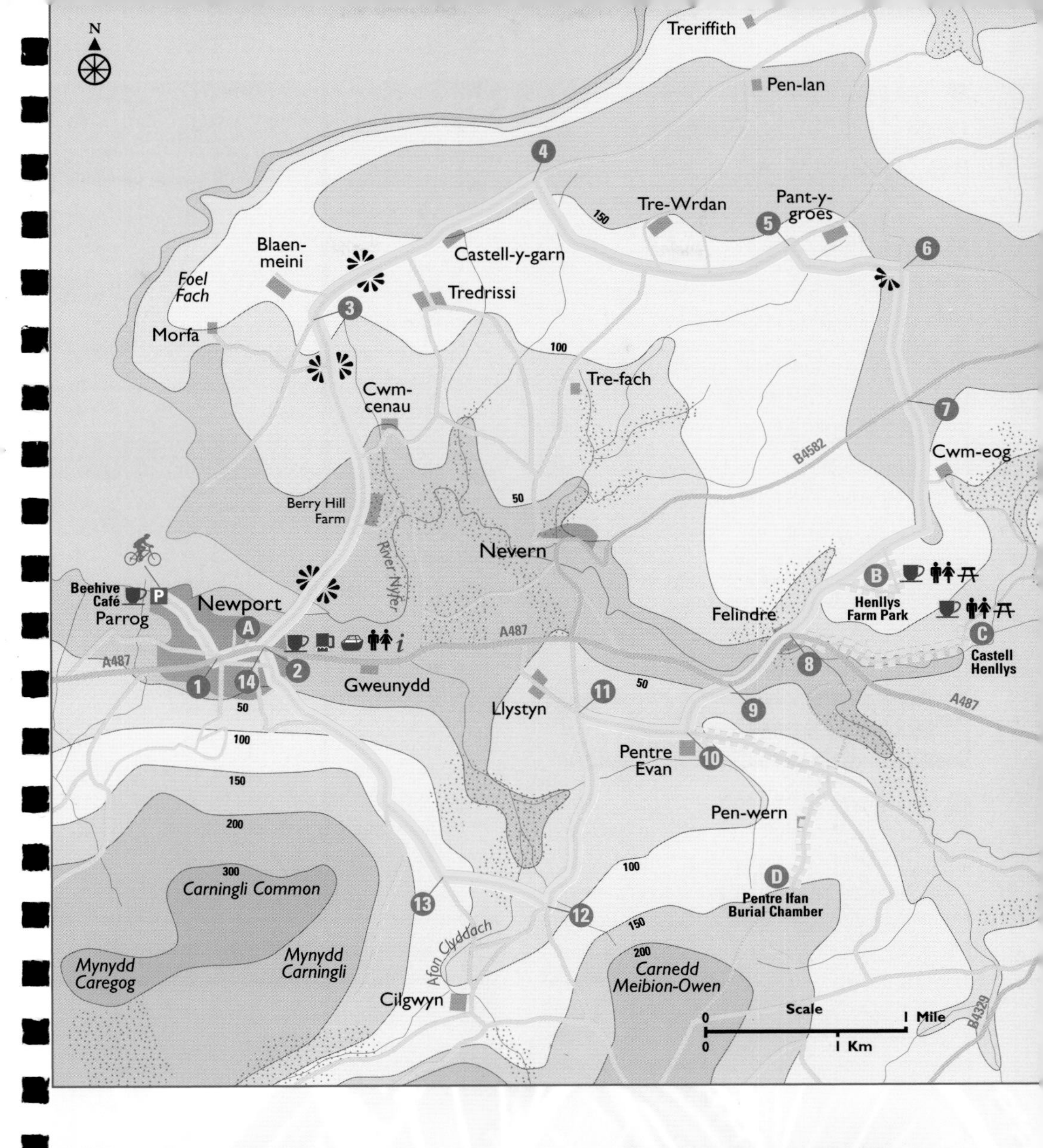

Otherwise, descend on a bumpy road into Felindre Farchog and on to junction with A487.

8 To visit Castell Henllys, TL onto A487 and take first TL, SP Castell Henllys.

Otherwise, TR (CARE) onto A487.

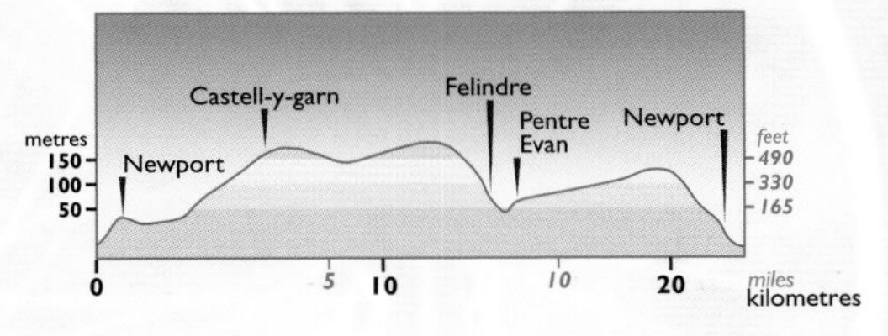

9 Take first TL, no SP (14.5km/9 miles). Climb steeply.

10 To visit Pentre Ifan, TL at TJ and follow SP.

Otherwise, TR at TJ, no SP.

11 TL at XR, SP Cilgwyn/Cwm Gwaun, and continue along this road to staggered XR.

12 TR at staggered XR, no SP except Ford (17.5km/11 miles). Continue along this rough road, across river (there is a footbridge) and on to TJ.

13 TR at TJ, no SP (18.5km/11.5 miles). Descend this narrow road towards Newport.

14 TL at junction and retrace route back to Parrog car park to finish the route.

22.5m (14 miles)

Places of interest along the route

A Newport

An attractive, small but busy town at the mouth of the River Nyfer, within the Pembrokeshire Coast National Park. There are the remains of a Norman castle and church on the slopes above the town. Newport is at one end of the Celtic Trail, a cycle route comprising sections of the National Cycle Network routes 4 and 47, and the Pembrokeshire Coastal Path. Newport's welsh name is Trefdraeth, which translates as 'town by the beach'. The sandy beach is protected by rocky headlands and is popular for swimming, windsurfing, sailing and canoeing. For more information contact the Tourist Information Centre (01239) 820912; www.newport-pembs.co.uk.

B Henllys Farm Park, Henllys

A working farm where visitors can walk around the farm, see the animals and enjoy wonderful views. Refreshments available. Open May to September, Tuesday–Sunday and Bank Holiday Mondays 1030–1700. Charge for farm walks only. Telephone (01239) 820578.

C Castell Henllys, Meline

A reconstructed Iron Age hill fort. The area is under excavation by archaeologists each summer, and the information uncovered has allowed the reconstruction of roundhouses and other buildings. Ancient breeds of livestock, herb garden, river walks and sculpture trails. Refreshments available and good picnic spots. Open Easter to October, daily 1000–1700. Charge. Telephone (01239) 891319.

D Pentre Ifan Burial Chamber, near Newport

A prehistoric burial chamber, dating back to circa 3500 BC and comprising a capstone supported on three uprights. The site is also know as Arthur's Quoit. Cadw property. Free access at all reasonable times. For more information telephone (029) 2082 6185; www.cadw.wales.gov.uk

Food and drink

Plenty of choice in Newport, including a café at the Parrog car park. Refreshments are available at Henllys Farm Park and Castell Henllys (during the holiday season only).

Beehive Café, Newport Sands

All day breakfasts available.

Route **2**

LLANDRINDOD WELLS AND NANT-GLAS

Route information

Distance 25.5km (16 miles)

Grade Moderate

Terrain Lanes and quiet A roads.The route is gently undulating with a climb out of and in to Llandrindod.

Time to allow 2–3 hours.

Getting there by car Llandrindod is on the A483. There is plenty of parking in the town.

Getting there by train Llandrindod is on the Heart of Wales line. Bicycle carriage is restricted to two bikes per train. Telephone (08457) 484950 or visit www.nationalrail.co.uk for travel information.

A scenic ride from Llandrindod to make a circuit through the countryside west of the town, passing through the villages of Llanyre, Nantmel and Nant-glas.

Places of interest along the route

A Llandrindod Wells

The site of spa waters well-known to the Romans, the town developed with the arrival of the railway in the mid 19th century. The waters can still be sampled in the original pump rooms at **Rock Park**. For more information, telephone (01597) 822997. Today Llandrindod has plenty of facilities for visitors. The Royal Welsh Show, the largest agricultural show in the UK, is held at Llanelwedd, just south of the town. The Radnor Ring (134.5km/84 miles) is part of the National Cycle Network (Route 25) and makes a circuit of mid Wales and the English border. Contact Sustrans (see page 8) for more information. The **National Cycle Collection** describes the history of the bicycle and cycling and has lots of fascinating memorabilia. Small admission charge. Open all year, daily from 1000. Telephone (01597) 825531. To the south of the town is **Llandrindod Lake**, built as a boating lake towards the end of the 19th century. Today there are attractive views of the surrounding area and lots of wildlife. Café, craft shop and picnic area.

Food and drink

There is plenty of choice is Llandrindod Wells, including the Herb Garden vegetarian café and the Metropole Hotel.

The Bell, Llanyre

Pub and restaurant serving a variety of meals.

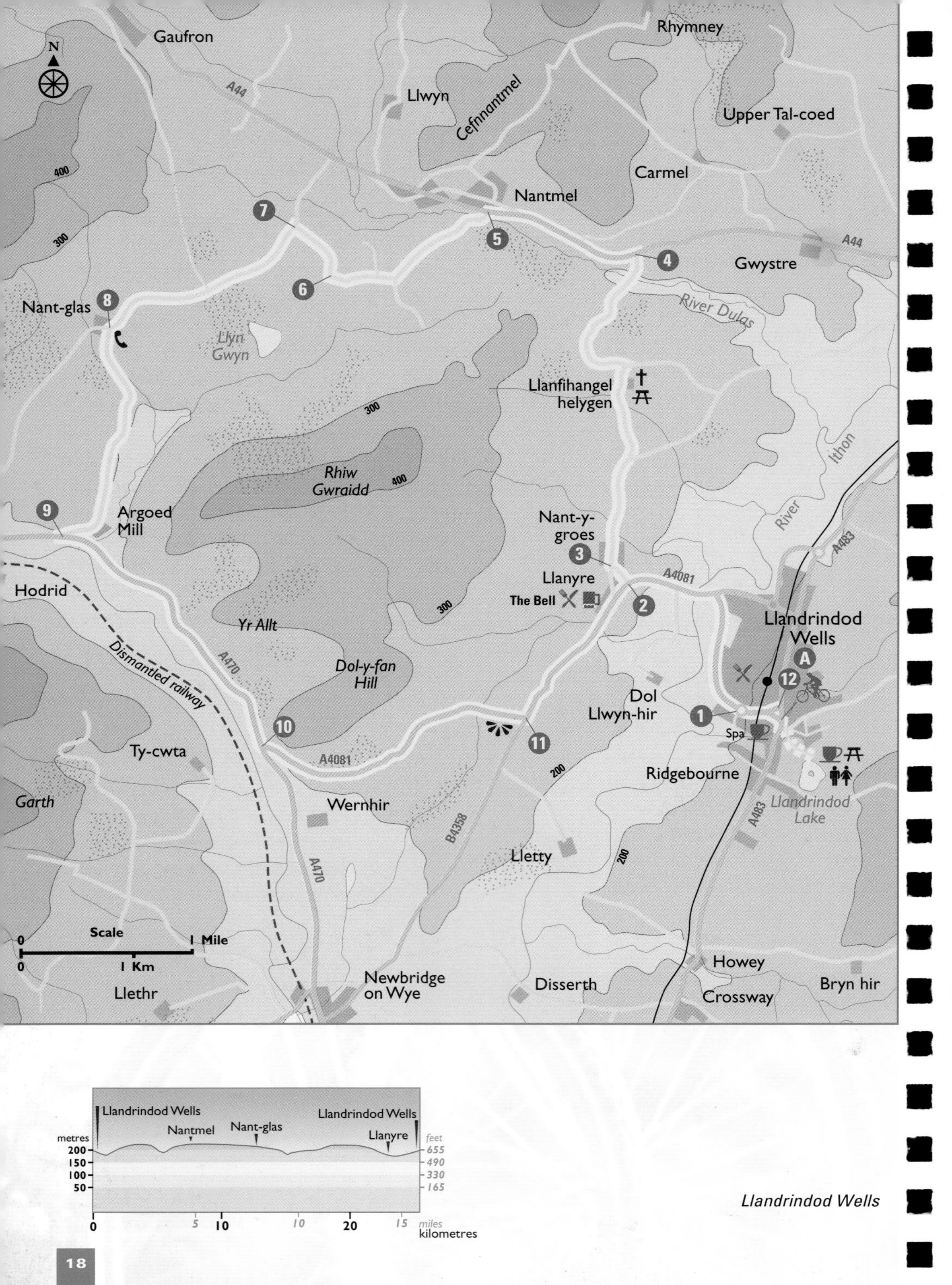

Llandrindod Wells

Route description

Start the route in Spa Road, which is the one-way street directly opposite the Automobile Palace/National Cycle Collection. Cycle along Spa Road, keeping to the left.

1 To visit the Spa, take first exit at roundabout. Spa entrance is immediately on LHS.

Otherwise, take second exit at roundabout into Ithon Road, SP Rhaeadr. Descend. Cross River Ithon and climb out of valley.

---

2 TR to Llanyre village, SP Highway Farm B&B.

---

3 TR at TJ, no SP (2.5km/1.5 miles). Continue along this road, passing picnic site and ancient chapel on RHS. Descend to junction with A44.

---

4 TL at TJ onto A44 (6.5km/4 miles). Continue along A44 into Nantmel.

---

5 TL (after war memorial on RHS), no SP (8km/5 miles). Cross River Dulas and continue along this lane.

6 Keep R at unmarked TJ, no SP.

10.5km (6.5 miles)

---

7 TL at TJ, no SP, and continue to outskirts of Nant-glas.

---

8 TL by telephone box, no SP (12.5km/8 miles). Descend to junction with A470.

---

9 TL at TJ, no SP (16km/10 miles). Continue along A470.

---

10 LHF, SP Llandrindod A4081, for gradual climb.

---

11 Keep L at top of climb, SP Llandrindod (good views here). Follow A4081 back into Llandrindod. Keep SO at roundabout and L at one-way system.

---

12 TR at TJ, SP Builth A483, and continue back to Spa Road to finish the ride.

25.5km (16 miles)

To visit the lake, TL before reaching National Cycle Collection, SP Lake. Immediately TR into Princes Road and continue for 1km (0.6 mile).

Route 3

HAUGHMOND HILL AND WROXETER

Route information

Distance 29.5km (18.5 miles)

Grade Moderate

Terrain The first 9.5km (6 miles) are flat. After Wroxeter, the lanes are quiet, but undulating, with splendid views across south and east Shropshire. There are some short hills which the novice cyclist may have to walk.

Time to allow 2–3 hours. Allow extra time to visit the places of interest.

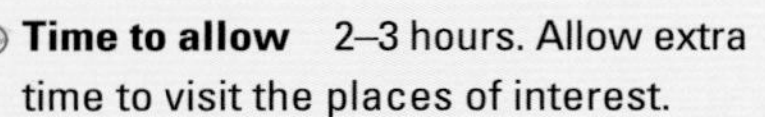

Getting there by car The start of the route, Haughmond Hill Forestry Commission car park is off the B5062, Shrewsbury/Newport road, approximately 5km (3 miles) north east of Shrewsbury. On the brow of the hill, TR (TL from Newport direction), SP Upton Magna/Withington. The car park is 400m on RHS.

Getting there by train The nearest railway station is in Shrewsbury (5km/3 miles). Telephone (08457) 484950 or visit www.nationalrail.co.uk for travel information. Cyclists will have to cross several busy road junctions to reach the start. From the station, follow A49 (Whitchurch road) to Heathgate roundabout. Take second exit at roundabout into Sundorne Road (B5062/Newport road). Cross mini roundabout at Featherbed Lane and SO at second roundabout (A49) to continue up Haughmond Hill to car park.

The route starts from Haughmond Hill and heads south to Atcham and Wroxeter. From here it turns east and then north to head back to Haughmond Hill via Withington. There are wonderful views from the Forestry Commission's site at Haughmond Hill, together with picnic areas and waymarked cycle routes.

Places of interest along the route

A St Lucia's Church, Upton Magna

The church has 12th century foundations, a bell tower, and contains interesting monuments. It is only one of two churches dedicated to St Lucia in this country. Contact Shrewsbury Tourist Information Centre for more details on (01743) 281200.

B Home Farm, Attingham

The original home farm to Attingham Hall, the working farmyard retains the traditional atmosphere of a Shropshire farm. Lots of different animals, including many rare breeds of pigs, sheep and cows. Also poultry and rabbits. Nature walk and special food to feed the animals. Tearoom with home baking and ice cream; picnic area. Open mid April to end September, weekends and Bank Holidays 1200–1730; Monday–Wednesday 1300–1730; open daily during local school holidays 1100–1730. Charge. Telephone (01743) 709243; www.openfarm.co.uk

C Attingham Park, Atcham

Atcham means 'land in a river bend belonging to the followers of Eata.' St Eata lived circa 640 AD and formed a small community at the river ford. The 11th-century church is dedicated to him. Attingham Park, managed by the National Trust, is a neo-classical mansion set in a landscaped deer park. The house features Regency interiors, with collections of silver, furniture, pictures and ceramics. Exhibition of the kitchen and servants' hall. The park has woodland and riverside walks, orchard and walled garden, and exhibitions on estate life. Tearoom. Grounds open daily, March to October 0900–2000; November to February 0900–1700. House open end March to end October, Friday–Tuesday 1300–1630, Bank Holiday Mondays 1100–1700. Telephone. Charge. Telephone (01743) 708123; www.nationaltrust.org.uk

D Wroxeter Roman City, Wroxeter

Known as *Viroconium*, this is the excavated centre of the largest city in Roman Britain. It would have originally been home to over 6000 men and several hundred horses. Later, the thriving settlement attracted traders and retired legionaires. An on-site museum displays and explains the finds. Soft drinks and ice cream available. English Heritage property. Open November to March, Wednesday–Sunday 1000–1300 and 1400–1600; April to October, daily 1000–1700. Charge. Telephone (01743) 761330; www.english-heritage.org.uk

E Wroxeter Roman Vineyard, Wroxeter

The vineyard, planted on 2.5ha (6 acres) of the area once covered by the Roman city, produces award-winning red and white wines. Also lavender fields, flock of Roman breed of sheep and farm shop. Guided vineyard tours and tastings (charge). Open all year, Monday–Saturday 1100–1700, Sunday 1200–1730. Admission free. Telephone (01743) 761888; www.wroxetervineyard.co.uk

F Withington

The Shrewsbury Canal, opened in 1797 and abandoned in 1944 ran close by. It was originally constructed to carry coal from the Ketley area to Shrewsbury. Near the old Post Office in Withington, there was a wharf which received over 30,402 kg (30 tons) of coal a month. The remains of two lift bridges may be seen in nearby fields. A trust has recently been created to work towards the restoration of the canal.

G Haughmond Abbey, near Upton Magna

Signposted from the top of the hill, the abbey was founded in 1135 by William Fitzalan, on a beautiful sloping site on Haughmond Hill. There are impressive remains, including parts of the chapter house and the infirmary. English Heritage property. Open daily April to September, 1000–1800; October 1000–1700. Charge. Telephone (01743) 709661; www.english-heritage.org.uk

Roman road near Wroxeter

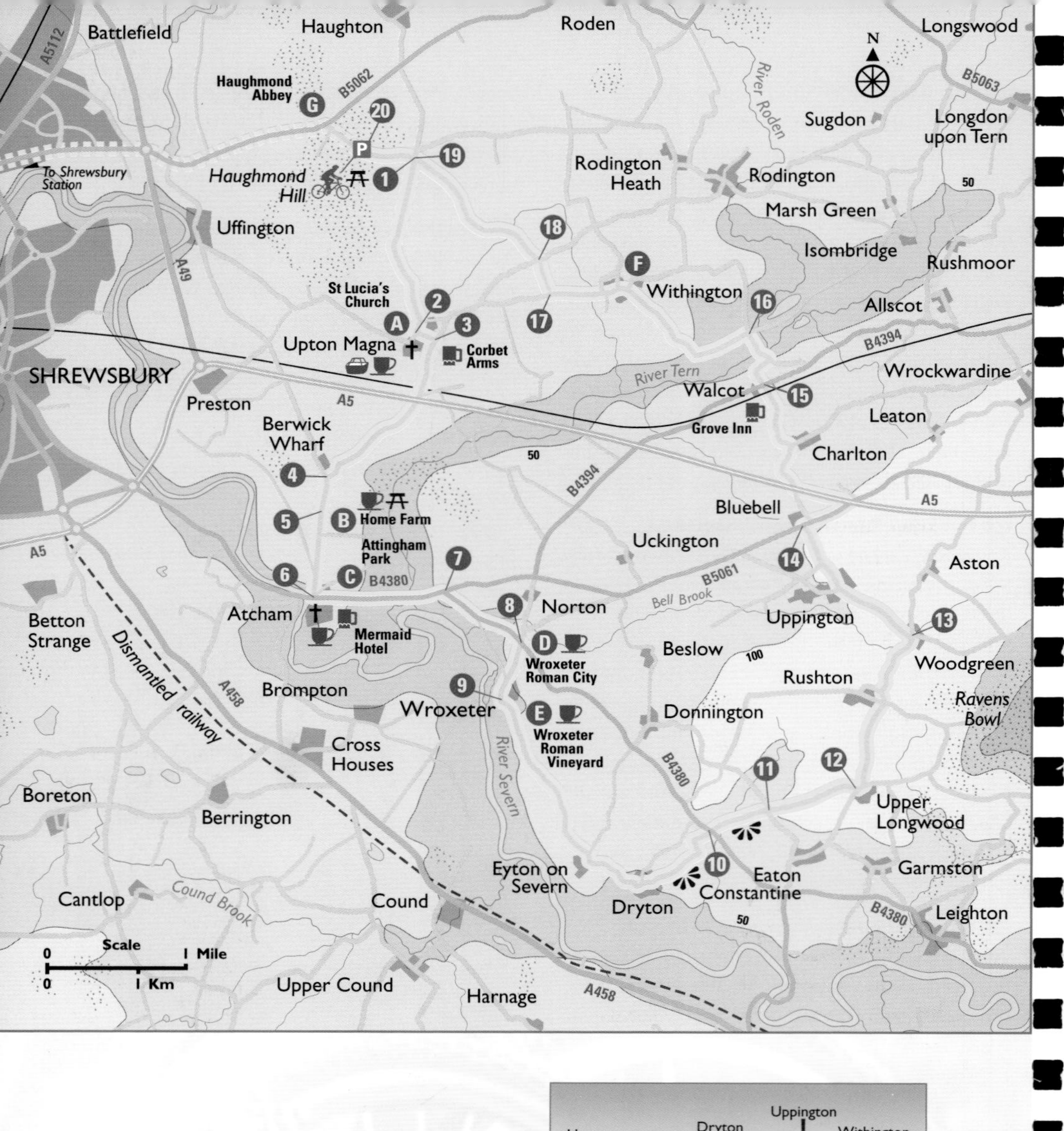
Battlefield
A5112
Haughton
Roden
Longswood
N
Haughmond Abbey
G
B5062
20
River Roden
B5063
Sugdon
Longdon upon Tern
P
19
To Shrewsbury Station
Haughmond Hill
1
Rodington Heath
Rodington
50
Marsh Green
Uffington
18
Isombridge
Rushmoor
A49
F
Withington
St Lucia's Church
2
16
Allscot
A
3
17
Upton Magna
Corbet Arms
B4394
SHREWSBURY
Wrockwardine
River Tern
Preston
A5
Walcot
15
Berwick Wharf
Grove Inn
Leaton
Charlton
50
4
B4394
Bluebell
A5
5
B
Home Farm
Attingham Park
Uckington
A5
7
14
6
C
B4380
B5061
Aston
Bell Brook
Norton
8
Betton Strange
Atcham
Uppington
13
Mermaid Hotel
D
Beslow
Wroxeter Roman City
100
Dismantled railway
Woodgreen
Rushton
A458
Brompton
9
Ravens Bowl
Wroxeter
E
Donnington
Wroxeter Roman Vineyard
Cross Houses
River Severn
B4380
11
12
Boreton
Upper Longwood
Berrington
10
Eyton on Severn
Eaton Constantine
Garmston
Cantlop
Cound Brook
Cound
Dryton
B4380
50
Leighton
Scale
0
1 Mile
0
1 Km
Upper Cound
Harnage
A458

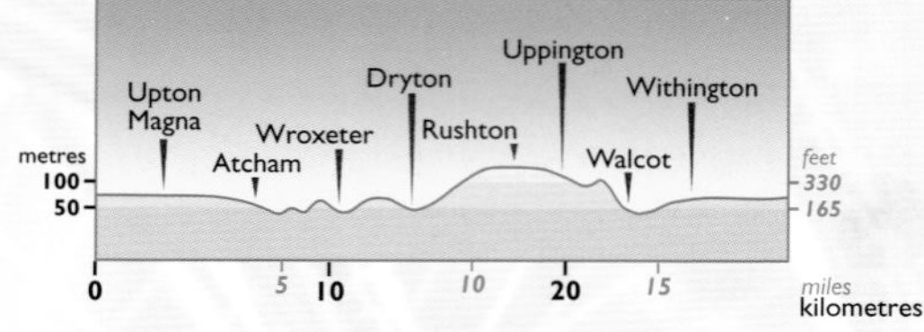
Upton Magna
Atcham
Wroxeter
Dryton
Rushton
Uppington
Walcot
Withington
metres
100
50
feet
330
165
0
5
10
10
20
15
miles
kilometres

Route description

TR out of car park. Cycle to XR.

1 TR, SP Upton Magna/Atcham.

2 Arrive Upton Magna. TL, SP Rodington/ Atcham. Continue to TJ opposite Corbet Arms pub.

3 TR at TJ, SP Berwick Wharf/Atcham.

4 Arrive Berwick Wharf. TL, SP Atcham.

5 Pass Home Farm on LHS.

6 Arrive Atcham and TJ with B4380. TL, SP Ironbridge/Telford (B5061). Continue and cross River Tern (Attingham Park on LHS).

7 TR onto B4380, SP Wroxeter Roman City/ Ironbridge. ***8.5km (5 miles)***

8 TR at Wroxeter Roman City XR, SP Wroxeter village/ Eyton on Severn.

9 Pass Wroxeter Roman Vineyard on LHS as leaving village. Follow lanes through hamlet of Eyton on Severn for steep downhill. Climb to Lower Longwood XR with B4380.

10 SO at XR, SP Longwood/Wellington.

11 SO at Longwood XR, SP Longwood/Rushton. Continue into Upper Longwood.

12 TL at TJ, no SP (16km/10 miles). SO through Rushton to Wood Green XR.

13 TL at XR, SP Uppington. Follow road as it skirts Uppington to arrive at XR with B5061.

14 TR, SP Wellington. Cycle under road bridge and immediately TL, SP Walcot/Charlton. Continue SO through Charlton to Walcot XR with B4394.

15 SO at XR. Pass confluence of River Roden and River Tern.

16 TL at XR, SP Withington/Upton Magna (24km/15 miles). Continue through Withington.

17 TR after village, no SP. ***26.5km (16.5 miles)***

18 SO at XR, SP Haughmond Hill/ Shrewsbury.

19 SO at XR, no SP.

20 Arrive Haughmond Hill car park. To visit Haughmond Abbey, continue SO.

Otherwise, TL into car park to finish the route. ***29.5km (18.5 miles)***

Food and drink

There is plenty of choice in the first half of the ride, with pubs, shops and tearooms. Refreshments are also available at Attingham Home Farm, Attingham Park, Wroxeter Roman City and Wroxeter Roman Vineyard (drinks only, no food).

Route 4

RHAYADER AND THE ELAN VALLEY

Route information

Distance 31.5km (19.5 miles)

Grade Moderate

Terrain Quiet, undulating roads with one long climb out of Rhayader at the start of the route.

Time to allow 2–3 hours.

Getting there by car Rhayader is 18km (11 miles) north of Builth Wells, at the junction of the A470 and A44. Park in the free car park off the A470.

Getting there by train The nearest railway station is at Llandrindod on the Heart of Wales line, approximately 19km (12 miles) from Rhayader along main roads. Telephone (08457) 484950 or visit www.nationalrail.co.uk for travel information.

A scenic ride from Rhayader, into the Elan Valley to pass three of the Elan Valley reservoirs, built by the Victorians to supply clean water to Birmingham. An optional extension of 15km (9.5 miles) takes in a fourth reservoir.

Route description

To start from Llandrindod Station, leave station and head out of town on A4081.Continue on this road to junction with A470, where TR and continue into Rhayader.

Start in Rhayader at free car park off A470. TR out of car park and immediately TL at TJ onto A470.

1 TR at clock tower, SP Elan Valley.

2 TR, SP Aberystwyth Mountain Road, for a long climb and steep descent.

3 TL, SP Elan Valley (9km/5.5 miles). Pass picnic site on RHS and continue around reservoir to dam.

4 To visit picnic site/toilets/information display, TL and cross dam.

Otherwise, TR, SP Rhaeadr (14km/8.5 miles). Follow road around Pen-y-garreg Reservoir, cross dam and follow road around Garreg ddu Reservoir.

5 To visit Claerwen Reservoir and dam (an additional 15km/9.5 miles), TR across Garreg ddu dam, SP Claerwen Dam. After visit, retrace route and TR, SP Rhaeadr.

Otherwise, continue along road, SP Rhaeadr, to Elan village.

6 To visit Elan Valley Visitor Centre, TR, SP Visitor Centre. ***25km (15.5 miles)***

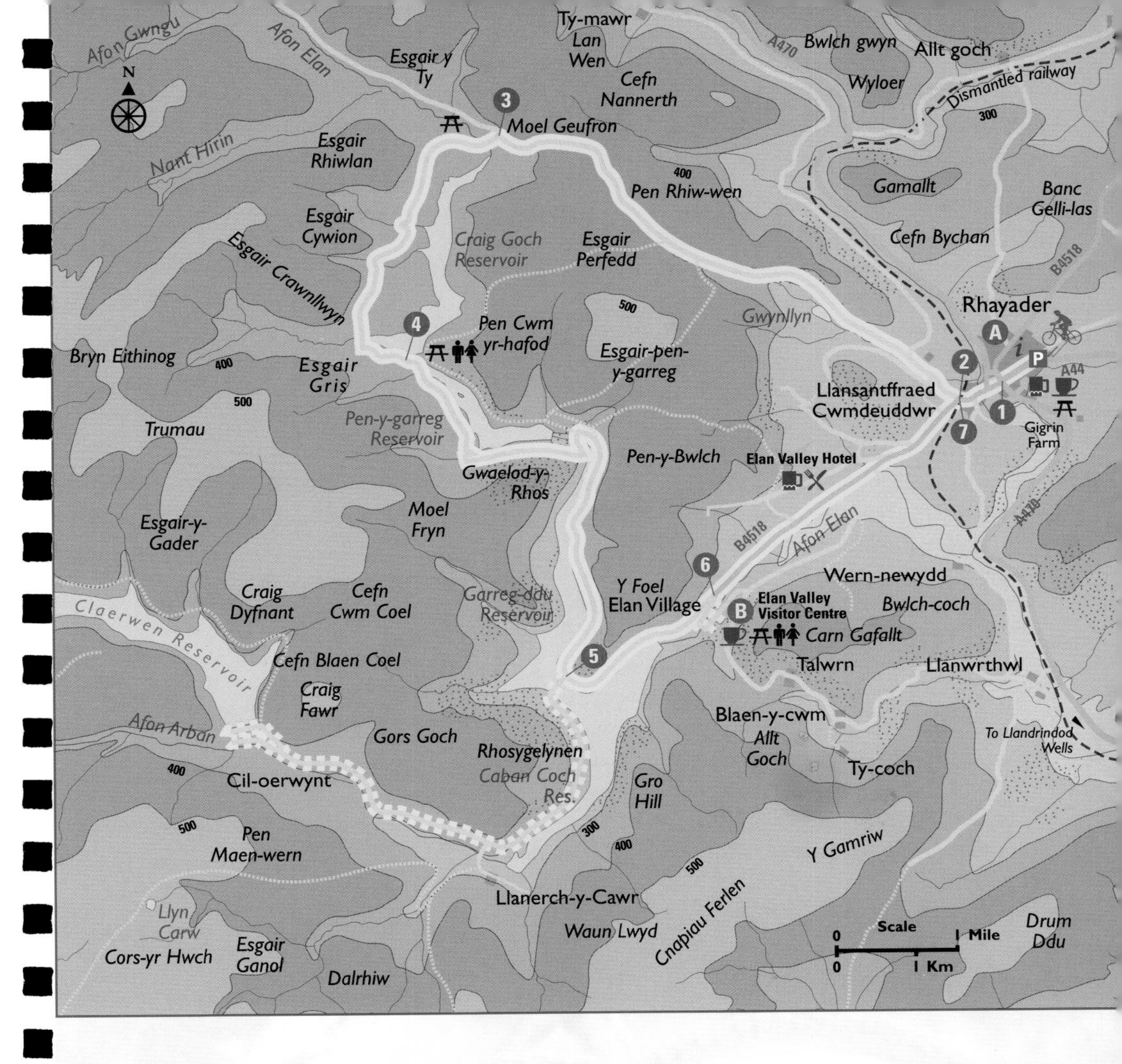

Otherwise, SO to continue route. Pass Elan Valley Hotel and continue to junction.

7 TR and retrace route back into Rhayader to finish the ride. ***31.5km (19.5 miles)***

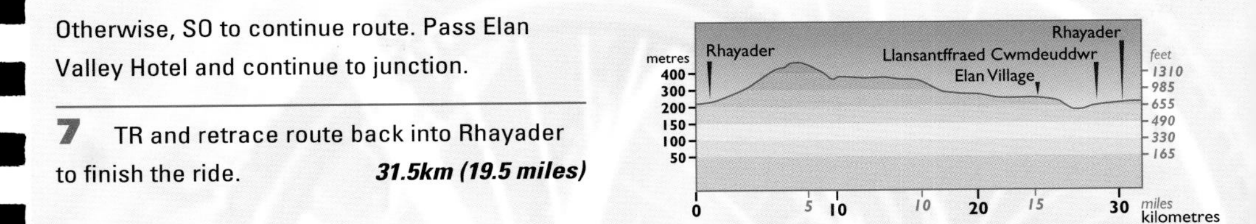

Places of interest along the route

A Rhayader

A small town on the River Wye. During the Middle Ages the area was known for the export of wool to Europe, and farming and sheep rearing made the town an import market centre. Today the town's market is held each Wednesday. **Welsh Royal Crystal** produces hand crafted lead crystal tableware. Visitors can take a tour of the manufacturing process. Café and shop. Open daily, 0900–1700. Charge for tours only. Telephone to confirm tour times on (01597) 811005; www.welshcrystal.co.uk. Also in the town is the **Marston Pottery** where an experienced potter creates hand thrown pottery for the home. Showroom open at most times, telephone to confirm on (01597) 810875. Just outside Rhayader is **Gigrin Farm**, where visitors can see Red Kites fed daily: summer 1500; winter 1400. Also nature trail, bird reserve, children's play area and picnic site. Charge. Telephone (01597) 810243; www.gigrin.co.uk. Rhayader is at the centre of several cycle routes including a section of the National Cycle Network, NCR 8, and the Radnor Ring which links Rhayader, Newbridge and Wye. Contact the Tourist Information Centre for more details on (01597) 81059.

B Elan Valley Visitor Centre, Elan village

The Elan Valley estate comprises 112 square km (70 square miles). The visitor centre contains an exhibition showing the local and natural history of the area. Also audio-visual show, shop, café, children's play area and large picnic areas. Open mid-March to end October, daily 1000–1730. Free admission to visitor centre. Telephone (01597) 810898; www.elanvalley.org.uk

Food and drink

There are plenty of pubs and cafés in Rhayader. Refreshments are available at the Elan Valley Visitor Centre.

Elan Valley Hotel, near Rhayader

Hotel with bar offering home cooked snacks and full meals.

Reservoir, Elan Valley

Route 5

BISHOP'S CASTLE AND THE SOUTH SHROPSHIRE MARCHES

Route information

Distance 32km (20 miles)

Grade Strenuous

Terrain Approximately 9.5km (6 miles) of B road, otherwise quiet narrow lanes. Three tough climbs make this route strenuous for its length.

Time to allow 2–3 hours.

Getting there by car Bishop's Castle is 19km (12 miles) north west of Craven Arms, just off the A488. There are two car parks in the town centre.

Getting there by train The nearest main line station is at Craven Arms, 19km (12 miles) from Bishop's Castle but only 4.5km (3 miles) from the route. Telephone (08457) 484950 or visit www.nationalrail.co.uk for travel information.

A route taking in the countryside of south Shropshire close to the Welsh border. From Bishop's Castle the route heads south and then east as far as Edgton. Here it turns south as far as Twitchen before turning back to Bishop's Castle. The quiet lanes are particularly attractive when the spring flowers are in bloom in the hedgerows.

Places of interest along the route

A Bishop's Castle

A small market town (market day is Friday), with several antique shops. The High Street and Castle Street lie on the site of a Norman road. The **House on Crutches Museum**, High Street, is housed in a half-timbered 16th century house. The museum illustrates the town's history and describes the surrounding area, much of the collection donated or loaned by local inhabitants. Open Easter to October, weekends 1200–1600, Bank Holidays 1100–1500. Also open at any other time by arrangement. Telephone (01588) 630007. **Bishop's Castle Rail and Transport Museum** is located in a renovated 15th-century property off the High Street. It describes the history of the town's railway and local transport. Telephone the Tourist Information Centre (TIC) on (01588) 638467 to confirm opening times. The **Three Tuns Brewery** Museum, Salop Street, describes the history of beer and brewing and is open by arrangement at any time (ask in the bar of the Three Tuns pub). Tours are available of the working Victorian tower brewery, but must be booked in advance. Telehone (01588) 638797 for more information. Brewery tours are also available (by appointment only) at the **Six Bells Brewery**, on the site of a 16th-century coaching inn. Telephone (01588) 638930. For more information on Bishop's Castle and the surrounding area, contact the TIC or visit www.bishopscastle. co.uk

B Walcot Hall and Arboretum, Lydbury North

The former home of Lord Clive of India. The arboretum comprises approximately 12ha (30 acres) of specimen trees and walks. Hall open once a year under the National Scheme, telephone for details. Arboretum open May to October, Friday–Monday 1200–1630. Charge. Telephone (01568) 610693; www.walcothall.com

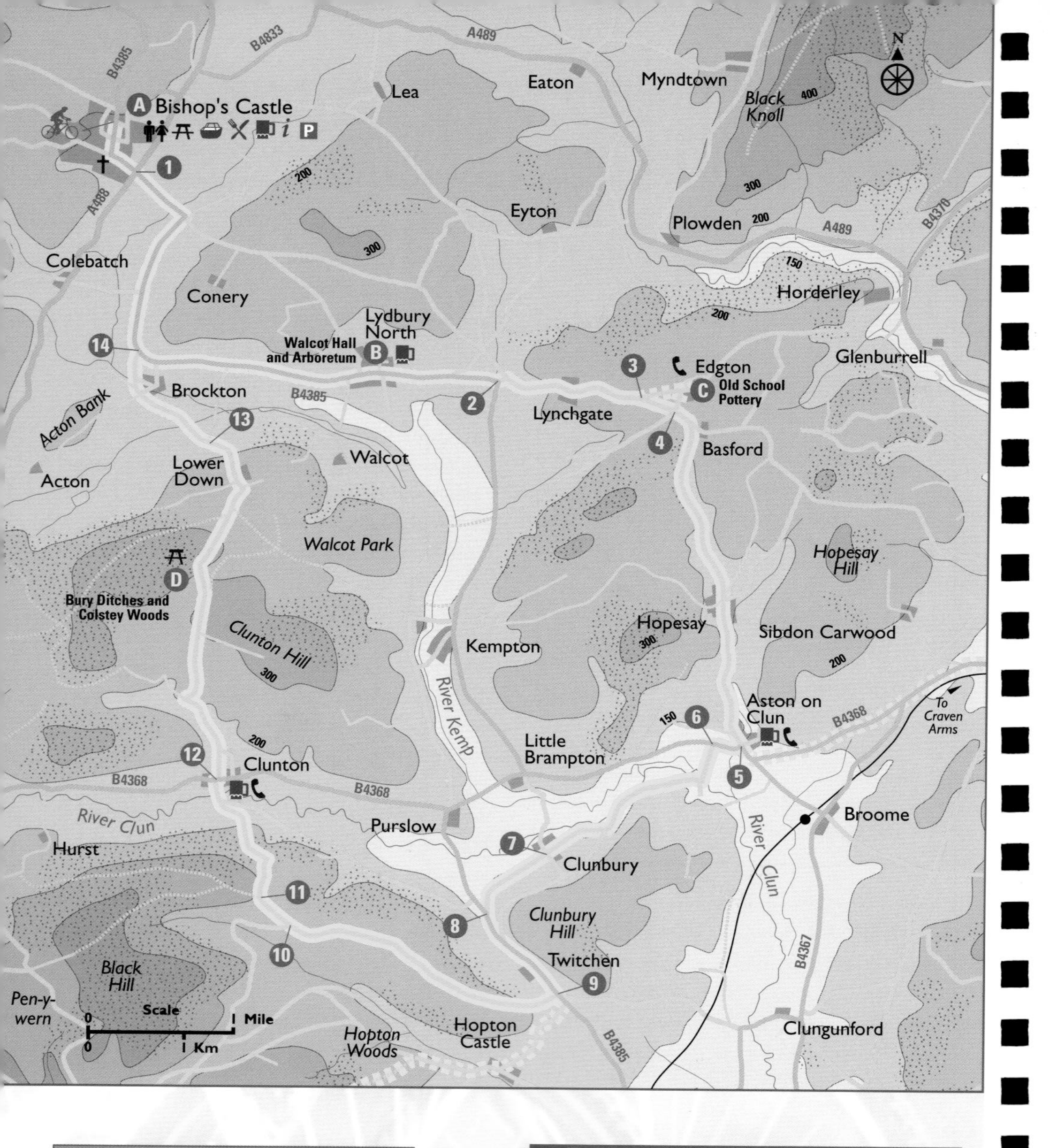

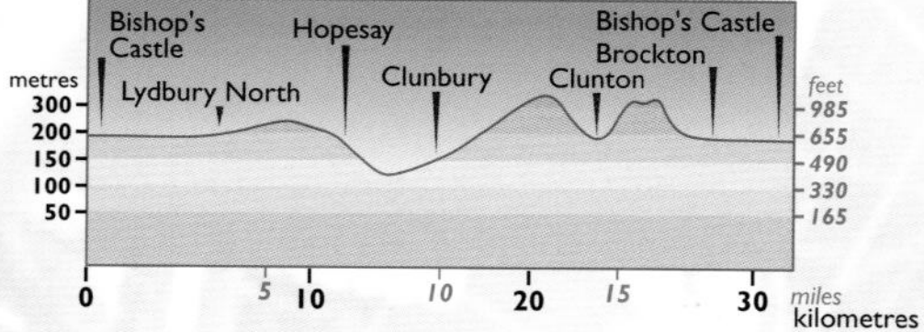

Food and drink

Plenty of choice in Bishop's Castle. There are pubs at Lydbury North, Aston on Clun and Clunton.

Ⓒ Old School Pottery, Edgton
Signposted from the centre of the village, and located in the old school. The potter produces glazed stoneware and frostproof garden pots. Open at all reasonable times. Telephone (01588) 680208.

Ⓓ Bury Ditches and Colstey Woods, near Bishop's Castle
A well preserved Bronze Age hill fort at the summit of Forestry Commission woodland (access on foot only). Panoramic views, walks and nature trail. Picnic area. For more information, telephone the forest ranger on (01889) 586593 or visit www. forestry.gov.uk

Off-road cycling enthusiasts will find a full range of waymarked routes in Hopton Woods, approximately 3km (2 miles) from the southernmost point of the route. There is also a waymarked forest trail through Bury Ditches to Colstey Wood which allows an alternative route back to Bishop's Castle through Colebatch on the A488. Contact Bishop's Castle TIC for more information.

Route description

To start the route from Craven Arms, take the B4368 west to Aston on Clun and start the route at direction 5, where SO, SP Clun/Bishop's Castle.

From Bishop's Castle, leave town centre down Church Street (continues from High Street). TL at the foot of Church Street, opposite church, SP Craven Arms/Knighton.

1 SO at XR with A488, onto B4385, SP Craven Arms/Lydbury North. Continue on this road through Lydbury North.

2 TL on RH bend and immediately TR, SP Edgton. Continue as road climbs around 100m in approximately 1.5km (1 mile). Shortly after road levels out:

3 To visit Old School Pottery, Edgton, take LHF and follow SP.

Otherwise, take RHF SP Hopesay.

9km (5.5 miles)

4 Take RHF, SP Hopesay/Aston on Clun. Descend pleasant quiet valley, through Hopesay to Aston on Clun.

5 To return to Craven Arms and railway station, TL.

Otherwise TR, SP Clun/Bishop's Castle B4368.

6 TL, SP Beambridge. Cross River Clun and continue along its valley on rather rough lane into Clunbury.

7 SO at XR, SP Twitchen.

16km (10 miles)

8 TL at TJ, SP Twitchen/Hopton Heath.

9 TR at XR, SP Llan/Cwm. Otherwise, to visit Hopton Woods for off-road routes, keep SO. Take next TR to Hopton Castle, then TR.

10 Take RHF, SP Clunton.

11 TR at TJ and descend very steeply to Clunton.

12 SO at XR (23km/14.5 miles) and climb 3km (2 miles) to pass access for Bury Ditches, Colstey Wood and waymarked cycle trail on LHS. Continue for descent to Lower Down.

13 SO on RH bend, no SP (20km/18 miles), and climb gently through Brockton to reach B4385.

14 TL at TJ and retrace route to Bishop's Castle to complete the ride.

32km (20 miles)

Route **6**

LUDLOW AND TENBURY WELLS

Route information

Distance 34km (21 miles)

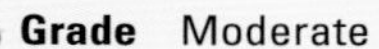

Grade Moderate

Terrain Reasonably quiet B roads, a short stretch of A road and country lanes. There is one steep section of the route.

Time to allow 2–3 hours.

Getting there by car Ludlow is 44km (27 miles) south of Shrewsbury, on the A49. From the A49, follow B4361, SP Town Centre. There is parking off Castle Street, a short distance from the start of the route at the Tourist Information Centre (TIC).

Getting there by train There is a railway station in Ludlow, approximately 1.5km (1 mile) from the start of the route.

From Ludlow the route heads south to Brimfield. After a short stretch of the A49, the route follows lanes tracing the River Teme to Tenbury Wells, before turning back to Ludlow.

Route description

If starting from the railway station, TR out of station. TL onto B4361 and up hill to pedestrian crossing. TR at crossing (one-way, SP Ludlow Castle). The TIC is on LHS in market square.

To start from the TIC, TL downhill, SP Shrewsbury/Leominster (A49). TL into Bell Lane and follow SP A49 to Broad Street.

1 TR through Broad Gate.

2 Arrive traffic lights on Lower Broad Street and SO over bridge, SP Richards Castle B4361/ Leominster A49.

3 TR, SP Richards Castle/Presteigne. Continue on this road through Overton and Richards Castle.

4 TL, SP Tenbury B4362 (8km/5 miles). Continue to Woofferton.

5 TR onto A49, SP Leominster. Continue, ignoring first TL.

6 Take second TL, SP Brimfield/Wyson. Continue into Brimfield.

7 TL, SP Tenbury/Kidderminster A456.

8 TR (before A456), SP Upton/Middleton-on-Hill.

9 TL at TJ, SP Little Hereford/Tenbury.

10 TR, SP Berrington (15.5km/9.5 miles). Continue into Berrington.

11 TL, SP Tenbury. Follow road to outskirts of Tenbury Wells.

12 TL at TJ into Teme Street. Follow main road, SP Kidderminster A456/Cleobury B4214 (WC on RHS). Cross bridge into Shropshire.

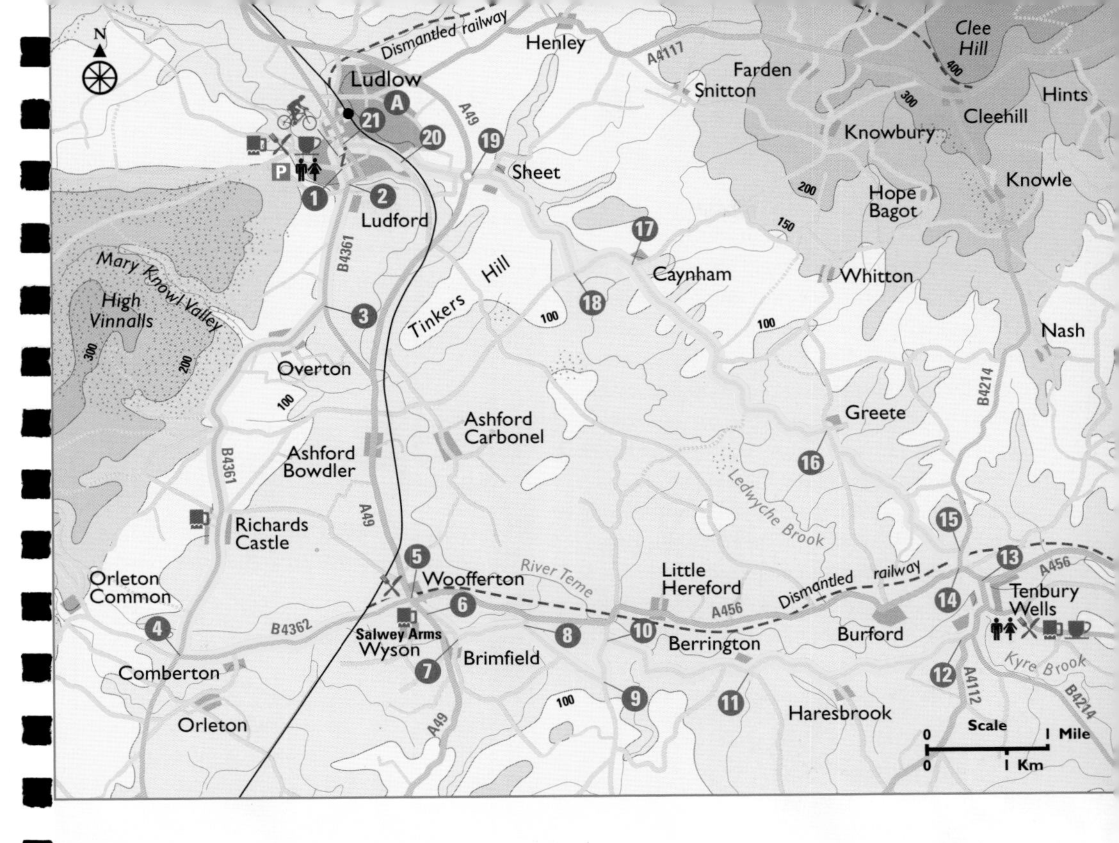

13 TL, SP Shrewsbury/Leominster A49/ Burford Industrial Estate. Continue, ignoring first TR.

14 Take second TR on LH bend after Rose and Crown pub, SP Clee Hill B4214/Burford Industrial Estate.

15 TL, SP Greete/Whitton. Continue into Greete.

16 TL at XR, SP Caynham/Ludlow (25.5km/16 miles). Continue into Caynham.

17 TL at TJ, SP Ashford Carbonel/Ludlow. Descend, cross bridge and:

18 TR, SP Ludlow. Cycle through Sheet.

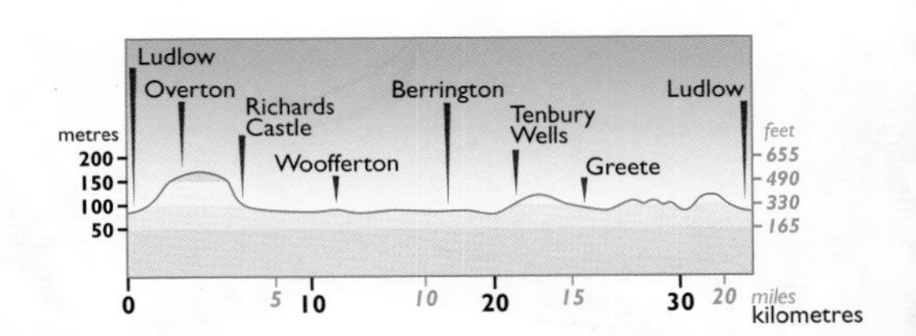

19 SO at roundabout with A49, SP Ludlow (32km/20 miles). Cycle under railway to TJ with Galdeford Road.

20 DISMOUNT and TL. Walk past Post Office.

21 SO at XR, SP Ludlow Castle, and finish the ride by the TIC. ***34km (21 miles)***

Places of interest along the route

Ⓐ Ludlow

A small town on the hill about the River Teme, well-known for its festival held each June. Craft and food fairs are also held during the year. **Ludlow Castle** was built in the late 11th century and features medieval and Tudor architecture. Open daily, February to April and October to December, 1000–1600; May to September, 1000–1700. Charge. Telephone (01584) 873355. Below the castle is **Linney Riverside Park**, with picnic area, children's playground and rowing boats for hire May to September. **Castle Lodge**, of medieval origin, was home to the officials of the Council of the Marches. It is open to the public. The **parish church** was rebuilt during the 15th century and contains fine stained glass. There is a memorial to A E Housman, author of *A Shropshire Lad*, in the churchyard. Stewards are on duty spring, summer and autumn. Open all year, daily 1000–1700. Donation requested. Telephone (01584) 872073 for information. **Ludlow Museum** describes the town's history, from the building of the castle to the present day. Telephone the TIC for more information, particularly opening times, on (01584) 875053 or visit www.ludlow.org.uk

Food and drink

There is plenty of choice in Ludlow and Tenbury Wells, and a Little Chef in Woofferton.

Salwey Arms, Woofferton
Bar meals served.

Ludlow

Route 7

NEWTOWN AND THE RHIW VALLEY

Route information

Distance 37km (23 miles)

Grade Moderate

Terrain Lanes and quiet B roads. The route is undulating in places, with a gradual climb along the Rhiw Valley. There is a steep climb before the descent to Newtown at the end of the ride.

Time to allow 3–4 hours.

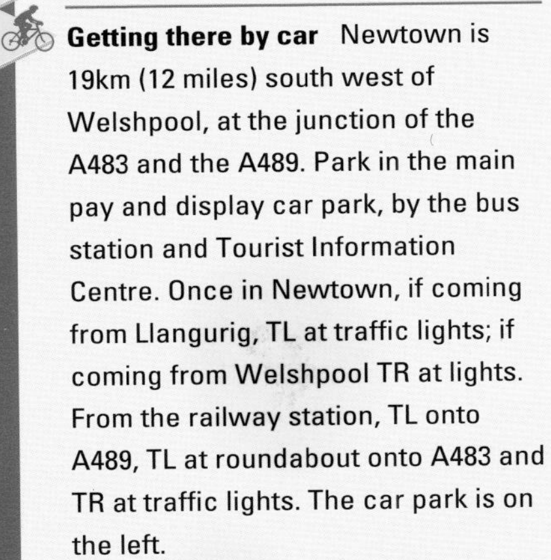

Getting there by car Newtown is 19km (12 miles) south west of Welshpool, at the junction of the A483 and the A489. Park in the main pay and display car park, by the bus station and Tourist Information Centre. Once in Newtown, if coming from Llangurig, TL at traffic lights; if coming from Welshpool TR at lights. From the railway station, TL onto A489, TL at roundabout onto A483 and TR at traffic lights. The car park is on the left.

Getting there by train There is a main line railway station in Newtown, on the Shrewsbury to Aberystwyth line. Telephone (08457) 484950 or visit www.nationalrail.co.uk for travel information.

From Newtown the route heads north to Berriew and then follows the Rhiw Valley around to New Mills. Here there is an optional extension of 13km (8 miles) to Llanfair Caereinion and the Welshpool and Llanfair Railway. From New Mills the route heads south, through the hamlet of Highgate for a steep climb and descent back to Newtown.

Places of interest along the route

A Newtown

The town dates back to the 13th century, when it was an important market town on the River Severn. Today's market is held every Tuesday. The town was the birthplace of Robert Owen (1771–1858), a social reformer and trade unionist who founded the Co-operative Society. The **Robert Owen Museum**, Broad Street, tells his story. Charge. Open all year, Monday–Friday 0930–1200 and 1400–1530; Saturday 0930–1130. Telephone (01686) 626345. Visitors can also see Owen's **tomb** in St Mary's church and a **statue** of him in Shortbridge Street. The **Textile Museum**, Commercial Street, describes the town's prominence in spinning and weaving flannel and tweeds. Open all year, Saturday and Monday 1400–1700. Telephone (01686) 622024. **Oriel 31** is an art gallery housed in the Davies Memorial Gallery, showing a varied programme of visual art and craft exhibitions through the year. Telephone (01686) 625041 for more information.

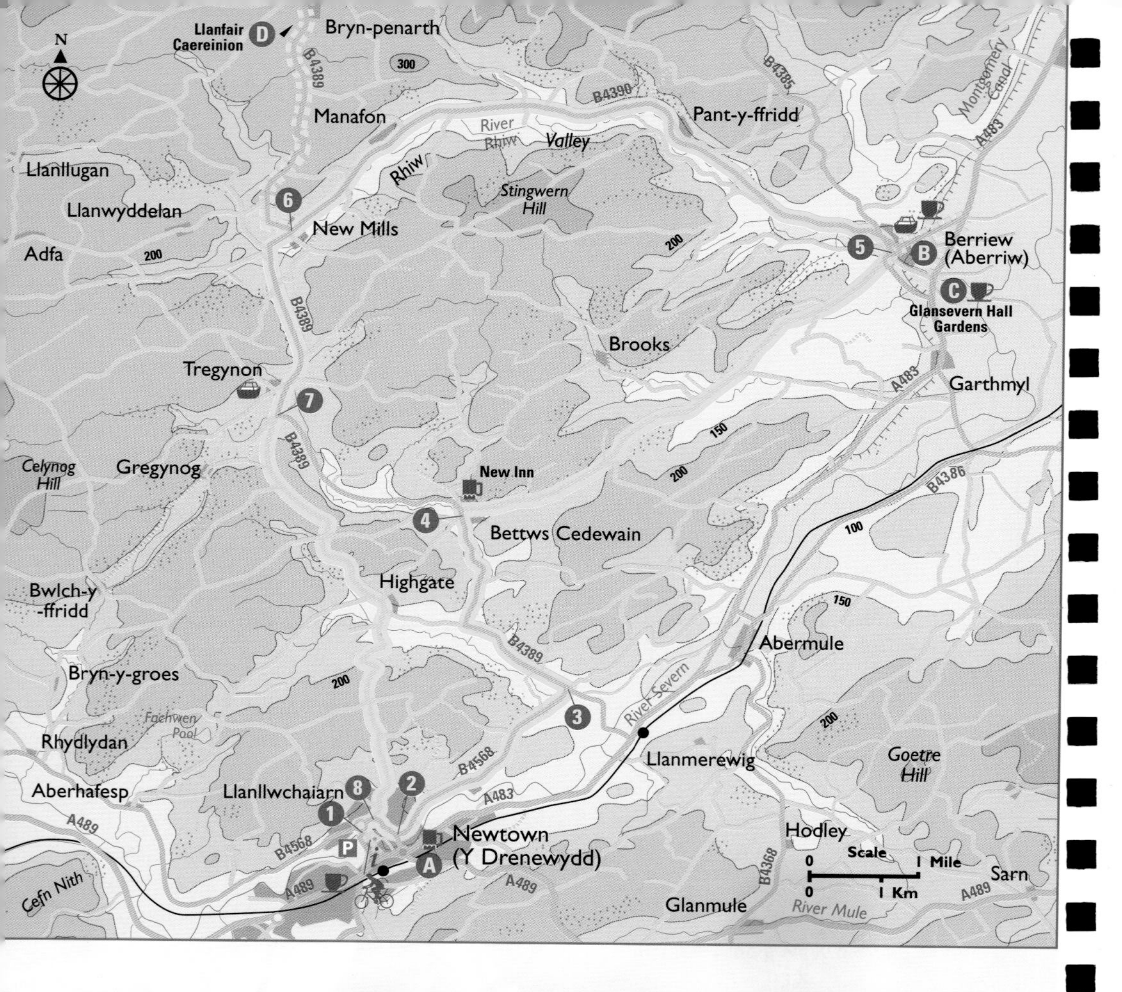

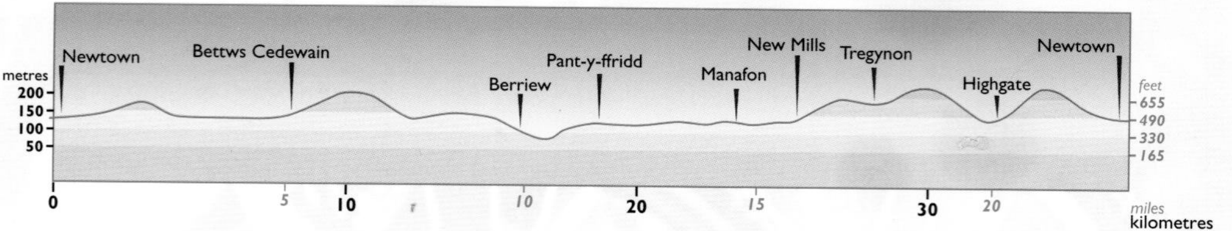

Ⓑ Berriew

On the Montgomeryshire/Shropshire border, this is an attractive village of traditional Welsh black and white houses. **The Museum of Sculpture** contains a collection of works by Andrew Logan, famous as the founder of the Alternative Miss World Competition. Open Easter, May–October, Wednesday–Sunday 1200–1800; November and December, weekends 1200–1800. Small charge. Café and gift shop. Telephone (01686) 640689; www.andrewlogan.com

C Glansevern Hall Gardens, Glansevern

A 7ha (18 acre) garden on the banks of the River Severn. There are formal gardens, walled and rose gardens, lakes, woodland and water gardens. Tearoom and gift shop. Open May–September, Friday, Saturday and Bank Holiday Mondays 1200–1800. Charge. Telephone (01686) 640200.

D Llanfair Caereinion

The small town of Llanfair Caereinion was once a flannel-making centre. Today it is the main terminus of the Welshpool and Llanfair Railway. This narrow gauge railway was first opened in 1903 and carried passengers and goods until its closure in 1956. In 1963 the railway was purchased by the preservation society who have restored the railway along its full length. Steam trains run April to October and during December. Telephone (01938) 810441 for details.

Route description

TL out of car park, no S[illegible]L at TJ into Broad Street and cross River Severn.

1 Take third exit at roundabout into Commercial Street, SP Bettws Cedewain. Continue SO at fork, SP Bettws Cedewain.

2 TL, SP Bettws Cedewain B4568, and continue to TJ.

3 TL at TJ, SP Llanfair Caereinion B4389. Continue to Bettws Cedewain.

4 Cross river in village and TR, Berriew (7km/4.5 miles). Continue into Berriew. To visit Museum of Sculpture and picnic area, TR, SP Museum.

5 To visit Glansevern Gardens, ignore TL, SP New Mills. Continue to TJ and TR. Follow road to TJ where TR onto A483. Entrance to gardens is on LHS.

Otherwise, to continue route, TL in Berriew, SP New Mills (15.5km/9.5 miles), and immediately TL at TJ, no SP. Follow B4390 along Rhiw valley to New Mills.

6 Arrive New Mills (25.5km/16 miles). To visit Llanfair Caereinion, TR, SP Llanfair Caereinion. Continue into town, cross River Banwy and TR, SP Welshpool/A458. The station is immediately on RHS.

Otherwise, to continue route, TL at TJ, SP Tregynon. Continue through Tregynon.

7 Continue SO (ignore TL SP Newtown). Descend to Highgate for steep climb out of hamlet, followed by steep descent into Newtown.

8 TR at TJ, no SP, and return to car park to finish the ride. **37km (23 miles)**

Food and drink

There is plenty of choice in Newtown, including the Severn Café in the car park at the start of the ride. Refreshments are also available at the Museum of Sculpture, Glansevern Hall Gardens and Llanfair Caereinion Station.

The New Inn, Bettws Cedewain

Open for meals at lunch times.

Route
8

ELLESMERE AND WEM

Route information

Distance 38.5km (24 miles)

Grade Easy

Terrain Mainly quiet lanes and several short sections of A road. The stretch of route along the canal towpath is rough in places.

Time to allow 2–3 hours.

Getting there by car Ellesmere is at the junction of the A528 (Shrewsbury/ Wrexham) and the A495 (Oswestry/ Whitchurch). There is car parking at The Mere.

Getting there by train The closest railway station is at Wem, on the route. There is also a station at Gobowen, but it is 12.5km (8 miles) from Ellesmere. Telephone (08457) 484950 or visit www.nationalrail.co.uk for travel information.

Getting there by bus The bus company Arriva carries two bicycles per bus on the number 501 service between Shrewsbury and Ellesmere. Telephone (0870) 608 2608 for more information.

A scenic route through the countryside of north Shropshire, between Ellesmere, on the Llangollen Canal, and Wem, on the River Roden, following quiet lanes and a section of the canal. The route can be shortened to 25.5km (16 miles) by returning from Loppington.

Places of interest along the route

A The Mere, Ellesmere
One of several meres in the district. The meres were formed at the end of the last Ice Age. Hollows left in the land by the melting glaciers filled with water to form lakes. The Visitor Centre describes the natural history of the area. Also restaurant, gardens, childrens' play-gound and rowing boats for hire. Telephone Shropshire County Council for more information (01743) 252363; www.ellesmere.co.uk

B Rue Wood Nature Reserve, near Wem
One of several nature reserves managed by Shropshire Wildlife Trust. For more information visit www.shropshirewildlifetrust.org.uk.

C Lowe Hall, Lowe
The hall was built in 1666 and was the home of Judge Jeffreys, the Hanging Judge. As Chief Justice of England in the 17th century, he hung 330 prisoners and transported 800 to the colonies.

D Colemere Country Park, near Ellesmere
Mature woodland and grazing pasture surrounds the mere. This is a Site of Special Scientific Interest with important bogland, vegetation and wildlife. Walks and a picnic area. Telephone Shropshire County Council for more information (see A above).

Ellesmere

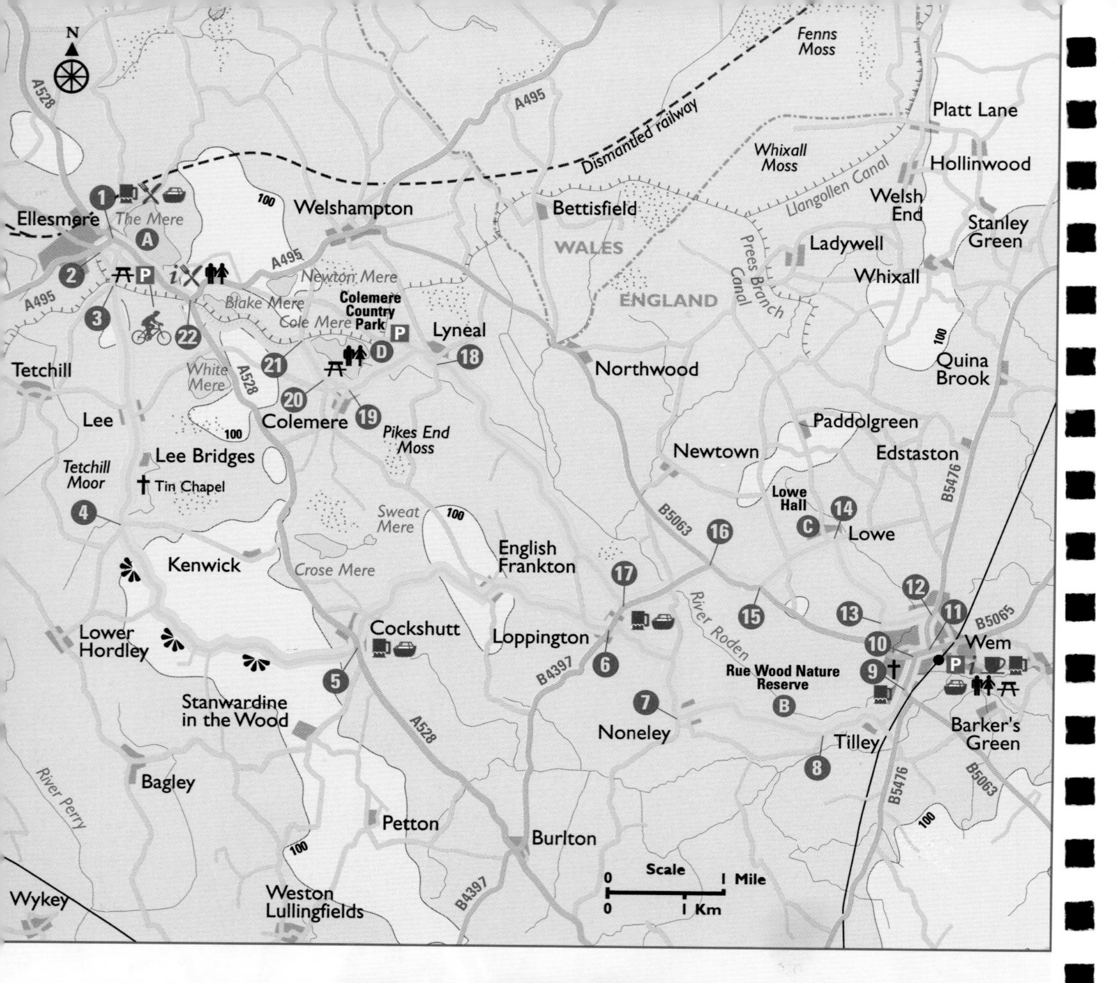

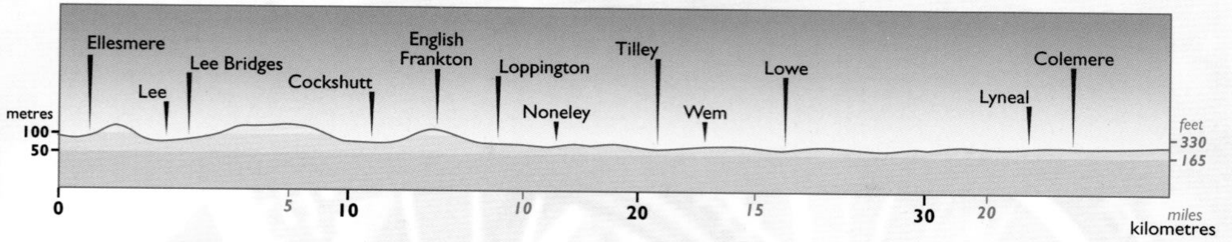

Route description

To start the route from Wem Station, leave station on B5065 towards town centre. TR at direction 11, SP Tilstock/Whixall.

From Ellesmere, start at the car park and picnic site opposite The Mere. TL out of car park towards town centre.

1 TL after garage, SP Tetchill/Ellesmere College.

2 Take second TL, SP Wharf, and follow canal towpath. TL and walk over footbridge (1.5km/1 mile). Return to road at next bridge, where TR over bridge.

3 TL, SP Lee/Lower Hordley/Bagley. Continue through Lee and Lee Bridges, passing tin chapel on LHS. ***4.5km (3 miles)***

4 Take second TL, SP Kenwick Park/ Cockshutt.

5 TL onto A528, SP Ellesmere (9.5km/ 6 miles). Soon TR (CARE), SP English Frankton/ Loppington. Follow this road through English Frankton into Loppington.

6 TL in Loppington, SP Newtown/Wem. To shorten route, SO to pond where TL, no SP, and continue from direction 18 in Lyneal.

Otherwise, to follow main route TR by Dicken Arms (note bull ring in road).

7 TL by Noneley Hall, no SP (16.5km/ 10.5 miles). Continue, passing Rue Wood Nature Reserve on LHS.

8 TL at TJ, SP Wem. Pass 17th-century black and white houses in Tilley and bear L into Wem.

9 TL at TJ in Wem onto B5063, no SP. ***20.5km (12.5 miles)***

10 TR at TJ by church, SP Whitchurch (car park on RHS, shops and toilets in town centre).

11 If you started from Wem Station, SO and return to station to complete the route.

Otherwise, TL opposite car park into New Street, SP Tilstock/Whixall. Pass Hawkstone Arms.

12 TL after Hawkstone Arms (Pyms Road), no SP.

13 TR at TJ, no SP (22.5km/14 miles). Continue into Lowe.

14 TL at TJ, SP Loppington/Whixall. Pass access to Lowe Hall on RHS.

15 TR at TJ onto B5063, SP Ellesmere. ***(25km/15.5 miles)***

16 TL, SP Loppington. Continue on this road towards Loppington, ignoring first TR.

17 Take second TR (by pond), no SP (27km/17 miles). Continue on this road into Lyneal.

18 SO at XR in Lyneal, no SP (32km/ 20 miles). Shortly TL at TJ, no SP, and TL, SP Colemere. Pass Colemere Country Park on RHS.

19 TR, no SP, and again TR, no SP.

20 TR at TJ, no SP (35km/21.5 miles). Continue and cross bridge over canal.

21 TR onto towpath. TR under bridge. Continue alongside canal.

22 Leave canal just before tunnel. TL then TR onto A528, SP Ellesmere, and return to car park on LHS to finish the route. ***38.5km (24 miles)***

Food and drink

There are numerous cafés and pubs in Ellesmere and Wem. The following villages have pubs serving meals: Cockshutt, Loppington and Tilley. There are convenience stores at Cockshutt and Loppington.

Route 9

A CIRCUIT FROM WHITCHURCH

Route information

Distance 41km (25.5 miles)

Grade Easy

Terrain Mostly quiet lanes with a few demanding hills.

Time to allow 2–3 hours.

Getting there by car Whitchurch is 29km (18 miles) north of Shrewsbury, on the A41/A49 from the north or south, and the A525 from the east or west. Park by Tesco supermarket, Bridgewater Street.

Getting there by train The Crewe/Shrewsbury service stops at Whitchurch. The route can also be accessed from Prees Station (request) and Wem. Telephone (08457) 484950 or visit www.nationalrail. co.uk for travel information.

Getting there by canal Whixall Marina is on the Prees Branch and offers mooring. Telephone (01948) 880540 for information.

Starting from Whitchurch the route heads east and then south to Edstaston, where an optional extension will take you to Wem (an additional 6.5km/4 miles) for shops, cafés and toilets. From here the route follows the line of the old Prees Branch Canal before turning north east and following the Llangollen Canal back into Whitchurch. The route passes two splendid lift bridges on the canal.

Places of interest along the route

A Whitchurch

First settled by the Romans, today Whitchurch is a busy market town (market every Friday). Whitchurch is on Shropshire's Regional Cycle Route 31, a 45km (28 mile) route between Oswestry, Ellesmere and Whitchurch. The route is part of the National Cycle Network and links with National Cycle Route 45 and the National Byway (a country-wide leisure cycling route) at Whitchurch. Contact Shropshire County Council for more information on (01743) 253035. Whitchurch TIC houses the Heritage Centre, which describes local history. Displays include Roman treasures, and information on J B Joyce, the world's oldest tower clock makers, Randolph Caldecott (1846–86) illustrator and author of children's books, and Edward German (1862–1936) the composer. Interactive displays. Open all year, Monday–Thursday 0900–1700, Friday closes 1630, Saturday opens 1000. Admission free. Telephone (01948) 665432; www.shropshire-tourism.com

B Brown Moss Nature Reserve, near Edgeley

Managed by Shropshire County Council, the nature reserve comprises attractive pools, marsh, heath and woodland. Free access at all reasonable times. Contact Shropshire County Council for further information (see above).

C Prees Branch Canal, near Prees

A branch of the Llangollen Canal, which never actually reached Prees. It was used for access to nearby clay pits – the clay was used to repair the local canals. After disuse for several years, the arm now gives boaters from the Llangollen Canal access to Whixall Marina, constructed in the old clay pit. The nature reserve, administered by Shropshire Wildlife Trust, covers 2.4ha (6 acres). The isolated stretch of water is home to water birds, damsel and dragonflies and aquatic plants. For more information visit www.shropshirewildlifetrust.org.uk

Food and drink

Plenty of choice in Whitchurch and Wem. There is a convenience store at Ightfield and in Prees.

Old Jack, Calverhall
Bar meals available.

Waggoners, Platt Lane
Pub in a tiny settlement. Meals available. Outside seating.

Whitchurch

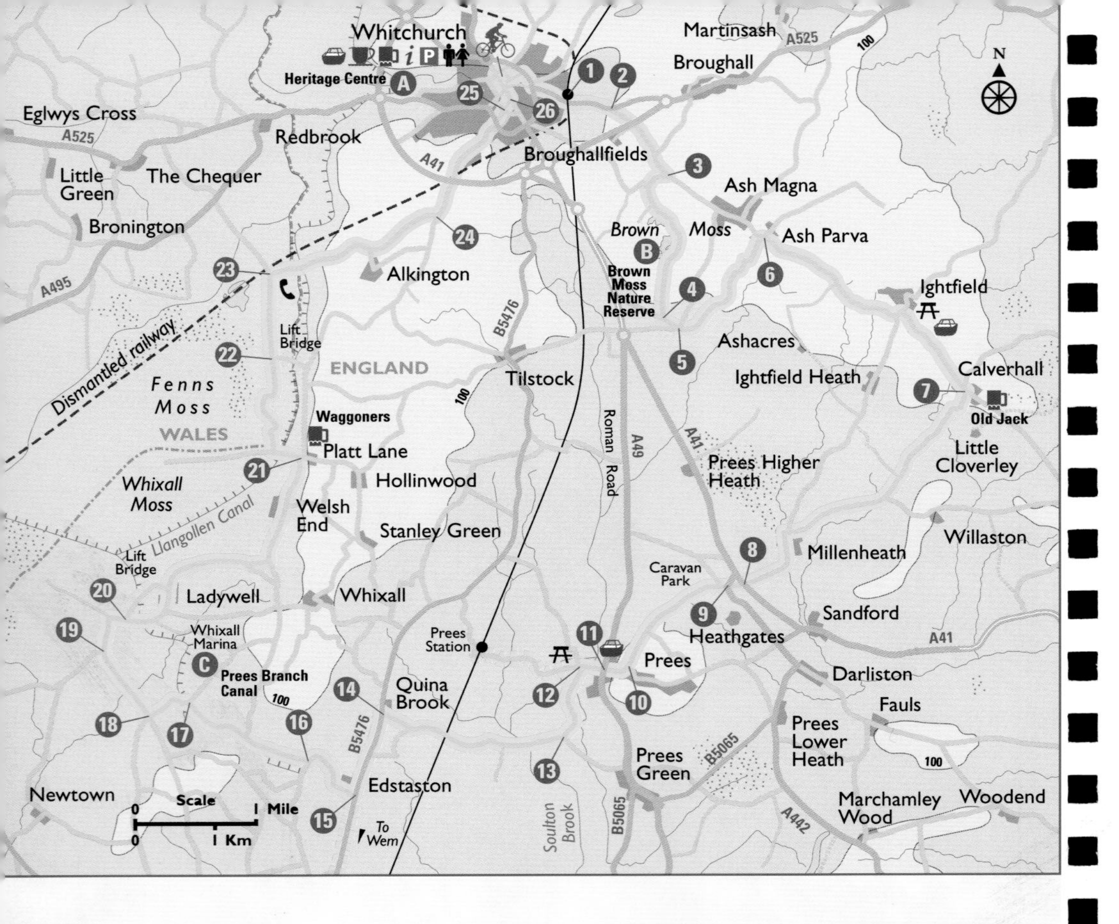

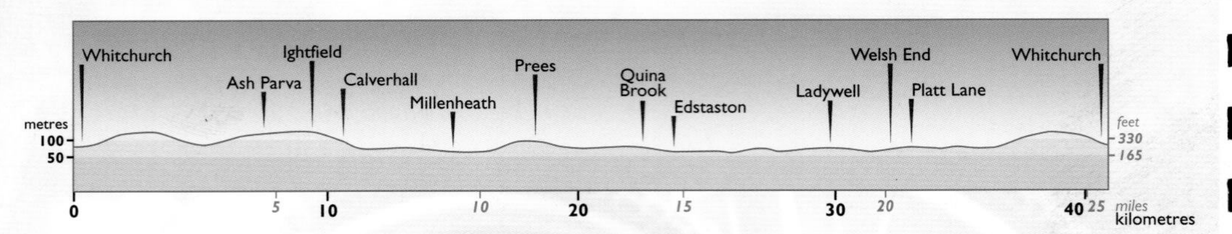

Route description

To start from Whitchurch Station, TL from station and continue route at direction 2.

To start from Prees Station, TL out of station and join route in Prees, at direction 12, where TR.

To start from Wem Station, TL out of station towards town centre. TR to Edstaston, where join route by bearing L at direction 15.

From Whitchurch start by the TIC/Heritage Centre in St Mary's Street. Head south east and TL into St John's Street. TR at TJ into Brownlow Street, no SP. Continue to traffic lights where take second TL into Station Road.

1 Note Joyce's clock factory on LHS and pass railway station.

2 Before roundabout, take path on R through industrial estate. Exit estate to roundabout and take second exit, SP Ash/Ightfield/Calverhall.

3 TR, SP Brown Moss. Continue through nature reserve to TJ with grass triangle.

4 TL at TJ, SP Ash.

5 SO at XR. Continue to Ash Parva.

6 TR at TJ, SP Ightfield/Calverhall. Continue through Ightfield. There is a playground and picnic table on LHS just before shop (10km/6 miles). Follow road SO into Calverhall. (John Pemberton Heywood, owner of the Shavington Estate is commemorated by the wooden bus shelter dated 1885, and the almhouses attached to the church built in 1887 for £1,400. Note the plaque on the old smithy dated 1884 with the motto 'Strike while the iron is hot'.)

7 TR, SP Prees. Continue to junction with A41

8 SO at A41, SP Prees.

9 SO at A442, no SP but caravan park on RHS (16km/10 miles). Continue for climb into Prees (note old cottage on LHS just before church 'Thomas and Martha Webb 1759').

10 TR at TJ, SP Wem.

11 SO at XR, SP Whixall.

12 If you started from Prees Station, continue SO to return to the station and finish the ride.

Otherwise, TL into Brades Road (playground and picnic table on RHS).

13 TR at TJ, no SP. ***19.5km (12 miles)***

14 TL onto B5476, no SP.

15 To visit Wem, or return to Wem Station, continue SO along B5476. For station, TL at TJ to town centre.

Otherwise, to continue route, TR, SP Edstaston.

16 TR, no SP (24km/15 miles) along Prees Branch Canal and through the nature reserve.

17 TL at TJ over Prees Branch Canal.

18 TR at XR, SP Northwood/Ellesmere.

19 TR at TJ, SP Whixall/Whitchurch. Continue on this road, ignoring first TL.

20 To see lift bridge, TL onto a no through road (except for pedestrians and cyclists). Pass bridge. TR at TJ, no SP, then TL at TJ and continue to direction 21.

Otherwise, continue SO, passing turn to Whixall marina on RHS.

21 TL at XR by Waggoners Inn, SP Fenns Bank (33km/20.5 miles).

22 TR here to see lift bridge.

23 TR after public telephone, SP Blackoe (on LHS, note steam engine on weather vane above old station).

24 TL at TJ, no SP. ***38.5km (24 miles)***

25 SO at XR into Bark Hill.

26 TL at mini roundabout into Watergate Street. Dismount and walk through the Bullring (note clock built by Joyce on RHS). TL into High Street then TR into St Mary's Street to finish the ride at the Heritage Centre.

41km (25.5 miles)

Route **10**

SHREWSBURY AND MORETON CORBET

Route information

Distance 42km (26 miles)

Grade Moderate

Terrain Quiet, undulating country lanes and a short section of cycle track. Two long hills rewarded by excellent views.

Time to allow 3–4 hours.

Getting there by car Approach Shrewsbury from the A49/A53 (Battlefield Island) to the north. The routes starts at the railway station, where there is parking. Alternatively, follow the one-way system in a right hand circuit around the town and park in the Raven Meadows car park (continue SO from here and follow SP Station).

Getting there by train There are regular services to Shrewsbury from Birmingham, Manchester, Chester, and all parts of Wales. Yorton, en route, is a request stop on the Crewe line. Telephone (08457) 484950 or visit www.nationalrail.co.uk for travel information.

This route starts in Shrewsbury and makes a circuit to the north of the town, heading up to Bomere Heath and onto Clive before turning east to pass Corbet Wood and Grinshill Quarry. The route then heads south through Shawbury and Roden before turning west, past Haughmond Hill and Abbey, and using a section of cycle track for the return into Shrewsbury. Shrewsbury has approximately 32km (20 miles) of cycle routes, both on- and off-road. Contact Shrewsbury and Atcham Borough Council for a map of the cycle routes and car parks on (01743) 281000.

Places of interest along the route

A Shrewsbury

Evidence of the town was first recorded in 901. Today Shrewsbury is a busy county town, located in a loop of the River Severn. The town centre contains many attractive timber-framed buildings, including Tudor, Jacobean and Georgian buildings. There is lots for the visitor to see, including **Shrewsbury Castle and the Shropshire Regimental Museum**, originally built in the 12th century. Open February to Easter, Wednesday–Saturday 1000–1600; Easter to September, Tuesday–Saturday 1000–1700 and Sundays/Bank Holidays 1000–1600. Telephone to confirm winter opening. Small charge. Telephone (01743) 358516; www.shrewsburymuseums.com. **Shrewsbury Abbey**, familiar to readers of Ellis Peters' **Brother Cadfael** books, was founded by the Saxons, rebuilt by the Normans and modified by the Tudors. Open daily, end March to end October 0930–1730; November to March 1030–1500. Admission free. Telephone (01743) 232723. **Rowley's House Museum**, housed in a 16th-century timber-framed warehouse, describes local history. Open January to Easter, Tuesday–Saturday

1000–1600; Easter to end September, Tuesday–Saturday 1000–1700, Sunday, Monday and Bank Holidays 1000–1600. Admission free. Telephone (01743) 361196; www.shrewsburymuseums.com. Contact the Tourist Information Centre for information on other places of interest in Shrewsbury on (01743) 281200; www.shrewsbury.ws.

B Corbet Wood and Grinshill Quarry Trail, near Clive
A wooded sandstone hill with sandstone outcrops and abandoned and working quarries. Grinshill Quarry was the site of the 19th-century discovery of fossilised bones, named rhynchosaurs and believed to have lived around 245 to 215 million years ago. Picnic area. Free access at all reasonable times.

C Moreton Corbet Castle, Moreton Corbet
The ornate ruin of a 13th-century keep and gatehouse, later merged with an Elizabethan manor house. The house was never completed and changed hands four times during the Civil War. English Heritage property. Free access at all reasonable times. Telephone (01743) 281200; www.englishheritage.co.uk

D Haughmond Hill, near Upton Magna
Forestry Commission land with wonderful views, picnic areas and waymarked cycle routes.

E Haughmond Abbey, near Upton Magna
The abbey was founded in 1135 by William Fitzalan, on a beautiful sloping site on Haughmond Hill. See route 3 for more information.

Food and drink

Plenty of choice in Shrewsbury, with numerous cafés and pubs. Bomere Heath and Clive have a convenience store and a pub and there is a convenience store in Shawbury. There are three garden centres, at Black Birches, Edgebolton and Roden, all just off the route but with tearooms and cafés

Railway Inn, Yorton
The pub serves sandwiches and fine beer.

Haughmond Abbey

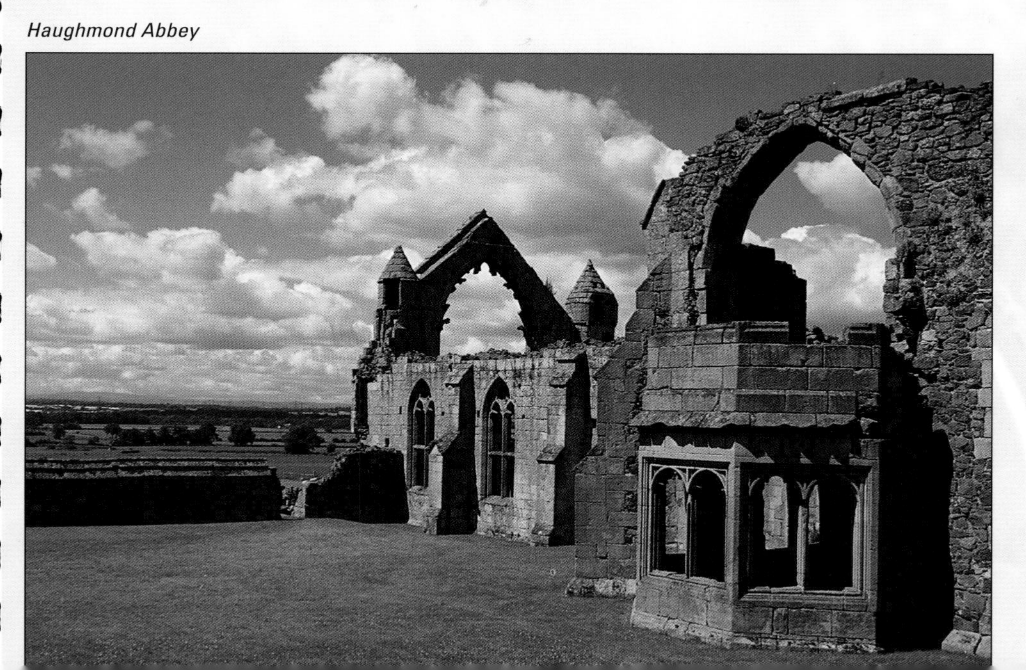

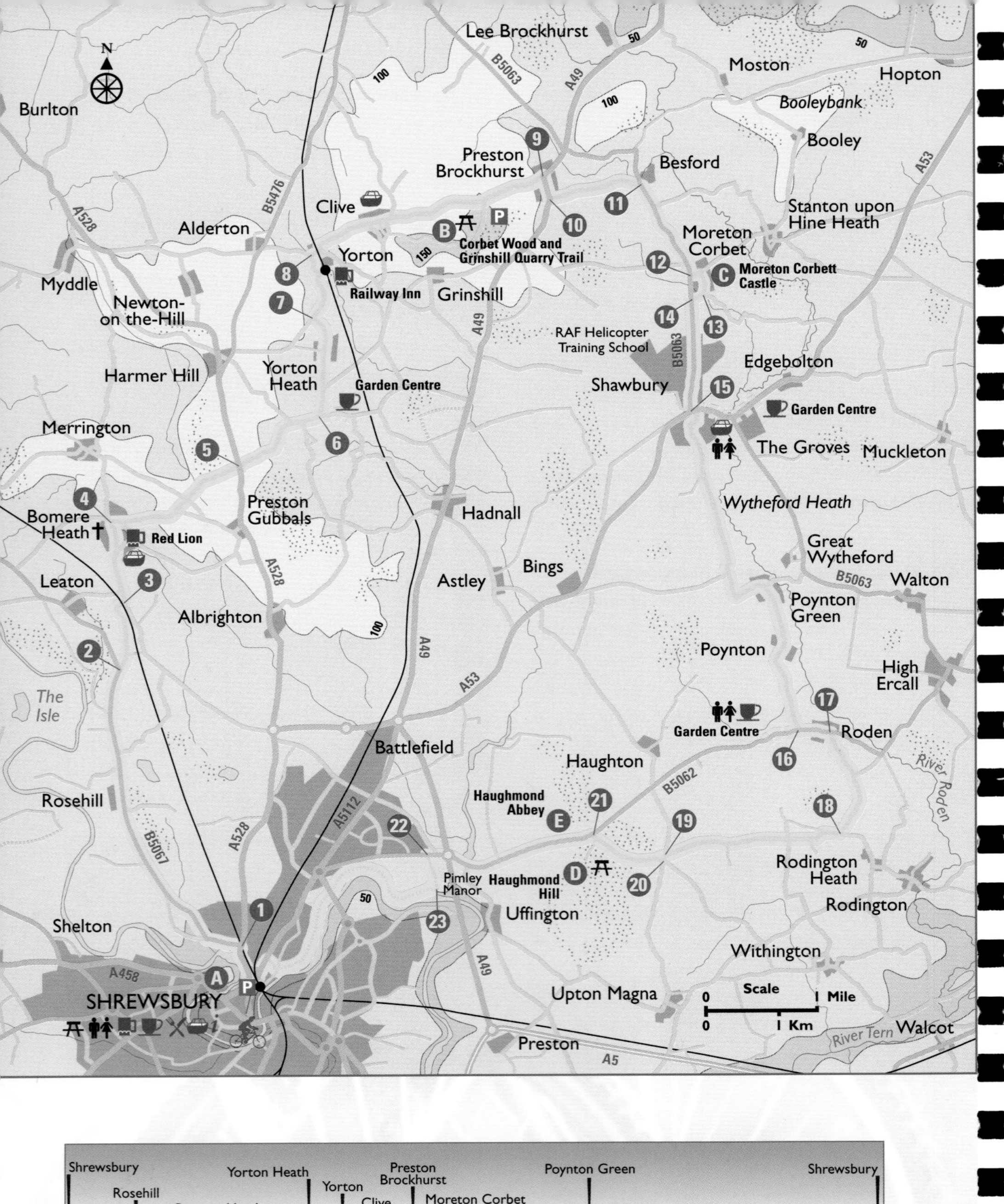

N
Burlton
Lee Brockhurst
B5063
A49
50
100
Moston
Hopton
Booleybank
Booley
A53
Preston
Brockhurst
Besford
9
10
11
B5476
Clive
Alderton
A528
P
B
Corbet Wood and
Grinshill Quarry Trail
Stanton upon
Hine Heath
Moreton
Corbet
150
Yorton
Railway Inn
Grinshill
C
Moreton Corbett
Castle
12
8
7
Myddle
Newton-
on the-Hill
14
13
RAF Helicopter
Training School
Edgebolton
Harmer Hill
Yorton
Heath
Garden Centre
Shawbury
15
Garden Centre
Merrington
5
6
The Groves
Muckleton
4
Bomere
Heath
Red Lion
Preston
Gubbals
Hadnall
Wytheford Heath
Great
Wytheford
Leaton
3
Bings
Astley
B5063
Walton
Albrighton
Poynton
Green
2
Poynton
High
Ercall
The
Isle
17
Garden Centre
Roden
Battlefield
16
Haughton
River
Roden
Rosehill
A5112
B5062
Haughmond
Abbey
E
21
18
22
19
B5067
Rodington
Heath
Pimley
Manor
Haughmond
Hill
D
20
Rodington
1
23
Uffington
Shelton
Withington
A458
A
SHREWSBURY
Upton Magna
Scale
0
Mile
0
Km
River Tern
Walcot
Preston
A5

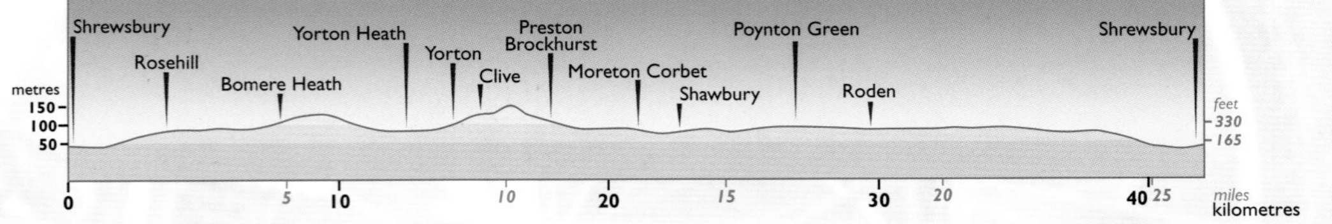

Shrewsbury
Rosehill
Bomere Heath
Yorton Heath
Yorton
Clive
Preston
Brockhurst
Moreton Corbet
Shawbury
Poynton Green
Roden
Shrewsbury
metres
150
100
50
feet
330
165
0
5
10
10
20
15
30
20
40
25
miles
kilometres

Route description

Start from outside the railway station at the traffic lights. SO, then immediately TR into Chester Street (one-way), SP Ellesmere/ Baschurch A528. Keep River Severn on LHS and climb.

1 TL at top of hill into Berwick Road, SP Baschurch B5067. Continue, ignoring first TR.

2 Take second TR, SP Bomere Heath/ Merrington.

3 TL at TJ under railway bridge. Continue into Bomere Heath.

4 TR at XR by chapel (after shop and Red Lion pub), SP Hadnall/Preston Gubbals.

8km (5 miles)

5 SO at XR with A528 (CARE), SP Hadnall. Continue, ignoring first TL.

6 To visit tearoom at Black Birches garden centre, SO then TL into drive.

Otherwise, take second TL, SP Yorton Heath/ Sansaw Heath/Yorton.

7 TR at TJ, no SP. ***13km (8 miles)***

8 TR at TJ, SP Clive/Grinshill. Pass Yorton Station and Railway Inn. Climb up through Clive to top of the hill. TR to visit Corbet Wood and Grinshill Quarry Trail. ***17km (10.5 miles)***

Otherwise, continue down hill towards Preston Brockhurst and junction with A49.

9 TR at TJ with A49 (CARE), SP Shrewsbury.

10 Soon TL into lane (by black and white house), no SP. ***18.5km (11.5 miles)***

11 TR at TJ, no SP. Continue towards Moreton Corbet, ignoring first TL.

12 Take second TL, SP Stanton/Booley. Immediately TR, no SP. Pass Moreton Corbet Castle.

13 TR, SP Shawbury/Wem.

14 TL at TJ onto B5063. Pass RAF Shawbury (helicopter training school) on RHS.

15 TL at traffic lights. To visit Edgebolton Garden Centre continue on A53 towards Market Drayton for short distance.

To continue route, immediately TR, SP Poynton/ Roden to pass church and toilets (24km/15 miles). Continue along this road into Roden.

16 To visit Roden garden centre, TR at TJ. It is on LHS.

Otherwise, to continue route, TL at TJ in Roden, SP High Ercall.

17 TR, SP Rodington/Walcot.

18 TR at TJ, SP Upton Magna/Shrewsbury.

31.5km (19.5 miles)

19 TL at TJ, SP Upton Magna/Atcham.

20 TR at XR, no SP (34.5km/21.5 miles). Haughmond Hill is on LHS.

21 TL at TJ onto B5062, SP Shrewsbury. Haughmond Abbey is on RHS. Continue to junction with A49. Take second exit at roundabout, then first exit at mini roundabout.

22 TL into Pimley Manor.

23 Just before farm, TR onto line of old canal and follow cycle route into town centre. After weir pass under Castle Walk footbridge and take steep TR to road. TL along the Howard Street (prison on RHS) to traffic lights on Castle Foregate. TL to return to station and finish the ride. ***42km (26 miles)***

Route

11

LLANON AND MYNYDD BACH

Route information

Distance 42.5km (26.5 miles)

Grade Strenuous

Terrain A hilly route over quiet roads with some 762m (2500 feet) of climbing, much of this concentrated into the first 14.5km (9 miles) of the route.

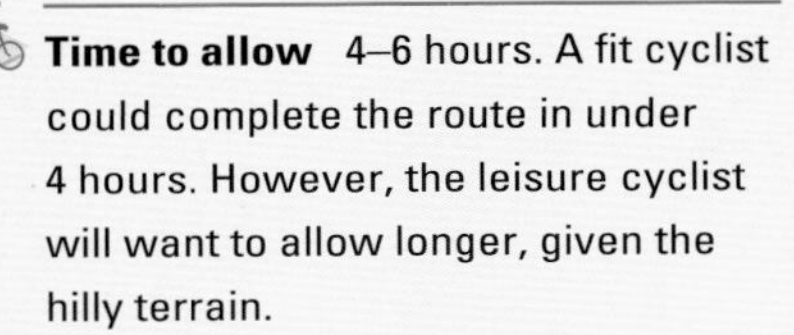

Time to allow 4–6 hours. A fit cyclist could complete the route in under 4 hours. However, the leisure cyclist will want to allow longer, given the hilly terrain.

Getting there by car Llanon is 8km (5 miles) north of Llanelli on the A487. Park in the small car park situated up a L turning off the A487 in the centre of Llanon (fish and chip shop on corner, street name Stryd y sgol). The car park is opposite the White Swan pub.

Getting there by train The nearest railway station is at Aberystwyth, 17.5km (11 miles) from Llanon. Telephone (08457) 484950 or visit www. national-rail.co.uk for travel information.

A ride almost entirely on quiet country lanes carrying little traffic, with natural attractions creating the main source of interest. It is possible to do most of this route without seeing a single vehicle outside settlements and the predominant sounds and sights are likely to be bird song and animals grazing in the fields. The route does involve a good deal of climbing, and a fair number of steep hills, but much of this is in the first 14.5km (9 miles), and there are spectacular views from the high point of the route above the village of Trefenter. After this point the route becomes much easier with a predominance of downhill cycling. There are two optional short cuts.

Places of interest along the route

A Llanon and Llansantffraid

Llanon and the adjoining settlement of Llansantffraid are small villages, with surviving examples of medieval strip field systems. Llansantffraid gives access to the beach. For a small village, Llanon has a reasonable number of shops, including a bakery, post office/stores, petrol station, pubs and a fish and chip shop.

B Mynydd Bach

The mountain of Mynydd Bach, a popular area for walking, reaches a height of 371m (1217 feet). You may see or hear skylarks, curlew, buzzards and the rare Red Kite in the area. At the highest point of the route, you will pass an interesting monument in a modern Celtic design, commemorating four local Welsh poets. There are fine views from here. Opposite the monument (on LHS of road) a path leads to a trig point, with more views of Cardigan Bay and the surrounding hills. Good places for picnics anywhere along this section of the route.

Route description

To start the route from Aberystwyth, leave railway station and head south out of the town on the A487. Continue into Llanon where TL into Stryd y sgol (fish and chip shop on corner). Start opposite the White Swan Inn.

In Llanon start from car park opposite White Swan Inn. With school and car park on RHS, face away from main road and cycle (or walk!) up steep hill. The climb is not that long, passing speed de-restriction signs and Llanon service reservoir before easing off. After a dip in the road and a further stretch of uphill, look for an unsigned TL.

1 TL, no SP. Road continues uphill, passing metal gates to Pentre and Ty Llwyd Farm, before levelling out to reach B4337.

---

2 TR onto B4337 and almost immediately TL, no SP. Follow this road, passing entrance to Hafodwnog Isaf on RHS. Continue to staggered XR (post box in hedge opposite).

---

3 SO at XR, no SP but TL SP Llanrhystud/ Llanon. Ignore no through road on RHS and TL to Llanrhystud and continue towards Llangwyryfon, over bridge and around double hair-pin with steep climb on second bend. Within a few hundred metres look out for TL.

---

4 **Optional route a** To avoid strenuous climb, SO at junction, passing Evan Bros Agricultural Dealers (just beyond R turn), then Fferm Cefnmabws on L. SO at XR (just beyond a farm) on B4576, SP Llangwyryfon. Continue on this road into Llangwyryfon and continue route from direction 6.

Otherwise, to continue main route, TL, SP Unsuitable for Heavy Goods Vehicles and Evan Bros Agricultural Dealers building in front on RHS (6.5km/4 miles). Continue down hill, quickly reaching steep downhill sharp R bend, followed by a further short stretch of steep downhill (1:5) with a sharp L bend at the bottom. CARE needed as this road can be slippery. Follow road along Cwm Mabws, cross bridge, pass cluster of houses, climb (short but steep) and arrive at B4337. ***9.5km (6 miles)***

---

5 TR onto B4337. To visit Llanrhystud, continue SO along B4337.

Great CARE is required on this short stretch of B road which is fast with poor visibility. You may prefer to walk the short distance between minor roads, keeping to the right of the road.

To continue route, shortly TR into minor road, SP Penrhos Golf and Country Club, for steep climb. At top of this uphill, road continues to rise, interspersed with level and downhill stretches, with a heavily wooded valley on LHS. Eventually you see a ridge ahead on RHS, topped with wind turbines – the high point of the route. Passing small chapel on LHS (12.5km/8 miles) and road levels out. Ignore TL by house, and follow road round to L. Continue, ignoring next TL (13.5km/8.5 miles). After couple of sharp bends, ignore next TL (SP road unsuitable for heavy goods vehicles – Cnwc y Barcud), and continue to R. In 30m take LHF. Continue along this road into Llangwyryfon to junction (church on LHS and village hall/ graveyard SO). ***15km (9.5 miles)***

NB: this climb is strenuous – the less fit are strongly advised to consider optional route **a** to reach Llangwyryfon.

---

6 TL down hill between church and village hall. Pass through centre of Llangwyryfon (water tap opposite post office/stores). SO at staggered XR across B4576 (opposite shop, school on RHS), SP Lledrod/Trefenter. There

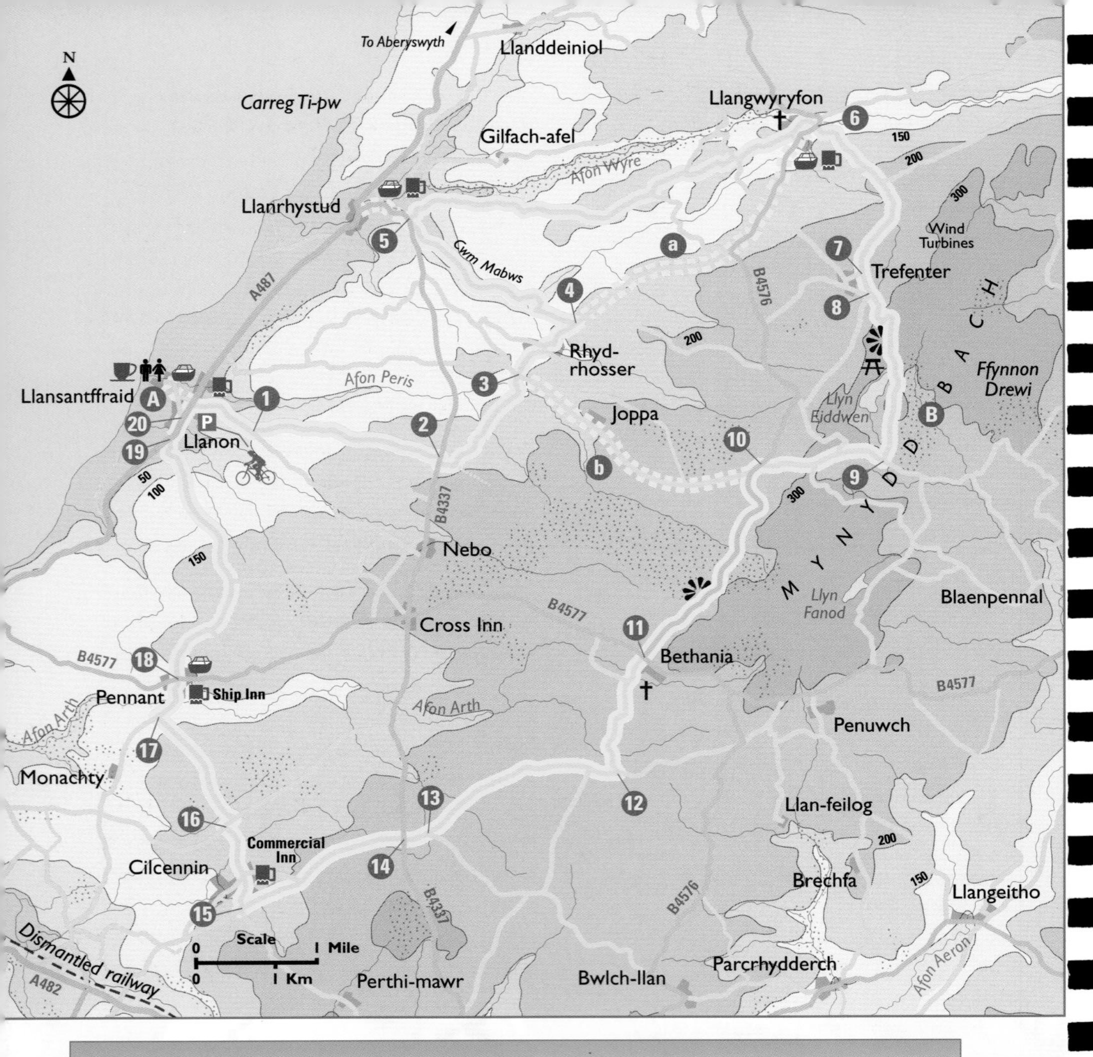

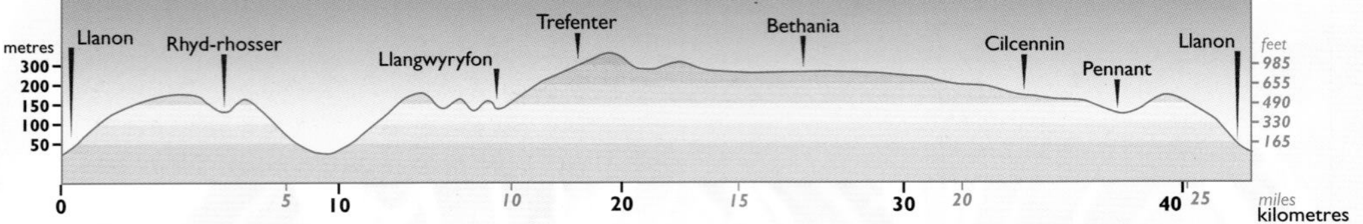

are a number of short steep climbs in next 2.5km (1.5 miles) with a height gain of over 183m (600 feet). Ignore TR then TL (SP Trefenter) and continue on this road (wind turbines visible on hill on LHS ahead) to Trefenter.

7 Arrive Trefenter (18.5km/11.5 miles) and continue, ignoring TL and TR.

8 Cross cattle grid and follow road as it bears R and climbs (good views on RHS, wind turbines on LHS). Pass monument on RHS (most of serious climbing is over now!) Cross second cattle grid (20km/12.5 miles) and continue to TJ. NB: ensure you are in a low gear at junction – steep climb ahead!

9 TR at TJ (21km/13 miles), SP Llanrhystud, for short, steep climb then downhill to TJ with B4576.

10 TL at TJ, SP Bethania.

Optional route b TR away from B4576, SP Llanrhystud. Continue downhill, past forestry on LHS and through Joppa village. Arrive XR (direction 3) and TL. Retrace route into Llanon.

Otherwise, to follow main route, shortly LHF to stay on B4576. Continue along this gently undulating road to XR at Bethania (post box directly ahead, bus shelter on LHS).

11 SO at XR, SP Trefilan/Talsarn B4337. Continue over hump back bridge. Pass Bethania chapel on LHS (26.5km/16.5 miles), then Moelfryn Mawr Stud Farm on LHS. Continue to TJ, passing old mill grid stone/machinery/mill pool dam in small group of trees in field on RHS, just before TJ.

12 TR at TJ, SP Cilcennin but SP is hidden (28km/17.5 miles). Pass large farm Croeswyntoedd at top of rise. Ignore turning to left, and continue to unsigned TJ.

13 TR at TJ, no SP but SP back the way Penuwch. Pass Pencwm Farm/Blaenpennal Stud where honey is sometimes for sale.

14 SO across B4337 (CARE), SP Cilcennin/Cycle Centre. Pass Cyclemart and continue downhill into Cilcennin, passing Commercial Inn.

15 Immediately past Commerical Inn, TR at XR, SP Pennant (33.5km/21miles). SO at staggered XR and continue to TJ.

16 TR at TJ, SP Cross Inn/Talsarn. Immediately TL, SP Pennant. Continue along wooded road towards Pennant.

17 TR at TJ, downhill to cross bridge over river (Ship Inn on RHS), then up hill to XR (shop and garage here).

18 SO at XR, SP Llanon. Stay on this road towards Llanon, ignoring LHF SP No Through Road, then ignoring two TR (at 37.5km/23.5 miles and 38.5km/24 miles).

As you continue, the sea will come into view ahead. The route is downhill all the way – beware of hairpin bend to right, immediately after Llanon village SP.

19 Arrive TJ with A487 (41km/25.5 miles). TR onto A487 and continue into Llanon, past post office on RHS.

20 To visit Llansanffraid, TL into Stryd yr Eglwys. Continue along this road, ignoring all turnings, into Llansanffraid.

To return to Aberystwyth railway station, continue on A487 and retrace route back to station.

Otherwise, TR into Stryd y sgol to finish the route by the White Swan pub.

42.5km (26.5 miles)

Food and drink

Pubs, stores and a fish and chip shop in Llanon. Llanrhystud and Llangwyryfon also have a post office/stores and a pub. There are also pubs in Cilcennin and Pennant. The village shops are not generally open on Sunday and close early on either Wednesday or Thursday. Cyclemart in Cilcennin sells canned drinks and confectionary. Cyclists may wish to carry refreshments to sustain them during this ride.

Route
12

CARDIGAN AND ABERPORTH

Route information

Distance 43km (27 miles)

Grade Moderate

Terrain Mostly quiet lanes and two stretches of B road. The first part of the ride is quite hilly.

Time to allow 3–5 hours.

Getting there by car Cardigan is 54.5km (34 miles) south west of Aberystwyth at the junction of the A484 and A478. Although there are several car parks in the town, parking can be difficult. The route starts from Finch Square in the centre of Cardigan.

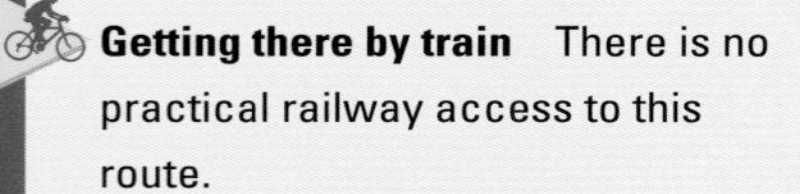

Getting there by train There is no practical railway access to this route.

An attractive route with superb coastal scenery. From the market town of Cardigan, the route heads north west towards Cardigan Island, before turning east and following the coast to Aberporth. Here the route continues east for a short distance before turning inland for the return to Cardigan.

Places of interest along the route

A Cardigan Island Coastal Farm Park, near Gwbert

Located on a headland overlooking Cardigan Bay, the farm park is home to both wild and farm animals. Among many different animals, visitors can see ponies, cattle and llamas, and get good views of seals and dolphins from the coast. Also numerous seabirds and wild flowers. Café. Open March to November, daily 0930–1800. Charge. Telephone (01239) 612196.

B Mwnt Beach

Mwnt is one of many beautiful beaches in Cardigan Bay, where dolphins can often be seen. The beach is a sandy cove with rock pools and safe bathing. Seasonal café.

C Felinwynt Rainforest and Butterfly Centre, Felinwynt

A landscaped tropical house with waterfalls, ponds and a stream, containing free-flying exotic butterflies. The recorded sounds of the Peruvian Amazon provide a backdrop. Also rainforest exhibition and gift shop. Light refreshments and cold drinks available. Open end April to end September, daily 1030–1700. Charge. Telephone (01239) 810882.

D Aberporth

A small village with two sandy beaches and safe bathing. Seasonal café.

For more information on Cardigan and the surrounding area visit www.cardiganshirecoastandcountry.com

Food and drink 

Plenty of choice all year in Cardigan. Aberporth has several cafés open during the holiday season only. Refreshments are available at Cardigan Island Coastal Farm Park and Felinwynt Rainforest and Butterfly Centre.

Mwnt Beach

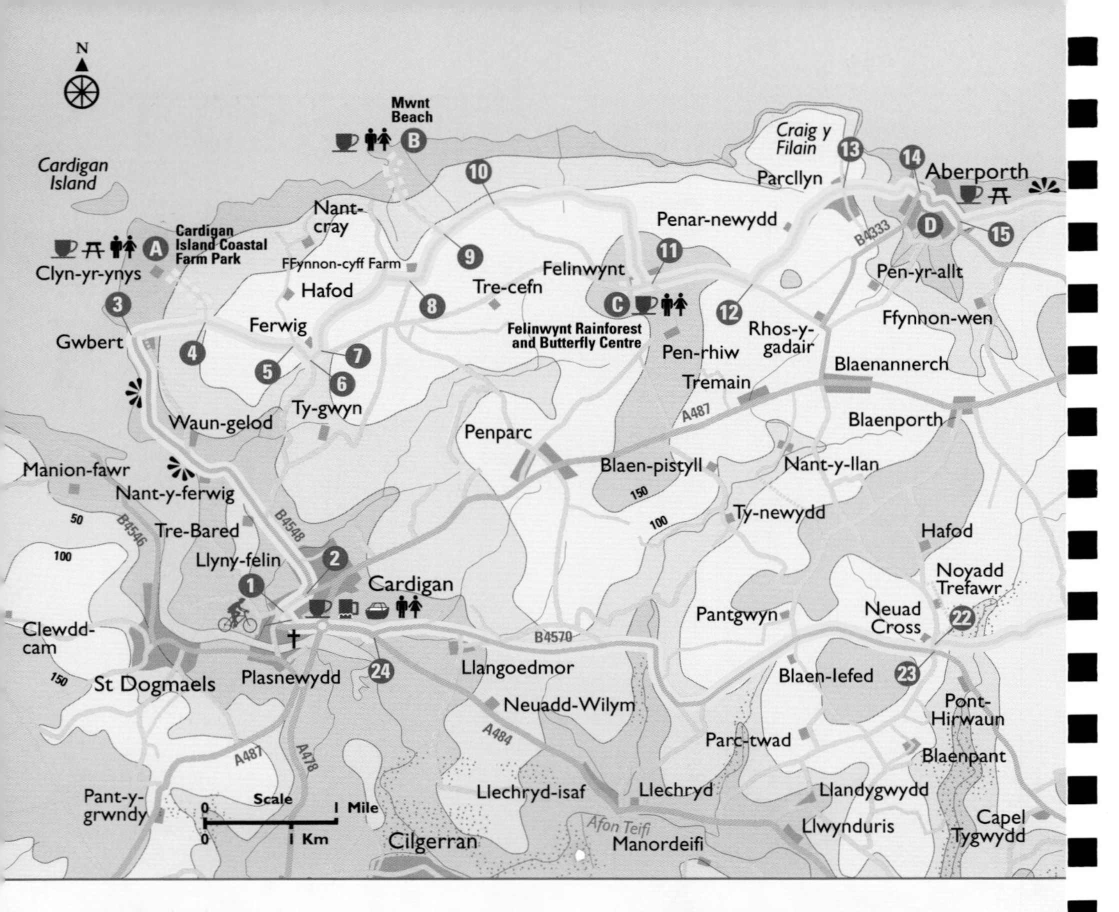

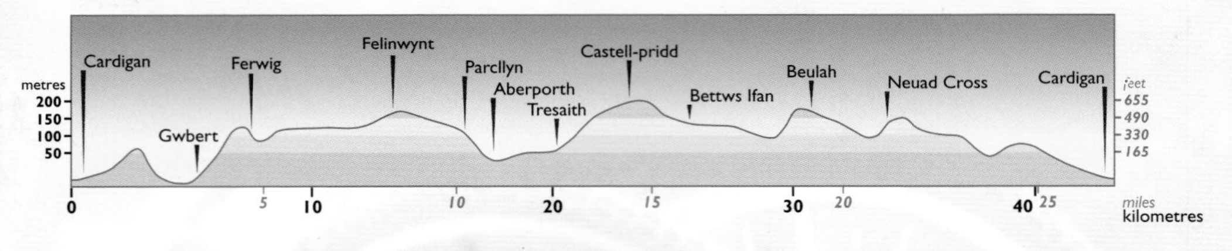

Route description

Start the route in Finch Square. TL out of Finch Square and cycle towards the guildhall (there is a clock on the building).

1 TR at TJ into main street.

2 LHF, SP Gwbert/Mwnt B4548. Almost immediately bear L, SP Gwbert. Continue on this road into Gwbert, with good views over the estuary

3 TR in Gwbert by entrance to Cliff Hotel, no SP (5km/3 miles). Climb.

4 To visit Cardigan Island Coastal Farm Park, TL.

Otherwise, continue SO.

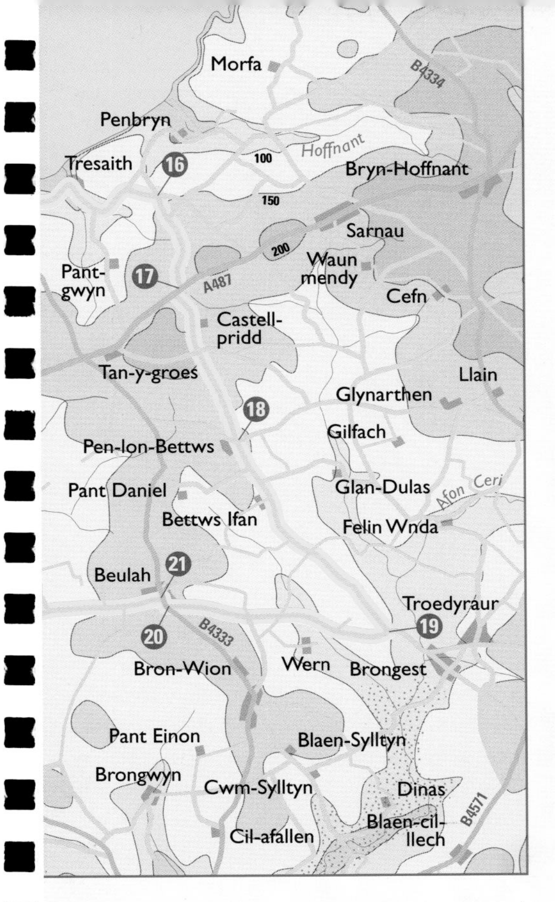

5 TR at junction and descend into Ferwig.

6 TL at TJ, no SP.

7 Take first TL, no SP (7km/4.5 miles). Continue for approximately 1km (0.6 mile) and TR (CARE) through Ffynnon-cyff Farmyard.

8km (5 miles)

8 SO at junction.

9 To visit Mwnt beach, TL.

Otherwise, continue SO.

10 LHF, SP Nant Mawr B&B, and continue along this road into Felinwynt.

11 To visit Felinwynt Rainforest and Butterfly Centre, TR at TJ.

Otherwise, TL at TJ, no SP.

12 TL, SP Parcllyn, and continue into Parcllyn.

13 TL into Pennar Road, no SP but after D.E.R.A. main entrance (15km/9.5 miles). Descend steeply.

14 TL at TJ into Aberporth. Keeping sea on LHS, climb out of Aberporth.

15 TL at junction, SP Tresaith. Continue through Tresaith and climb to XR.

16 TR at XR, SP Cardigan. Continue to junction with A487.

17 TR onto A487 and immediately TL, SP Brongest/Bettws Ifan. Continue towards Bettws Ifan.

18 SO at XR, SP Brongest (23.5km/14.5 miles). Continue towards Brongest.

19 TR at TJ, SP Beulah.

26.5km (16.5 miles)

20 TR onto B4333, SP Beulah, and continue into Beulah.

21 TL, SP Neuad Cross, and continue to Neuad Cross.

22 TL at TJ, no SP. ***32.5km (20 miles)***

23 TR at XR, SP Cardigan B4570. Continue along this road towards Cardigan.

24 TR at TJ, SP Cardigan A484. Take second exit at roundabout, SP Town Centre. Continue past hospital and church to Finch Square and the end of the ride.

43km (27 miles)

Route
13

LEOMINSTER, WEOBLEY AND BODENHAM

Route information

Distance 50km (31 miles)

Grade Easy

Terrain Mostly quiet lanes, a couple of short stretches of A road and a few gentle hills.

Time to allow 3–4 hours.

Getting there by car Leominster is 19km (12 miles) north of Hereford on the A49 and A44. There are several free car parks in the town, including one by the Tourist Information Centre (TIC), the start of the route.

Getting there by train There is a frequent rail service to Leominster. Telephone (08457) 484950 or visit www.nationalrail.co.uk for travel information.

An attractive circuit through rural Herefordshire, passing through Weobley and Bodenham

Places of interest along the route

A Leominster

A small market town on the River Lugg in the heart of the Marches, the borderlands between Wales and England. The regular market is held every Friday and the town is known as an important centre for antiques. **Leominster Folk Museum**, Efnam Street, houses an extensive collection of rural artefacts. Telephone (01568) 615186 for opening times. The **Lion Gallery**, Broad Street, is run by local artists and displays local arts and crafts. Telephone (01568) 611898 for more information. **Priory Church** was founded in 1123 and possesses a ducking stool. The last recorded use of a ducking stool in England was in Leominster in 1809. Contact Leominster TIC for more information on (01568) 615546.

B Weobley

An attractive village, past winner of the Village of the Year competition. To the south of the village, the remains of 12th-century **Weobley Castle** can still be seen. In the village, there is a **local history museum, craft centre** and **pottery**. Contact Leominster TIC for more information on (01568) 616460; www.weobley. org.uk

Route description

Start by the TIC. Head R past Woolworths. Take first exit at roundabout into South Street. Take second exit at next roundabout into Westbury. Then take first exit at roundabout into Rylands Road. Continue on this road to Bush Bank and junction with A4110.

1 TL onto A4110, SP Hereford, and shortly TR, SP King's Pyon/Weobley.

10.5km (6.5 miles)

---

2 TL at TJ, SP King's Pyon/Weobley. Take next TR, SP Weobley. Continue towards Weobley Marsh.

Weobley

3 TR at TJ, SP Weobley/Weobley Marsh/ Dilwyn. Shortly TL, SP Weobley.

4 To visit Weobley, TR then TL into village.

16.5km (10.5 miles)

Otherwise, TL, SP King's Pyon/Wormsley/ Canon Pyon.

5 TL, SP King's Pyon. Follow this road through Canon Pyon to junction with A4110.

6 TR onto A4110, SP Hereford (25.5km/16 miles). Pass Nags Head pub and TL, SP Wellington. Continue towards Wellington.

7 TL at TJ, no SP. Immediately TL again (broken SP).

8 TR at TJ, SP Dinmore.

9 TR opposite white house just before main road (A49). SO across A49 (CARE), SP Marden (31.5km/19.5 miles). Continue into Marden.

10 TL at TJ, SP Litmarsh/Bodenham.

11 TL, no SP (37km/23 miles). Continue towards Bodenham.

12 TR at TJ, no SP. Shortly TL no SP.

13 TR onto A417 then TL, SP Risbury/Stoke Prior. ***39km (24 miles)***

14 TL, SP Stoke Prior. Continue for descent.

15 TR at foot of hill, SP Leominster.

16 TL at TJ onto A44. Take second exit at roundabout, SP Leominster. Keep right past station and TR, SP Information Centre/Car Park, to finish the ride. ***50km (31 miles)***

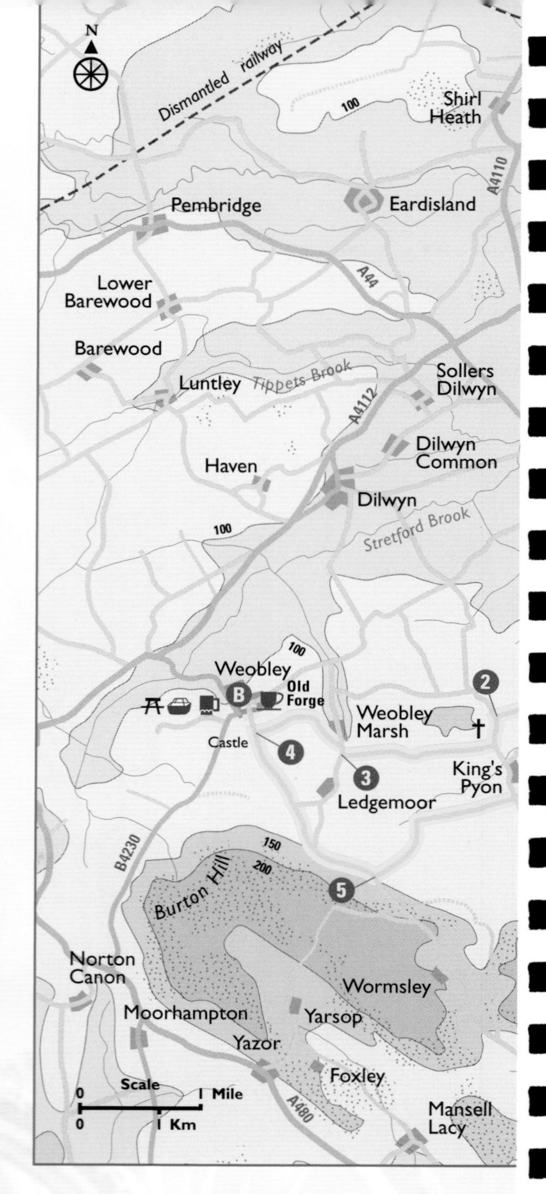

Food and drink

There are plenty of cafés, pubs and convenience stores in Leominster and Weobley. Several pubs are passed en route.

Old Forge, Weobley
Tearoom and gift shop off High Street.

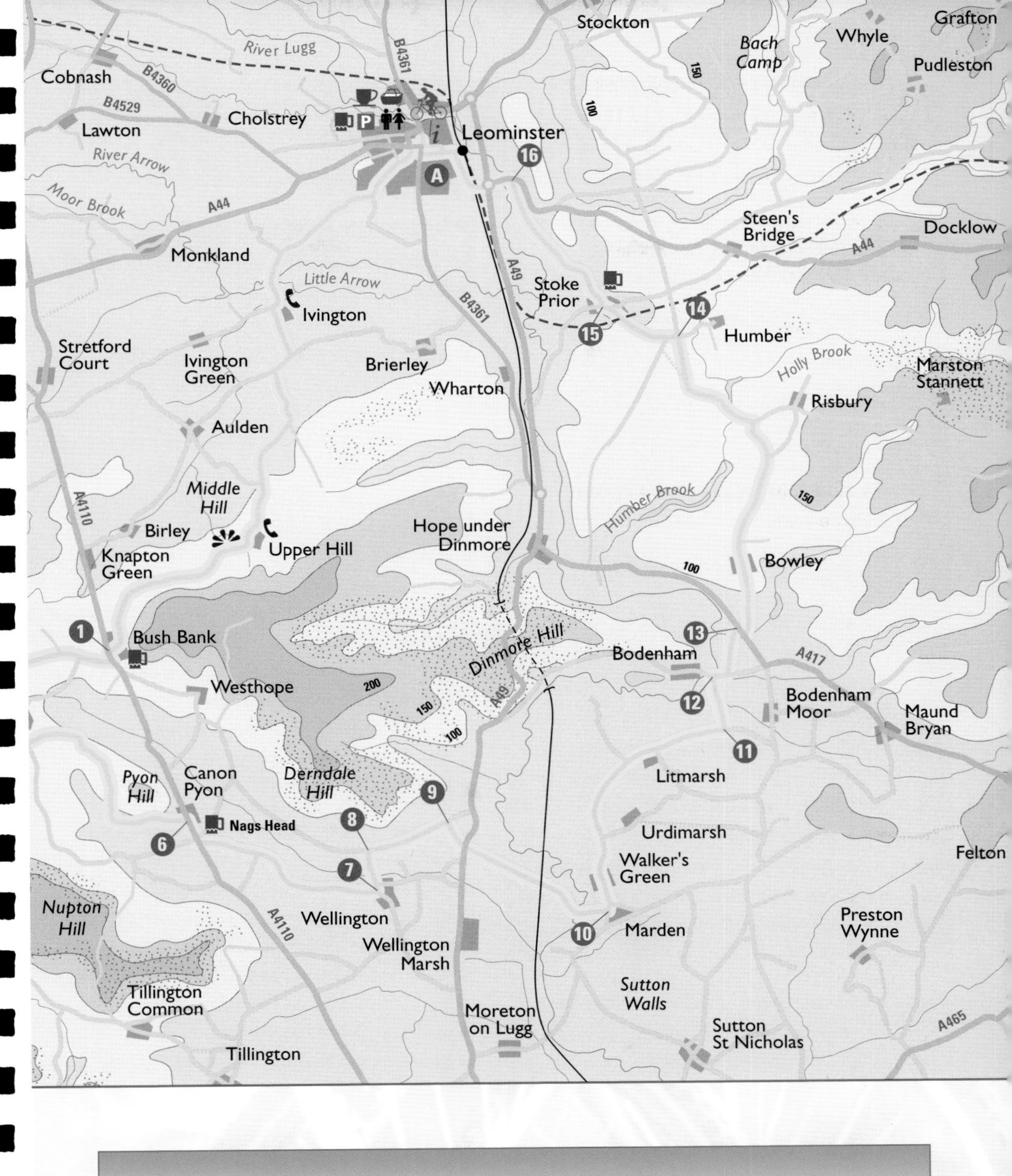
Stockton
Grafton
Whyle
Bach Camp
Pudleston
River Lugg
B4361
Cobnash
B4360
B4529
Cholstrey
Lawton
Leominster
River Arrow
Moor Brook
A44
Monkland
Steen's Bridge
Docklow
Little Arrow
A49
Stoke Prior
B4361
Ivington
Humber
Stretford Court
Ivington Green
Brierley
Holly Brook
Marston Stannett
Wharton
Risbury
Aulden
Middle Hill
Humber Brook
A4110
Birley
Upper Hill
Hope under Dinmore
Knapton Green
Bowley
Bush Bank
Dinmore Hill
Bodenham
A417
Westhope
Bodenham Moor
Maund Bryan
Pyon Hill
Canon Pyon
Derndale Hill
Litmarsh
Nags Head
Urdimarsh
Felton
Walker's Green
Nupton Hill
Wellington
Wellington Marsh
Marden
Preston Wynne
Sutton Walls
Tillington Common
Moreton on Lugg
Sutton St Nicholas
A465
Tillington

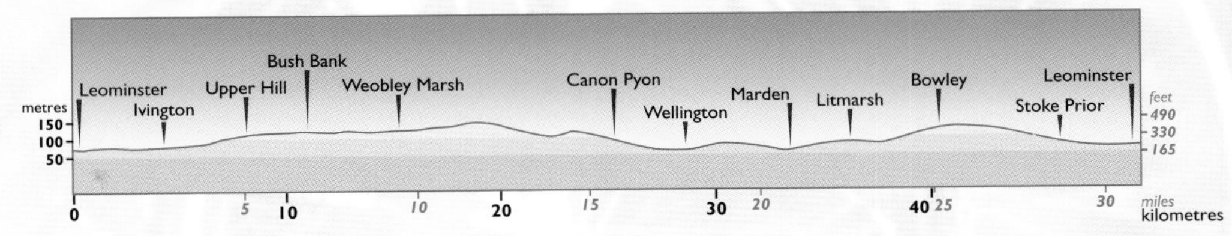
Leominster
Ivington
Upper Hill
Bush Bank
Weobley Marsh
Canon Pyon
Wellington
Marden
Litmarsh
Bowley
Stoke Prior
Leominster
metres
150
100
50
feet
490
330
165
0
5
10
10
20
15
30
20
40
25
30
miles
kilometres

Route **14**

THREE COUNTIES – SHROPSHIRE, POWYS AND HEREFORDSHIRE

Route information

Distance 57km (35.5 miles)

Grade Moderate

Terrain Quiet B roads and lanes.

Time to allow 3–4 hours.

Getting there by car Presteigne is 8km (5 miles) south of Knighton on the B4355 and B4362. There is car parking in the town.

Getting there by train The closest main line stations are at Leominster (27km/17 miles) and Ludlow (32km/20 miles). The Heart of Wales line stops at the following stations on the route – Bucknell, Knucklas and Llangunllo – but there is a limited service and limited space for carrying bicycles. Telephone (08457) 484950 or visit www.nationalrail.co.uk for travel information.

A scenic route. From Presteigne the route makes a circuit through Lingen, Bucknell, Knucklas and Llangunllo, following the valleys of the Rivers Lugg, Redlake and Teme. The route is crossed at intervals by several long distance footpaths (Offa's Dyke, Glyndwr's Way and the Jack Mytton Way). A section of the National Cycle Network, NCR 25 (the Radnor Ring) passes through Presteigne.

Places of interest along the route

A Presteigne

A small town on the River Lugg. There is a riverside walk and nature reserve. The **Judge's Lodging**, an award-winning museum, is housed in a Victorian townhouse. Visitors can see the courtroom, cells, judge's apartments and servants' quarters. The Tourist Information Centre is located in the same building. Open March to October, daily 1000–1800; November to February hours vary. Charge for museum only. Telephone (01544) 260650. **St Andrew's Church** is home to a superb 16th-century Flemish tapestry, one of only two pre-reformation tapestries left in the country's churches. On the edge of town is **Bryan's Ground**, a reconstructed Edwardian garden. Telephone (01544) 260001 for opening times.

B Lingen Nursery and Garden, Lingen

An intensively planted garden with alpine house, raised beds and rock, bog and scree gardens. Lots to see at all times of the year. Plant nursery, tearoom, children's play area. Nursery and garden open February to October, daily 1000–1700; tearoom open April to September 1000–1700. Small admission charge for garden only. Telephone (01544) 267720.

Route description

Start by the clock tower in the town centre. Follow SP Route 25 down Broad Street, passing Judge's Lodging on RHS and church on LHS. Cross 17th-century bridge over River Lugg and climb gently.

1 TR, SP Kinsham (away from Route 25). Follow north side of Lugg valley.

---

2 TL at TJ, SP Kinsham/Lingen (5km/3miles). Continue through Kinsham and Lingen, then climb to Birtley. Descend, looking out for next junction:

---

3 TL and shortly TR, SP Brampton Bryan. Continue into Brampton Bryan.

---

4 SO at XR, SP Buckton/Coxall. Pass church with notable yew hedge and cross River Teme at Parsons Pole Bridge. Dippers and the occasional kingfisher may be seen here.

---

5 TL at TJ shortly after bridge, onto narrow lane. ***15km (9.5 miles)***

---

6 TR at TJ onto B4367 – CARE here due to poor visibility.

7 Cross level crossing in Bucknell. TL at TJ, SP Chapel Lawn. Climb the valley of the River Redlake through Chapel Lawn.

---

8 LHF to New Invention (24km/15 miles). Continue into New Invention.

---

9 Arrive XR with A488 and SO, SP Purlogue.

---

10 After Purlogue TL uphill, no SP, for climb out of valley followed by steep descent, crossing Offa's Dyke.

---

11 Arrive Selley Cross XR and TL, SP Knighton. Descend into Teme valley and continue into Skyborry Green.

---

12 TR at TJ, SP Lloyney (32km/20 miles). Continue into Monaughty Poeth.

---

13 TL, rejoin Route 25. Cross River Teme. SO across B4355, SP Village Centre, and follow

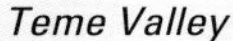

Teme Valley

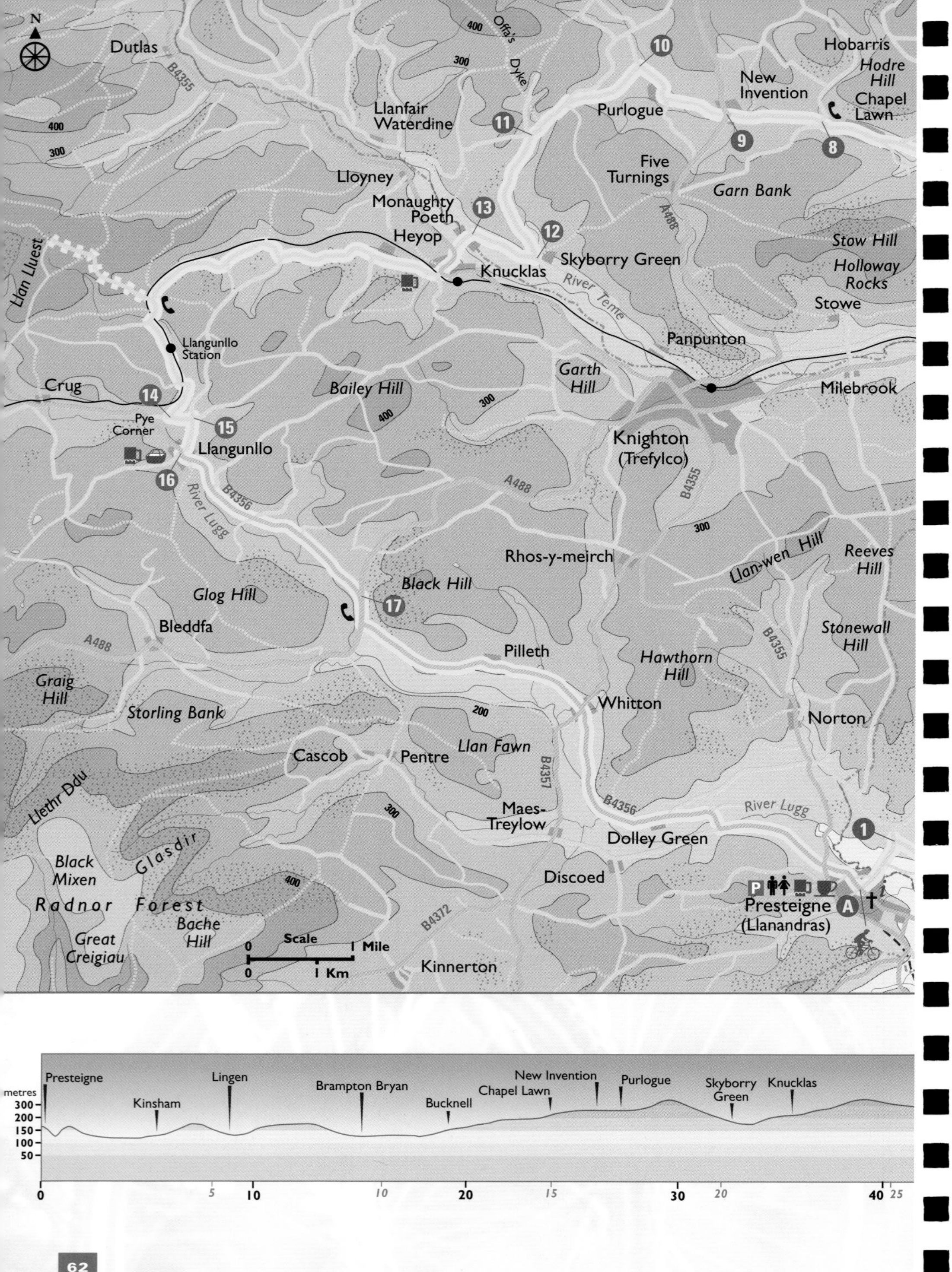

N
Dutlas
B4355
400
300
Offa's Dyke
Llanfair Waterdine
10
11
Purlogue
New Invention
Hobarris
Hodre Hill
Chapel Lawn
9
8
Five Turnings
Garn Bank
A488
Lloyney
Monaughty Poeth
13
Heyop
12
Skyborry Green
Stow Hill
Holloway Rocks
Knucklas
River Teme
Stowe
Llan Lluest
Llangunllo Station
Panpunton
Crug
14
Bailey Hill
Garth Hill
Milebrook
Pye Corner
15
Llangunllo
Knighton (Trefylco)
16
River Lugg
B4356
A488
B4355
Rhos-y-meirch
Llan-wen Hill
Reeves Hill
Black Hill
Glog Hill
17
Bleddfa
Stonewall Hill
Pilleth
Hawthorn Hill
Graig Hill
Storling Bank
Whitton
Norton
200
Cascob
Pentre
Llan Fawn
B4357
Llethr Ddu
Maes-Treylow
B4356
River Lugg
1
Dolley Green
Glasdir
Black Mixen
Discoed
Radnor Forest
Presteigne (Llanandras)
A
Bache Hill
B4372
Great Creigiau
Scale
0
1 Mile
0
1 Km
Kinnerton
metres
300
200
150
100
50
Presteigne
Kinsham
Lingen
Brampton Bryan
Bucknell
Chapel Lawn
New Invention
Purlogue
Skyborry Green
Knucklas
0
5
10
10
20
15
30
20
40
25

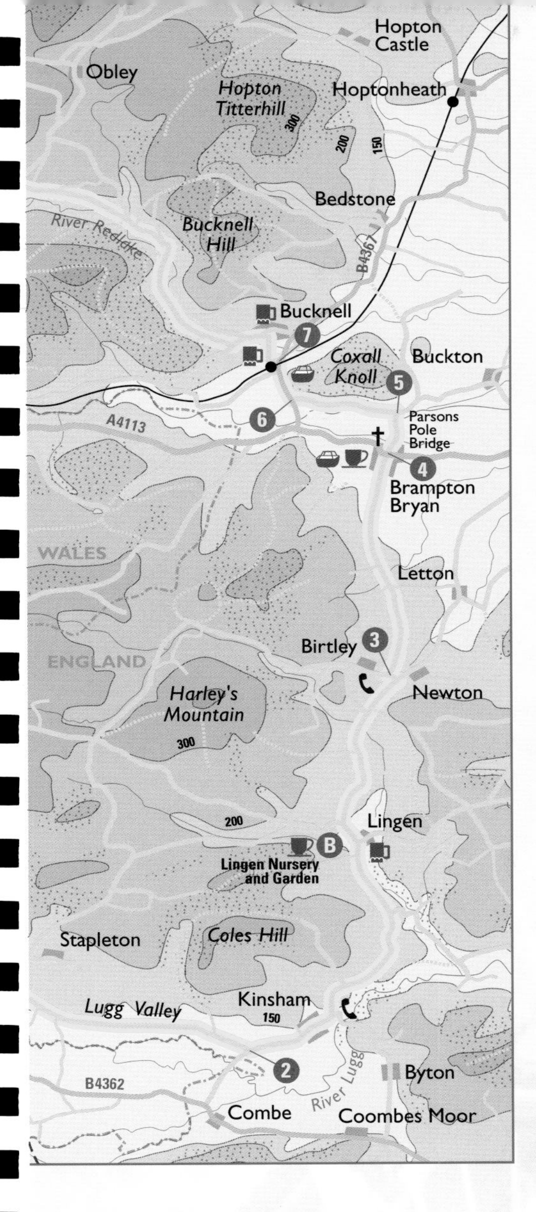

Llangunllo | Pilleth | Whitton | Presteigne

feet: 985, 655, 490, 330, 165

miles: 30, 35 — kilometres: 50

SP Route 25 under castellated railway viaduct. Continue through Heyop, over railway tunnel, and descend past Llangunllo Station to Pye Corner, leaving Route 25.

14 TL at TJ, SP Llangunllo/Knucklas/ Knighton. ***40km (25 miles)***

15 TR at XR, SP Llangunllo. Continue into Llangunllo.

16 TL at TJ onto B4356. Follow B4356 along valley of River Lugg to junction with A488.

17 TR at TJ with A488. Pass telephone box on RHS and TL onto B4356, SP Presteigne (47km/29 miles). Stay on this road past Pilleth (site of Welsh/English battle in 1402), through Whitton and Dolley Green, and arrive back in Presteigne to finish the ride.

57km (35.5 miles)

NB: There is a maze of tracks over Beacon and Wernygeufron Hills, accessible from above the railway tunnel. Between directions 13 and 14 TR onto tarmac lane (after farm and before telephone box on LHS). Climb to unfenced moorland by a conifer wood. Retrace to rejoin route. Cyclists should carry and be able to read a map of this area, particularly during poor weather.

Food and drink 

Plenty of choice in Presteigne. Lingen has a pub and refreshments are available at Lingen Nursery and Garden. There are various convenience stores and pubs in villages along the route. The pub in Llangunllo includes a shop, open each morning, Monday–Saturday.

Route 15

ABERYSTWYTH AND THE YSTWYTH VALLEY

Route information

Distance 58km (36 miles)

Grade Moderate

Terrain Mostly quiet lanes and B roads. There is one particularly steep climb and a steep descent, and some shorter, sharp climbs. However, there are two alternative sections of route to bypass these. This area is quite unpopulated and exposed, and the weather conditions can change rapidly, particularly during the winter. Cyclists are advised to carry appropriate clothing, and sufficient food and drink to sustain them during the ride.

Time to allow 4–5 hours.

Getting there by car Aberystwyth is 17.5km (11 miles) north of Llanon on the A487 and A44. Park in the town's long stay car park on the A487, opposite Somerfield supermarket.

Getting there by train There is a railway station at Aberystwyth. Telephone (08457) 484950 or visit www.nationalrail.co.uk for travel information.

A scenic ride through quiet, generally unpopulated countryside with wonderful views and the opportunity of possibly seeing birds of prey. From Aberystwyth the route heads south east, along a mountain road through the Ystwyth valley to Pont-rhyd-y-groes. Here the route turns south west to Ystrad Meurig before heading north west back to Aberystwyth.

Places of interest along the route

Ⓐ Aberystwyth

The town of Aberystwyth was established over 700 years ago on the site of a much older settlement. Today the town is dominated by the university, which each year adds 7000 students to the local population. **Aberystwyth Castle** was constructed by the Normans on the site of an Iron Age fort. The city council have created a park around the site and there is free access at all reasonable times. **Aberystwyth Cliff Railway** is the longest electric railway in Britain and climbs 110m (361 feet) to the summit of Constitution Hill, where there is the camera obscura. The original **camera obscura** was originally located at the castle circa 1880 and was rebuilt on the hill in 1896. Today's building was constructed in 1985. For information on opening times, contact the Tourist Information Centre on (01970) 612125.

Aberystwyth

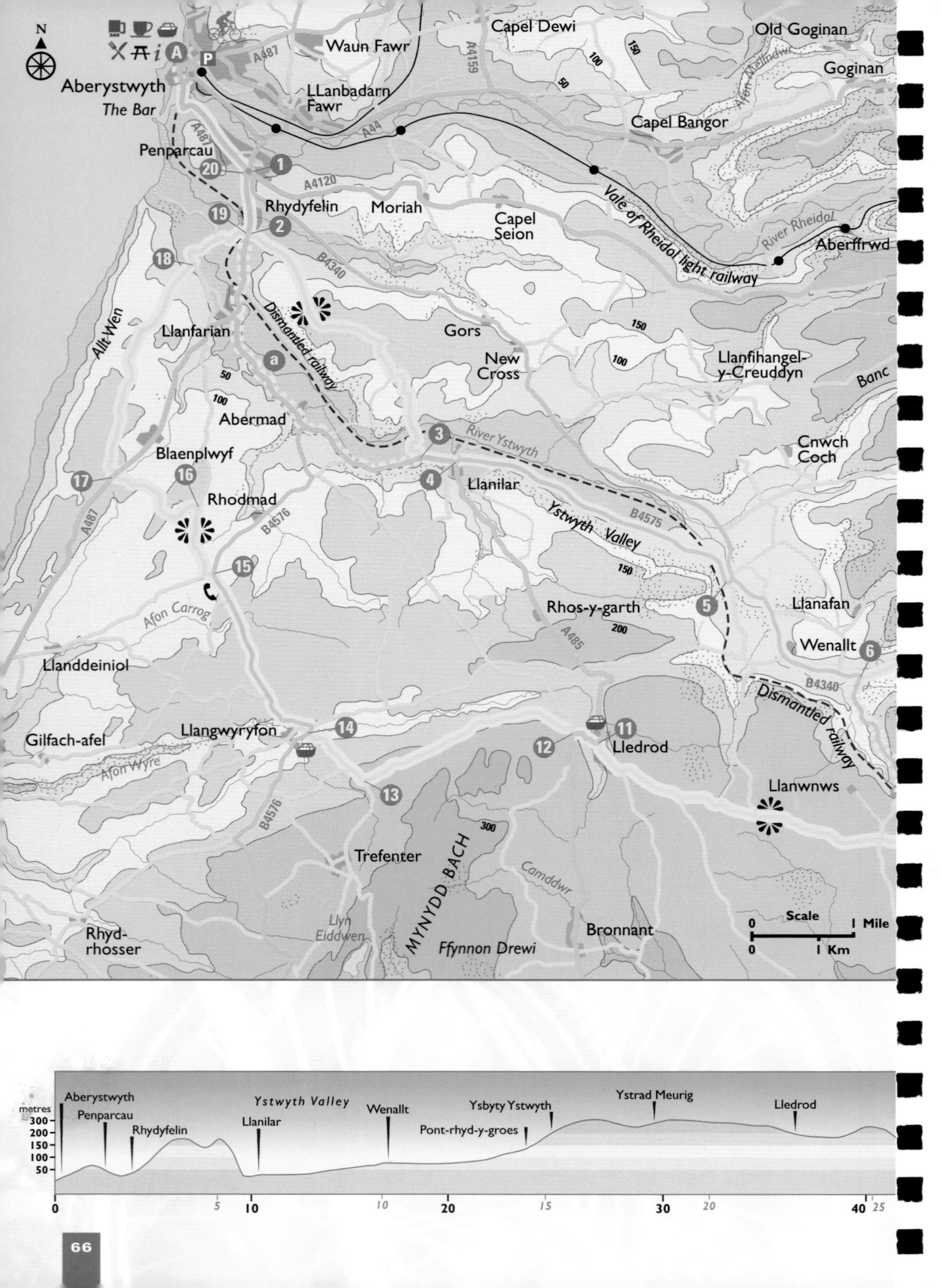

N
Aberystwyth
The Bar
Waun Fawr
Capel Dewi
Old Goginan
Goginan
LLanbadarn
Fawr
Capel Bangor
Penparcau
Rhydyfelin
Moriah
Capel
Seion
Vale of Rheidol light railway
River Rheidol
Aberffrwd
Afon Melindwr
Allt Wen
Llanfarian
Dismantled railway
Gors
New
Cross
Llanfihangel-
y-Creuddyn
Banc
Abermad
River Ystwyth
Cnwch
Coch
Blaenplwyf
Llanilar
Rhodmad
Ystwyth Valley
Afon Carrog
Rhos-y-garth
Llanafan
Wenallt
Llanddeiniol
Dismantled railway
Gilfach-afel
Llangwyryfon
Lledrod
Afon Wyre
Llanwnws
Trefenter
MYNYDD BACH
Camddwr
Llyn
Eiddwen
Ffynnon Drewi
Bronnant
Rhyd-
rhosser
Scale
0
1 Mile
0
1 Km
A487
A4159
A44
A4120
B4340
B4576
B4575
A485
metres
300
200
100
50
Aberystwyth
Penparcau
Rhydyfelin
Ystwyth Valley
Llanilar
Wenallt
Pont-rhyd-y-groes
Ysbyty Ystwyth
Ystrad Meurig
Lledrod
0
5
10
10
20
15
30
20
40
25

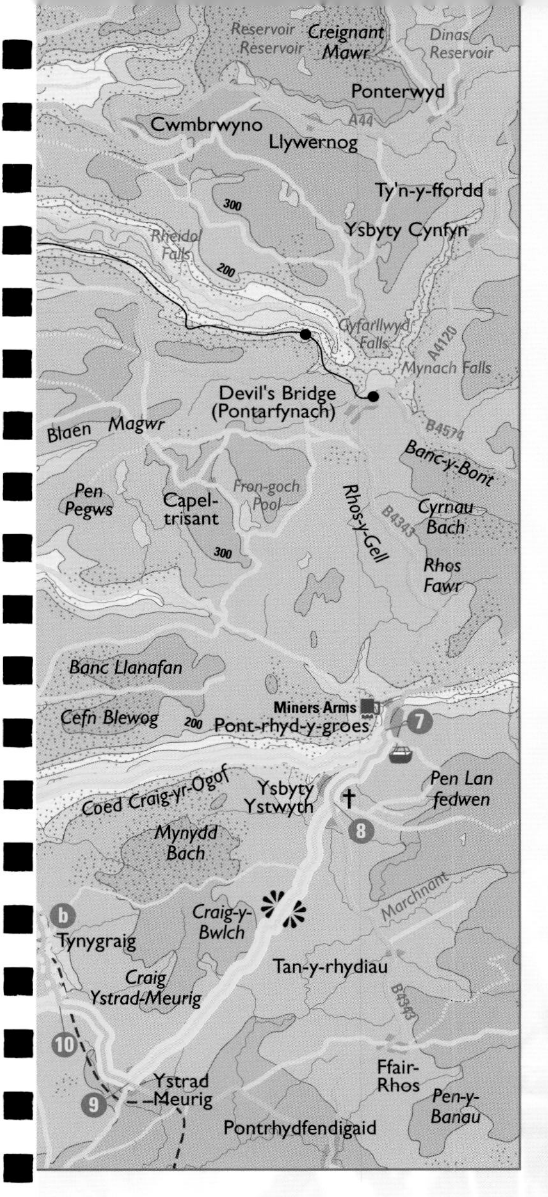

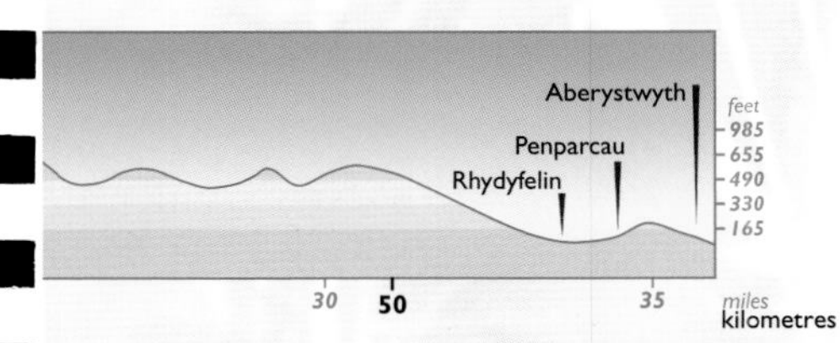

Route description

If starting from the railway station, exit station onto A487, SP Cardigan, and follow this road, continuing route at direction 1.

To start from the car park, TL out of car park. TL at mini roundabout, SP Cardigan A487. Keep L over bridge and gradually climb.

1 TR at roundabout (third exit), SP Cardigan. Continue into Rhydyfelin.

2 Alternative route **a** to avoid steep climb: SO at XR, staying on A487. TL, SP Tregaron A485, and rejoin route near Llanilar at direction 3, where TR at TJ onto A485.

Otherwise, to follow main route, TL at XR, SP Golf Course, and climb steeply. There are good views from the summit. Continue for long, steep descent and cross River Ystwyth (8km/5 miles). After short, steep climb away from river:

3 TL at TJ onto A485, no SP.

4 TL, SP Trawsgoed B4575. Continue along Ystwyth Valley.

5 TL and cross River Ystwyth, SP Pontrhydfendigaid. TR (after bridge), SP Pontrhydfendigaid. Continue, eventually re-crossing river.

6 After crossing river, immediately TL, no SP (17.5km/11 miles).

To follow alternative route **b**:
Continue SO on B4340, through Tynygraig. Rejoin route at direction 10, where TR.

Otherwise, to follow main route, gradually climb through Ystwyth Valley, through woodland and into Pont-rhyd-y-groes.

7 TR at TJ, SP Tregaron B4343. Pass village shop on L. Continue into Ysbyty Ystwyth.

8 TR by chapel, SP Ystrad Meurig (25km/15.5 miles). Climb past quarry for good views from summit. Descend to Ystrad Meurig.

9 TR at TJ, SP Aberystwyth B4340.

10 TL by post box (31.5km/19.5 miles). Follow this road along the ridge, looking out for Red Kites, buzzards and kestrels. Descend to Lledrod.

11 TL at TJ, SP Tregaron A485 (shop on RHS).

12 TR, SP Llangwyryfon and immediately TL, SP Llangwyfron. ***37.5km (23.5 miles)***

13 TR at TJ, SP Llangwyryfon. Descend to Llangwyryfon.

14 TR at TJ, SP Aberystwyth. Climb out of Llangwyryfon and descend. Pass public telephone on LHS and:

15 TL, SP Llanddeiniol. Then TR, no SP, and climb for excellent views from summit.

16 TL, no SP (47.5km/29.5 miles). Descend and climb to A487.

17 TR at TJ, no SP, and immediately TL, SP Morfa Bychan Holiday Site. Climb to communications mast and then descend.

18 TL at TJ, no SP.

19 TL at XR onto A487. Retrace route into Aberystwyth.

20 TL at roundabout, SP Aberystwyth. Cross river. To visit town centre and seafront, SO.

Otherwise, TR into Mill Street, SP Station. TR at mini roundabout and TR into car park to finish the ride. ***58km (36 miles)***

Food and drink

Plenty of choice in Aberystwyth. Cyclists are advised to carry sufficient food and drink to sustain them during this ride, as refreshments may be difficult to obtain along the route, particularly during the winter.

Miners Arms, Pont-rhyd-y-groes
Village pub selling traditional ales and home cooked food. Also B&B.

Ystwyth Valley

Route **16**

CARDIGAN, THE CYCH VALLEY AND NEVERN

Route information

Distance 62km (38.5 miles)

Grade Moderate

Terrain Mostly quiet but undulating lanes.

Time to allow 4–6 hours.

Getting there by car Cardigan is 54.5km (34 miles) south west of Aberystwyth at the junction of the A484 and A478. Although there are several car parks in the town, parking can be difficult. The route starts from Finch Square in the centre of Cardigan.

Getting there by train There is no practical railway access to this route.

This route offers excellent views across Cardigan Bay and over the Preseli Mountains. From Cardigan the route heads south east into the Cych valley, before turning west across country and through the Afon Nevern valley to the coast. The final section of the route follows the coast back to Cardigan. There is an optional 2km (1 mile) extension to visit Ceibwr Bay. The route follows a section of the Celtic Trail, a signed cycle route which forms routes 4 and 47 of the National Cycle Network.

Places of interest along the route

A Pentre Ifan Burial Chamber, near Newport
A prehistoric burial chamber, dating back to circa 3500 BC. See Route 1 for more information.

B Nevern
A picturesque village near the coast, it was once a stopping place for pilgrims on their way to the cathedral town of St David's. The Norman church has some 5th and 6th century inscriptions from earlier churches on the site and a large and ancient cross in the churchyard. Above the village are the remains of a large 11th-century castle.

C Ceibwr Bay
Within the Pembrokeshire Coast National Park. The beach is surrounded by spectacular scenery, but is unsuitable for swimming.

D Poppit Sands
This is a large sandy beach at the mouth of the River Teifi. The beach is patrolled by lifeguards during the summer and swimmers must be aware that there are unpredictable tidal and river currents at some stages of the tide, when swimming becomes dangerous. The mud flats and sand dunes at the southern end of the beach are fragile and visitor are asked not to walk across eroded areas. There is a picnic site above the beach.

E Y Felin, St Dogmaels
A water-powered, working corn mill, probably built in the late 18th or early 19th century. New milling machinery was installed in 1819 and the mill was restored during the early 1980s. Wholemeal and speciality flours are produced. Shop and tearoom. Open all year, daily 1030–1730. Small charge.

Churchyard, Nevern

Route description 

TR out of Finch Square and pass church and hospital on RHS.

1 Take second exit at roundabout, SP Newcastle Emlyn/Camarthen A484.

2 TL, SP Cwm-cou B4570.

3 Take first TR, no SP (2km/1 mile), along leafy lane to Llangoedmor. TR by church and pass through village.

4 SO at XR over A484, no SP. Follow road as it climbs, drops quite steeply through some sharp bends, before climbing through woodland.

5 Keep left on sharp corner – look out for deer along this road. After a steep descent through bends, arrive at Llechryd Bridge.

6 TR over bridge, SP Cilgerran, and immediately TL, no SP. Follow road as it passes between river and remains of a canal which used to service an old tin plate works. Pass Manordeif Church.

7 TL at TJ, no SP (9km/5.5 miles). After a short climb, continue along lane with good views of River Teifi on LHS.

8 TL SP Abercych. Continue through Abercych.

9 TL at TJ, SP Cenarth B4332. Descend and take first TR (by Nags Head pub), SP Cwmcych/ Clydau. Continue up Cych Valley.

10 TR at XR, SP Clydau/Bwlch-y-groes, for steep climb.

11 Take first TL, SP Clydau (15km/9.5 miles). Continue along this road for descent.

12 TL and descend into Star.

13 Take first TR, no SP but just before small bridge (19km/12 miles). Start to climb and continue along this road into Tegryn.

14 TR by Butchers Arms Pub, SP Boncath/ Crymych. This section of the route is part of the Celtic Trail (NCR 47). Continue out of Tegryn.

15 Take first TL, SP Crymych.

16 TL at TJ, SP Crymych (25km/15.5 miles), for a gradual climb then a nice descent to TJ.

17 TL at TJ onto A478 and continue into Crymych.

18 TR, SP Eglwyswrw.

19 TR at TJ, no SP (30km/18.5 miles). Take first TL by post box, SP Ffynnongroes/ Crosswell.

20 SO at XR, no SP. Keep L at next junction (31.5km/19.5 miles). Continue through Pontyglasier to Crosswell.

21 SO at XR in Crosswell, SP Trefdraeth/ Newport. Good views of northern flank of Preseli Mountains on LHS.

22 To visit Pentre Ifan burial chamber, TL at junction and follow SP.

Otherwise, continue SO.

23 TR at TJ, SP Nevern (40km/25 miles). Descend to XR with A487.

24 SO at XR (CARE), over A487, SP Nevern B4582. Drop down into Nevern.

25 Take first TL in Nevern, opposite phone box. Climb through bends and take first TL, no SP. Keep R at fork, no SP. Continue to Gethsemane Chapel.

N
Cardigan
Bay
Verwig
Waun-gelod
Ty-gwyn
Poppit
Sands
Cyppyn
Nant-y-ferwig
Tre-Bared
Hendre
Llyny-felin
Cardigan
Tre-Rhys
Y Felin
Ceibwr
Bay
St Dogmaels
Eagles
Inn
Llan
goedmor
Plasnewydd
Pant Saeson
Treriffith
Moylgrove
Hafod
Grove
Pant-y-
grwndy
River Teifi
Pen-lan
Peny-bryn
Cilgerran
Blaen-
meini
Castell-y-garn
Pant-y-groes
Glanrhyd
Bridell
LLantood
Morfa
Tredrissi
Cwm-cenau
Tre-fach
Trewilym
Croes-y-
forwyn
Hafod
Cwm-eog
Rhos-hill
Pen-cwm
Nevern
Bwlch-gareg
lwyd
Newport
Velindre
Llystyn
Gweunydd
Eglwyswrw
Boncath
Pentre
Evan
Bryn-bwa
Eithion-
duon
Llanfair
Nant Gwyn
Blaenffos
Carningli
Common
Pen-wern
Afon Nevern
Mynydd
Carningli
Afon Clydach
Pente Ifan
Burial Chamber
Crosswell
Whitechurch
Rhyd-du
Clover Hill
Carnedd
Meibion-Owen
Pont-faen
Cilgwyn
Pontyglasier
Cidigill
Llanerch
Tre-fach
Parc-y
maes
Dyffryn-
mawr
Rhyd-wen
Brynberian
Waun Mewn
Carn Alw
Crymych
Pen-trisil
Foeldrygarn
Afon
Tafarn-y-bwlch
Scale
0
1 Mile
0
1 Km
Mynydd
Bach
Carn Breseb
Pwll-glas
Waun Maes
Crug-yr-Hwch
B4546
B4548
A487
A484
B4582
A478
A487
B4332
B4329
A478
metres
200
150
100
50
Cardigan
Llangoedmor
Manordeifi
Abercych
Pen-yr-allt
Star
Tegryn
Crymych
Whitechurch
Crosswell
Nevern
Tredrissi
0
5
10
10
20
15
30
20
40
25

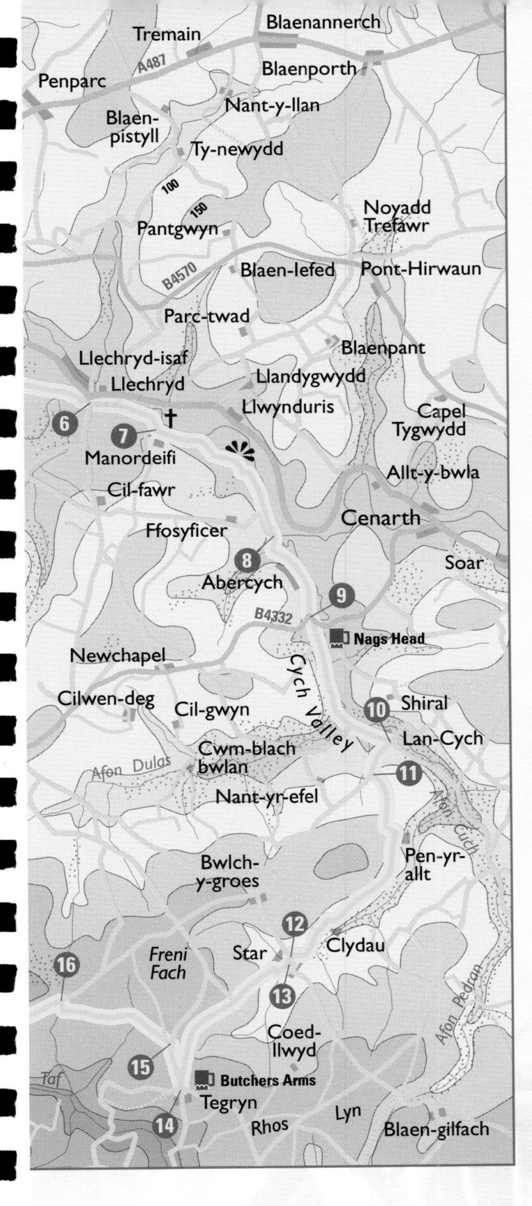

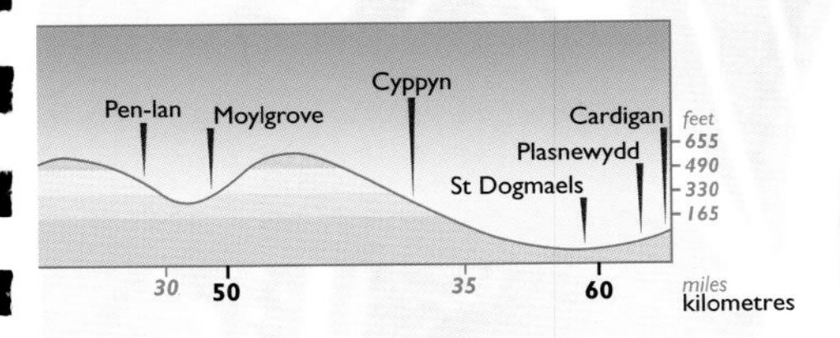

26 Keep R, no SP. ***44km (27.5 miles)***

27 TR at TJ, no SP, and continue towards Moylgrove.

28 To visit Ceibwr Bay, TL (before Moylgrove), SP Ceibwr. Follow this road to the coast and around to rejoin main route.

Otherwise, continue SO into Moylgrove.

29 Keep L in Moylgrove, SP St Dogmaels, and climb for spectacular views.

30 TL at TJ, SP Poppit. Pass through Cyppyn and descend steeply on narrow road into Poppit Sands.

31 TR at TJ onto B4546, no SP (57km/ 35.5 miles). Continue beside estuary, climb a short steep hill and enter St Dogmaels.

32 TL at TJ in village centre, SP Aberteifi (Cardigan) B4546.

33 TL at TJ by Eagles Inn, SP Canol Dref (Town Centre). Cross bridge and follow one-way system to Finch Square and the end of the ride. ***62km (38.5 miles)***

Food and drink

Cyclists may wish to carry refreshments with them on this longer route, although there is plenty of choice throughout the year in Cardigan.

Butchers Arms, Tegryn
Village pub serving snacks and meals.

Route **17**

LLANIDLOES AND THE DYLIFE GORGE

Route information

Distance 69km (43 miles)

Grade Strenuous

Terrain Undulating roads through a remote area, with several long climbs. The route follows a section of the National Cycle Network, NCR 7.

Time to allow 4–6 hours.

Getting there by car Llanidloes is 17.5km (11 miles) south west of Newtown on the A470. Park in The Gro free car park in the centre of the town.

Getting there by train The nearest railway station is at Newtown and the route can be started from Clatter, the closest point to Newtown. Telephone (08457) 484950 or visit www.nationalrail.co.uk for travel information.

A scenic route, starting from the small town of Llanidloes at the confluence of the Rivers Clywedog and Severn, and taking in the Clywedog reservoir and the dramatic Dylife Gorge. The route passes through remote areas and, particularly in winter, cyclists are advised to carry sufficient food and drink and appropriate clothing. Check the weather forecast as the weather can change rapidly in the hills. A couple of alternative sections are given within the route.

Places of interest along the route

A Llanidloes

A small town at the confluence of the Rivers Clywedog and Severn. The **Old Market Hall** was built in 1600 on timber stilts and is the only remaining building of its kind in Wales today. The hall houses a local history museum. Telephone the Tourist Information Centre on (01686) 412605 for more information, or visit www.llanidloes.com

B Clywedog Dam, near Llanidloes

The dam was constructed in 1967. It holds 11,000,000,000 gallons of water and is used to feed and relieve the River Severn, to reduce flooding. It is a dramatic site and is popular with walkers and fishermen. For more information, contact the Tourist Information Centre in Llanidloes (see above).

Food and drink

There are plenty of pubs and cafés in Llanidloes. During the summer there is a snack bar close to the dam.

Star Inn, Dylife

Open during the summer.

Dylife

Route description 

If starting the route from Newtown railway station, leave the station and follow A489 and then A470 to Clatter. Join the route at direction 12, where continue SO.

From Llanidloes start from the Gro car park. TL out of car park and pass Old Market Hall. TL at roundabout, SP Llyn Clewedog/Staylittle B4569. Cross river and:

1 Take first TL, SP Llyn Clewedog, for steady climb.

---

2 To shorten the route by 6.5km (4 miles) continue along B4518 to Staylittle and direction 4, where SO.

Otherwise, TL, SP Llyn Clywedog Scenic Route. Continue along this lane and cross River Clywedog. On L bend, TR for viewing point/WC/ snack bar. Otherwise, continue around dam.

---

3 TR at TJ, SP Staylittle/Llanbrynmair. Pass through forestry plantation and cross River Llwyd.

---

4 TL in Staylittle, SP Llanbrynmair (16.5km/10.5 miles).

NB: Alternatively, you can TR in Staylittle to make a short circuit of the dam and return to Llanidloes.

---

5 TL, SP Dylife Gorge/Machynlleth/Cycle Route 8.

---

6 Arrive at Dylife Gorge viewing point/ information board on RHS.

As an alternative to the full route, reducing the distance by 13km (8 miles), retrace route to TJ and TL, rejoining main route at direction 10, where TR.

To follow main route, continue through Dylife (21km/13 miles). Climb and descend, with spectacular panoramic views.

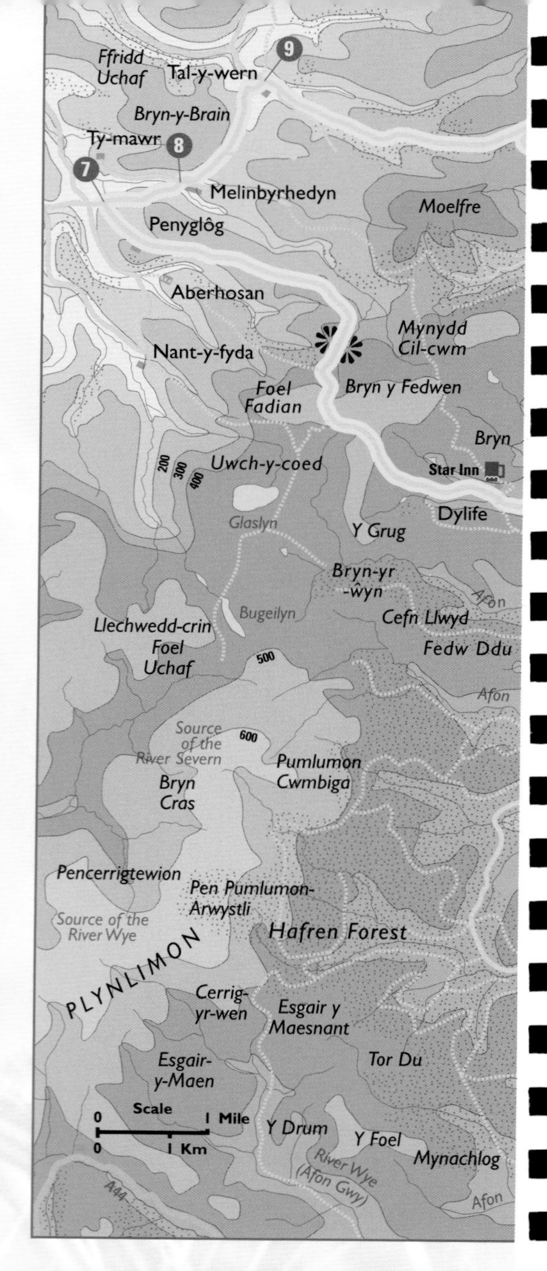

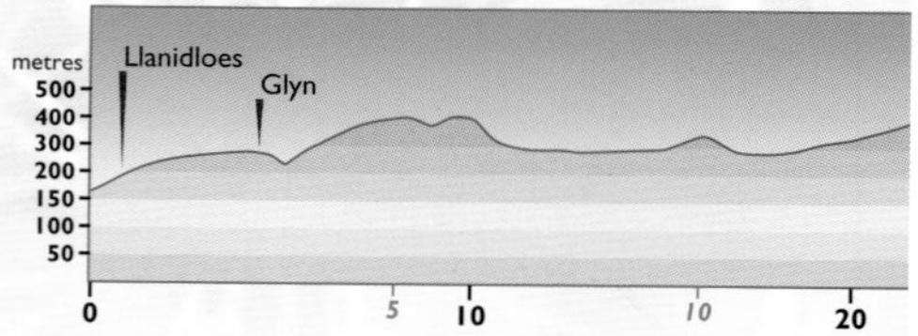

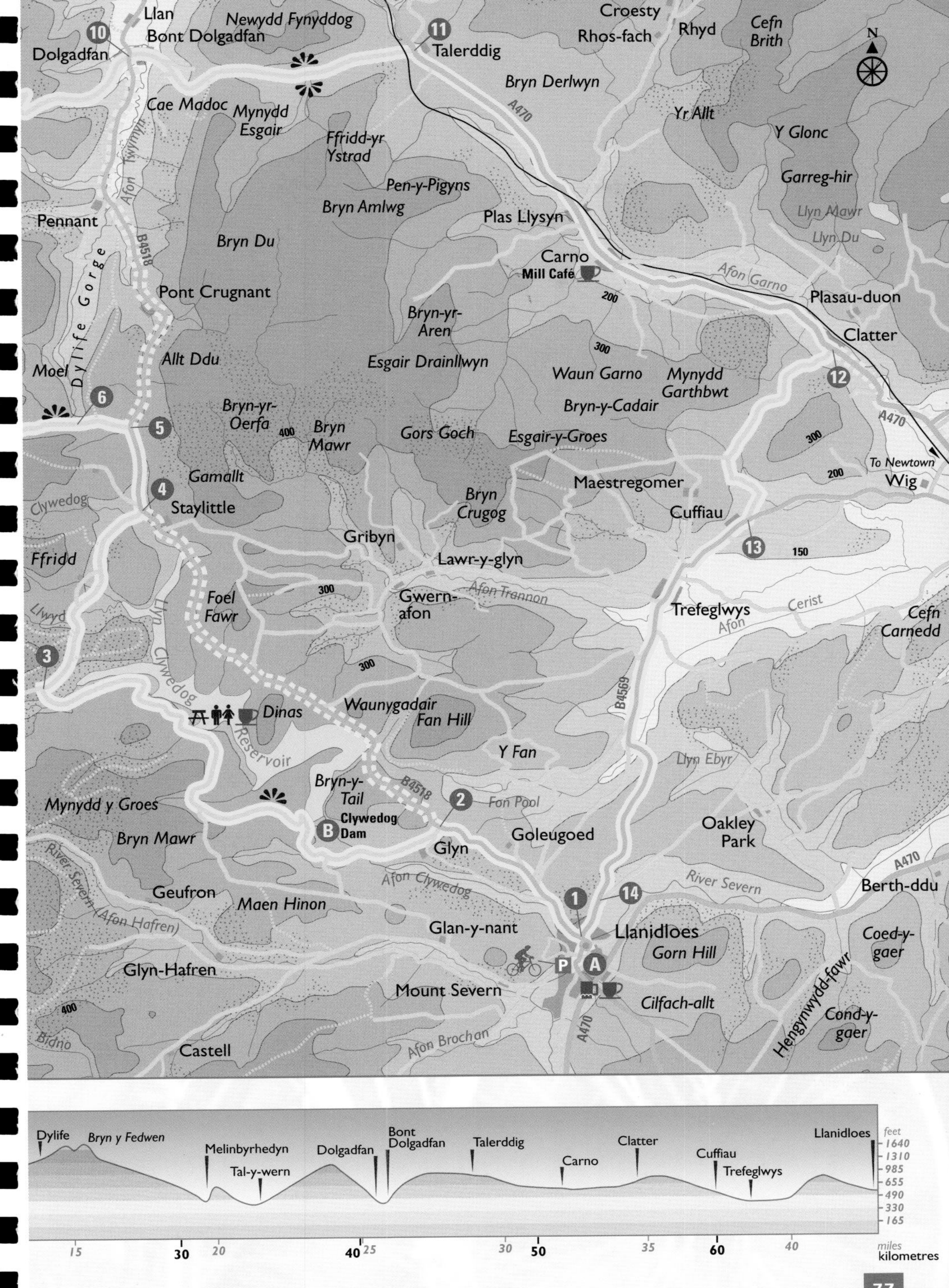

Llan
Newydd Fynyddog
Bont Dolgadfan
Dolgadfan
Talerddig
Croesty
Rhos-fach
Rhyd
Cefn Brith
N
Bryn Derlwyn
A470
Cae Madoc
Mynydd Esgair
Ffridd-yr Ystrad
Yr Allt
Y Glonc
Garreg-hir
Afon Twymyn
Pen-y-Pigyns
Bryn Amlwg
Plas Llysyn
Llyn Mawr
Llyn Du
Pennant
B4518
Bryn Du
Carno
Mill Café
Afon Garno
200
Plasau-duon
Dylife Gorge
Pont Crugnant
Bryn-yr-Aren
Clatter
300
Allt Ddu
Esgair Drainllwyn
Waun Garno
Mynydd Garthbwt
Moel
Bryn-y-Cadair
Bryn-yr-Oerfa
400
Bryn Mawr
Gors Goch
Esgair-y-Groes
A470
300
To Newtown
200
Wig
Gamallt
Maestregomer
Clywedog
Staylittle
Bryn Crugog
Cuffiau
Gribyn
150
Ffridd
Lawr-y-glyn
300
Foel Fawr
Gwern-afon
Afon Trannon
Trefeglwys
Cerist
Afon
Cefn Carnedd
Llwyd
Llyn Clywedog Reservoir
300
B4569
Dinas
Waunygadair
Fan Hill
Y Fan
Llyn Ebyr
Bryn-y-Tail
B4518
Fan Pool
Mynydd y Groes
Clywedog Dam
Goleugoed
Oakley Park
Bryn Mawr
Glyn
A470
River Severn (Afon Hafren)
Afon Clywedog
River Severn
Berth-ddu
Geufron
Maen Hinon
Glan-y-nant
Llanidloes
Gorn Hill
Coed-y-gaer
Glyn-Hafren
Mount Severn
Cilfach-allt
A470
Hengynwydd-fawr
400
Cond-y-gaer
Bidno
Castell
Afon Brochan
Dylife
Bryn y Fedwen
Melinbyrhedyn
Tal-y-wern
Dolgadfan
Bont Dolgadfan
Talerddig
Carno
Clatter
Cuffiau
Trefeglwys
Llanidloes
feet
1640
1310
985
655
490
330
165
15
30
20
40
25
30
50
35
60
40
miles
kilometres

7 TR, SP Tal-y-wern (29.5km/18.5 miles).

8 Pass through Melinbyrhedyn and keep L.

31.5km (19.5 miles)

9 TR in Tal-y-wern, SP Dolgadfan. TR at TJ, no SP. Continue, ignoring all turnings as far as XR.

10 SO at XR, SP Bont Dolgadfan (41km/ 25.5 miles). Continue through village and into Talerddig.

11 TR at TJ onto A470, no SP. Continue along A470 through Carno and into Clatter.

12 To return to Newtown railway station, continue SO along A470 and retrace route to Newtown.

To continue the route, TR in Clatter, no SP.

55.5km (34.5 miles)

13 TR at TJ onto B4569, no SP. Pass through Trefeglwys and descend to Llanidloes.

14 Take third exit at roundabout, SP Town Centre. Retrace route to car park to finish the ride. ***69km (43 miles)***

Route

18

OSWESTRY AND LLANRHAEADR

Route information

Distance 71.5km (44.5 miles)

Grade Strenuous

Terrain Quiet B roads and lanes. At times the route is remote, with some steep climbs.

Time to allow 4–5 hours. Allow an extra hour to visit the waterfall.

Getting there by car Oswestry can be reached via the A5 from Shrewsbury, and A483 from Welshpool and Chester. There is car parking by the Heritage Centre/Tourist Information Centre (TIC).

Getting there by train The regular rail service between Shrewsbury and Chester stops at Chirk (on the route) and Gobowen (1.5km/1 mile from the route). Telephone (08457) 484950 or visit www.nationalrail.co.uk for travel information.

From Oswestry the route circuits north and west, along the Ceiriog Valley, to eventually arrive at Llanrhaeadr, where there is an optional visit to Wales' highest waterfall at Pistyll Rhaeadr (an extra 16km/10 miles). From here the route continues south to Llanfyllin before turning north to return to Oswestry.

Llyn Clywedog

Places of interest along the route

A Oswestry

On the Welsh/English border, the ancient town of Oswestry grew up around King Oswald's Well. At varying times through history, Oswestry has been both Welsh and English. The town trail is a good way to explore – leaflets are available from the TIC. The town's market is one of the country's busiest, with over 120 stalls. Markets are held on Wednesdays throughout the year and on Saturdays during the summer. Oswestry was the headquarters of the old Cambrian Railway and at the centre of the network of the rail network serving north and mid Wales. The **Cambrian Museum of Transport** describes the railway's history and has a collection of memorabilia and a small number of bicycles and mopeds. Locomotives are regularly steamed up. Open all year: summer 10000–1600; winter 1000–1500. Nominal charge. Telephone (01691) 671749. Just north of the town is **Old Oswestry Hill Fort**, one of the best examples of an Iron Age hill fort, with massive earthwork ramparts. There are spectacular views from the top. **Oswestry Heritage Centre** has exhibitions on local history and is home to the TIC a craft shop and a café. Open all year, Monday–Saturday 0930–1700. Telephone (01691) 662753.

B Pistyll Rhaeadr, Llanhaeadr

The highest waterfall in Wales (74m/240 feet), at the head of the River Rhaeadr.

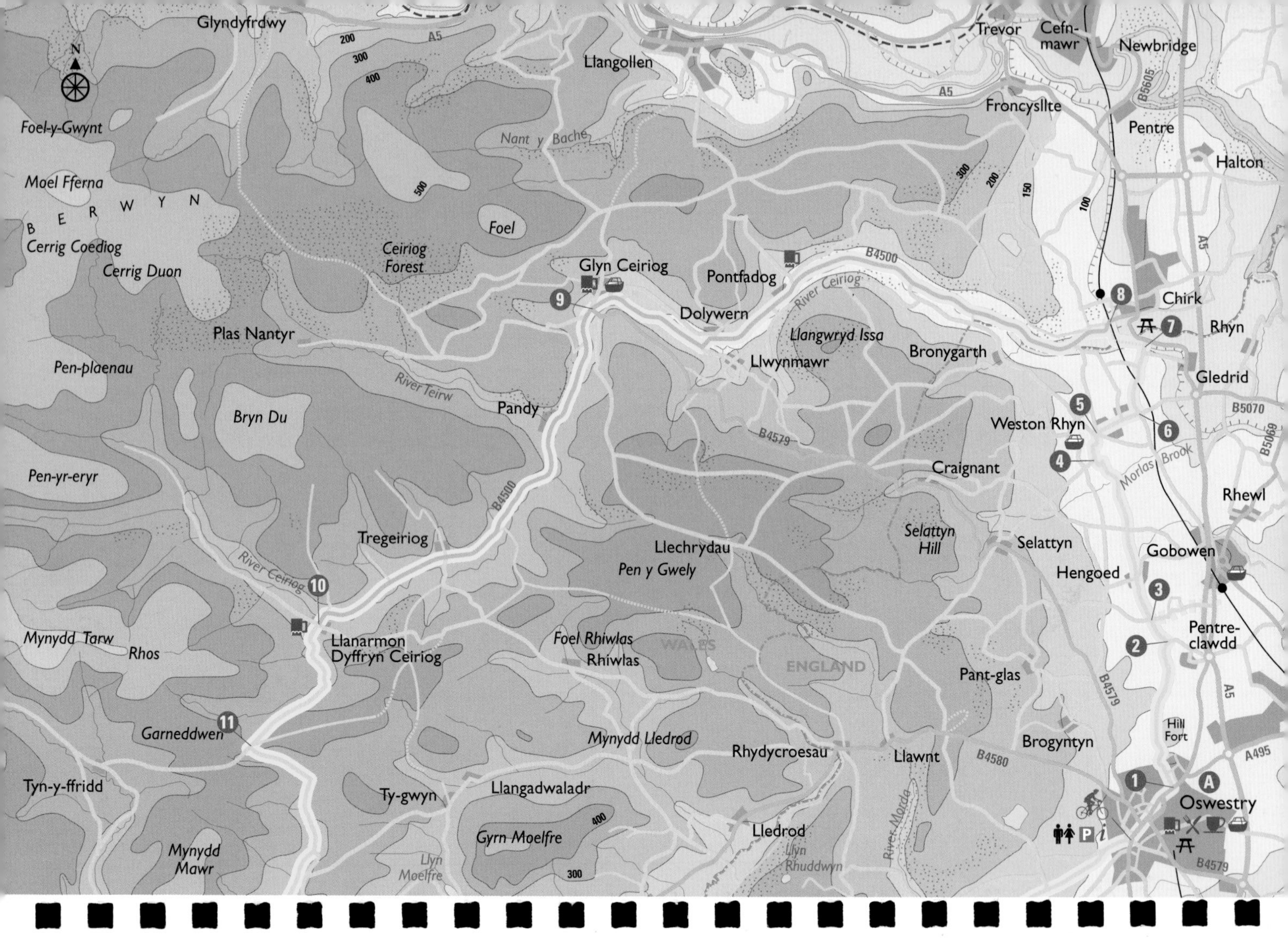

Glyndyfrdwy
A5
Llangollen
Trevor
Cefn-
mawr
Newbridge
B5605
Froncysllte
Pentre
Halton
Foel-y-Gwynt
Nant y Bache
Moel Fferna
B E R W Y N
Foel
Cerrig Coediog
Cerrig Duon
Ceiriog
Forest
Glyn Ceiriog
Pontfadog
B4500
River Ceiriog
Chirk
Dolywern
Rhyn
Plas Nantyr
Llangwryd Issa
Llwynmawr
Bronygarth
Gledrid
Pen-plaenau
River Teirw
Pandy
B5070
Weston Rhyn
B5069
Bryn Du
B4579
Craignant
Morlas Brook
Pen-yr-eryr
Rhewl
Selattyn
Hill
Tregeiriog
Selattyn
Llechrydau
Gobowen
Pen y Gwely
Hengoed
River Ceiriog
Pentre-
clawdd
Mynydd Tarw
Llanarmon
Dyffryn Ceiriog
Foel Rhiwlas
Rhiwlas
WALES
ENGLAND
Rhos
Pant-glas
Hill
Fort
Garneddwen
Mynydd Lledrod
Rhydycroesau
Llawnt
B4580
Brogyntyn
A495
Tyn-y-ffridd
Ty-gwyn
Llangadwaladr
Oswestry
Gyrn Moelfre
Lledrod
Mynydd
Mawr
Llyn
Moelfre
Llyn
Rhuddwyn
River Morda

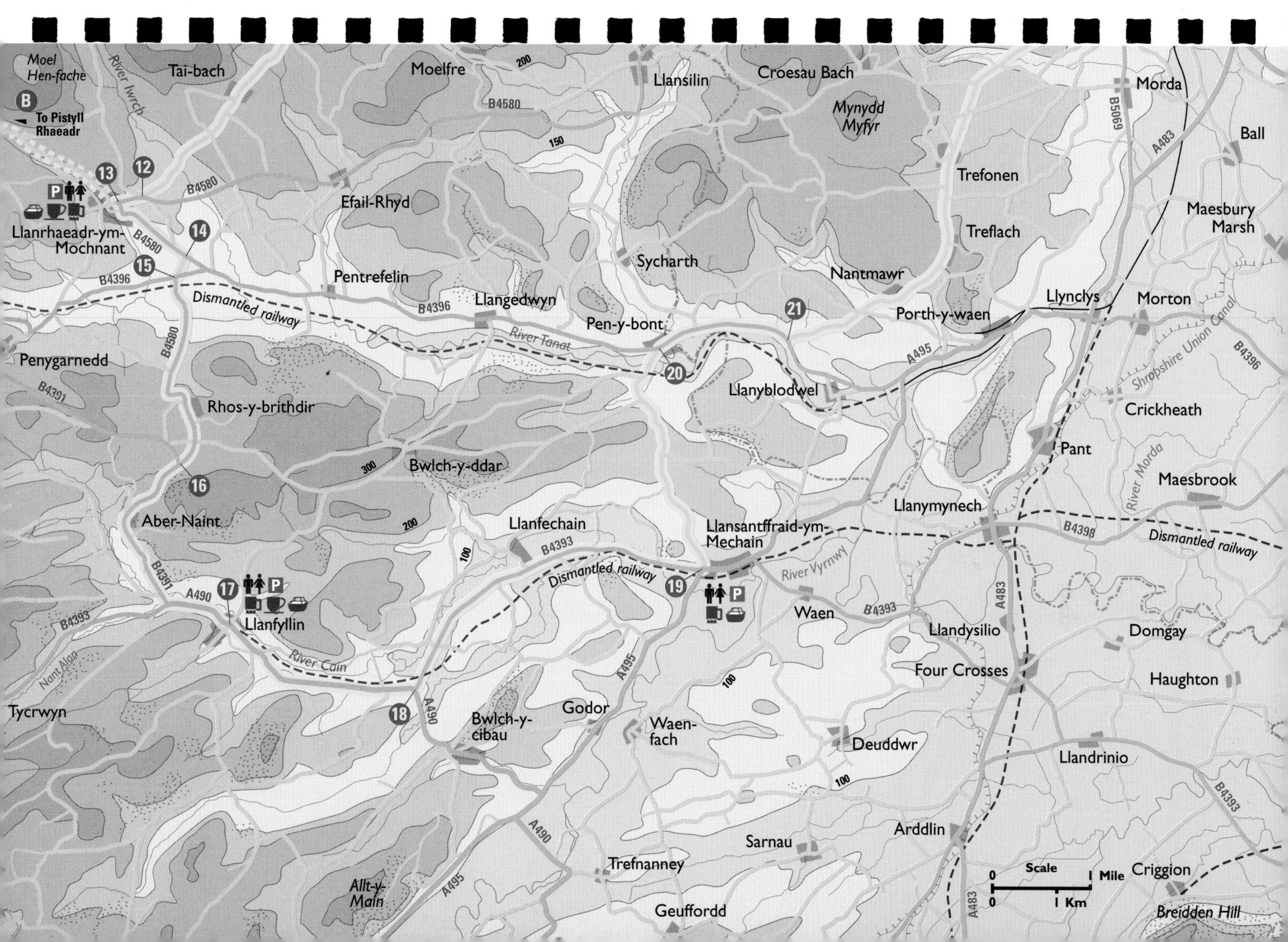

Moel Hen-fache
B
To Pistyll Rhaeadr
River Iwrch
Tai-bach
Moelfre
200
B4580
150
Llansilin
Croesau Bach
Mynydd Myfyr
Morda
B5069
A483
Ball
13
12
B4580
Efail-Rhyd
Trefonen
Maesbury Marsh
Llanrhaeadr-ym-Mochnant
B4580
14
Treflach
15
Sycharth
B4396
Pentrefelin
Nantmawr
Dismantled railway
B4396
Llangedwyn
21
Llynclys
Morton
Pen-y-bont
Porth-y-waen
River Tanat
Shropshire Union Canal
B4580
B4396
Penygarnedd
A495
20
B4391
Llanyblodwel
Rhos-y-brithdir
Crickheath
Pant
300
Bwlch-y-ddar
River Morda
16
Maesbrook
Llanymynech
Aber-Naint
200
Llanfechain
Llansantffraid-ym-Mechain
B4398
Dismantled railway
100
B4393
Dismantled railway
River Vyrnwy
B4391
17
19
A490
A483
Waen
B4393
B4393
Llanfyllin
Llandysilio
Domgay
Nant Alan
River Cain
Four Crosses
A495
100
Haughton
18
Tycrwyn
Godor
A490
Bwlch-y-cibau
Waen-fach
Deuddwr
Llandrinio
100
B4393
A490
Arddlin
Sarnau
Trefnanney
Scale
0
1 Mile
Criggion
A495
0
1 Km
Allt-y-Main
A483
Geufordd
Breidden Hill

Route description 

To start from Gobowen Station, TL out of station, TR at TJ and join route by TR at direction 3.

To start from Chirk Station, TL out of station and TR to join route at direction 8, where TR along Ceiriog Valley.

From the Heritage Centre in Oswestry, TR away from the town centre. Immediately TR along Welsh Walls. TL at TJ into Willow Street.

1 TR then immediately TL into York Street/ Liverpool Road/Old Fort Road. TL at mini roundabout.

---

2 TL at TJ, no SP.

---

3 To return to Gobowen Station, TR at XR, SP Gobowen, then TL at TJ, SP Gobowen, and finish the route at the station.

Otherwise, SO at XR, SP Hengoed.

---

4 TR at TJ, SP Weston Rhyn.

---

5 Take third exit at mini roundabout.

8km (5 miles)

---

6 TL at XR, SP Chirk Bank/Chirk.

---

7 TL onto canal bank, over aqueduct, and climb onto road.

---

8 TL in Chirk (10.5km/6.5 miles) and continue along Ceiriog valley, following river to Glyn Ceiriog.

9 In Glyn Ceiriog, take second exit at mini roundabout, SP Llanarmon (20.5km/12.5 miles). Continue into Llanarmon.

---

10 SO in Llanarmon, SP Llanrhaeadr.

28km (17.5 miles)

---

11 TL, SP Llanrhaeadr (30.5km/19 miles). Continue towards Llanrhaeadr.

---

12 TR at TJ onto B4580 and continue to centre of Llanrhaeadr.

---

13 To visit the waterfall SO then TR just before river bridge.

Otherwise, TL onto B4580, SP Llangedwyn/ Oswestry.

---

14 TR, SP Llanfyllin (B4396).

---

15 SO at XR with B4380, SP Llanfyllin.

39.5km (24.5 miles)

---

16 TL at TJ onto A490, SP Llanfyllin.

---

17 Continue SO through Llanfyllin.

---

18 TL onto B4393, SP Llansantffraid.

50km (31 miles)

---

19 TL at junction with A495 into Wyllan Road, no SP. ***56km (35 miles)***

---

20 TR at TJ onto B4396, SP Oswestry.

---

21 Take second TL, SP Nantmawr. Continue into Oswestry to finish the route at the Heritage Centre (LHS by church).

71.5km (44.5 miles)

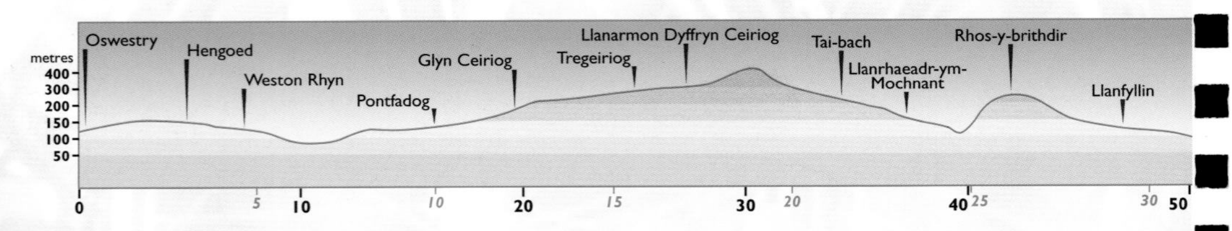

Ceiriog Valley

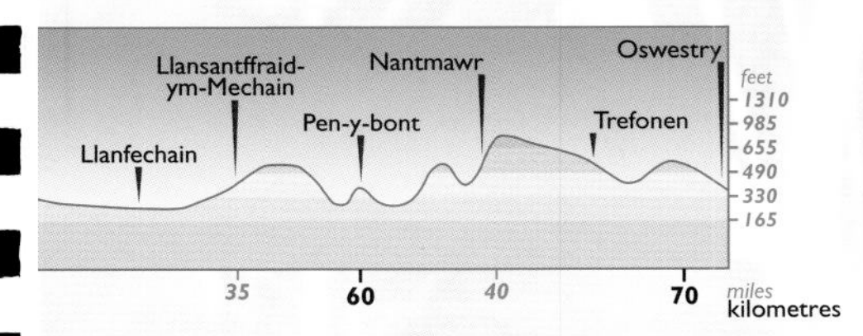

Food and drink

There are plenty of cafés, pubs and convenience stores in Oswestry, Llanrhaeadr and Llanfyllin. Weston Rhyn has a convenience store and there are pubs in Pontafadog, Glyn Ceiriog and Llanarmon

Route **19**

BORTH AND DEVIL'S BRIDGE

Route information

Distance 75.5km (47 miles)

Grade Strenuous

Terrain Quiet, undulating minor roads and some stretches of A road through a remote area. There are some steep climbs and descents.

Time to allow 5–8 hours.

Getting there by car Borth is 8km (5 miles) north of Aberystwyth, off the A487 on the B4353. Park in the car park, the start of the route.

Getting there by train There is a railway station at Borth and Aberystwyth. Telephone (08457) 484950 or visit www.nationalrail.co.uk for travel information.

An attractive ride which combines both sea views and mountain scenery. The ride starts at the seaside resort of Borth and heads south to Aberystwyth. From here the route climbs east to Devil's Bridge and then north to the remote Nant-y-moch Reservoir. During winter, cyclists are advised to carry sufficient food and drink with them, together with suitable clothing. Check the weather forecast, too – the highest point on the route is 400m (1300 feet) and the weather conditions can change rapidly.

Places of interest along the route

A Borth

Borth is an old fishing hamlet with a beautiful sandy beach, popular with families and wind-surfers. **Borth Animalarium** is well-known for the breeding of endangered species, and is part of the European breeding programme for Geoffroy's Cat, a rare native of South America. Visitors can see lots of animals, including lemures, monkeys, wallabies, polecats and less exotic creatures such as gerbils. Also aviaries, bat house and reptile house. Open mid-March to November, 1000–1800 (closed 1630 October and November). Charge. Telephone (01970) 871224.

B Aberystwyth

The town was established over 700 years ago, on the site of a much older settlement. See route 15 for more information.

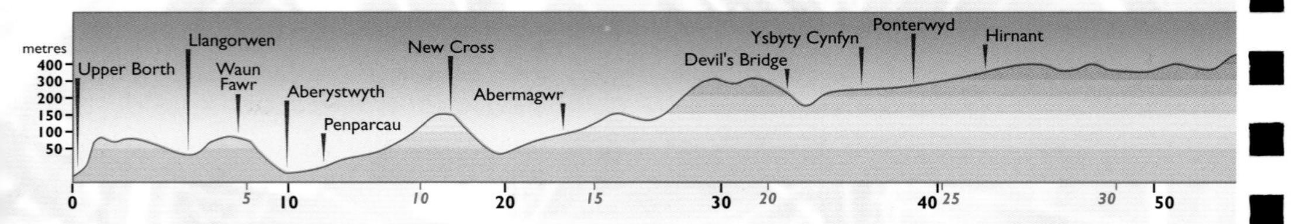

Borth

C Vale of Rheidol Railway, Devil's Bridge

This was the last steam railway owned by British Rail until it was privatised in 1989. The railway was originally opened in 1902 to serve the lead mines of the Rheidol valley. Today the line runs between Aberystwyth and Devil's Bridge. For more information telephone (01970) 625819; www.rheidolrailway.co.uk

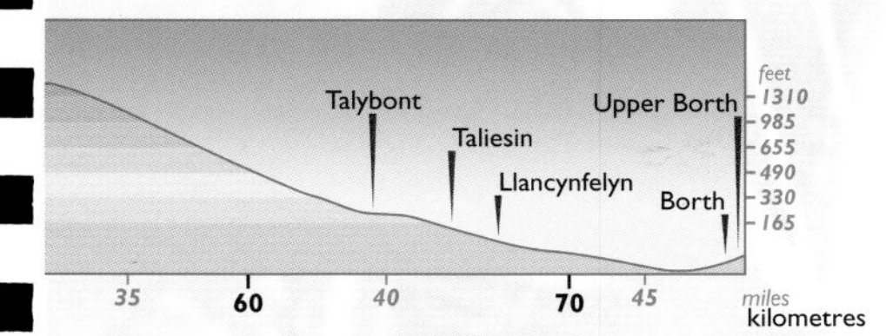

D Devil's Bridge

A popular area for walking, there are waterfalls and three superimposed bridges in the deep river valley. The lowest bridge dates from the 12th century.

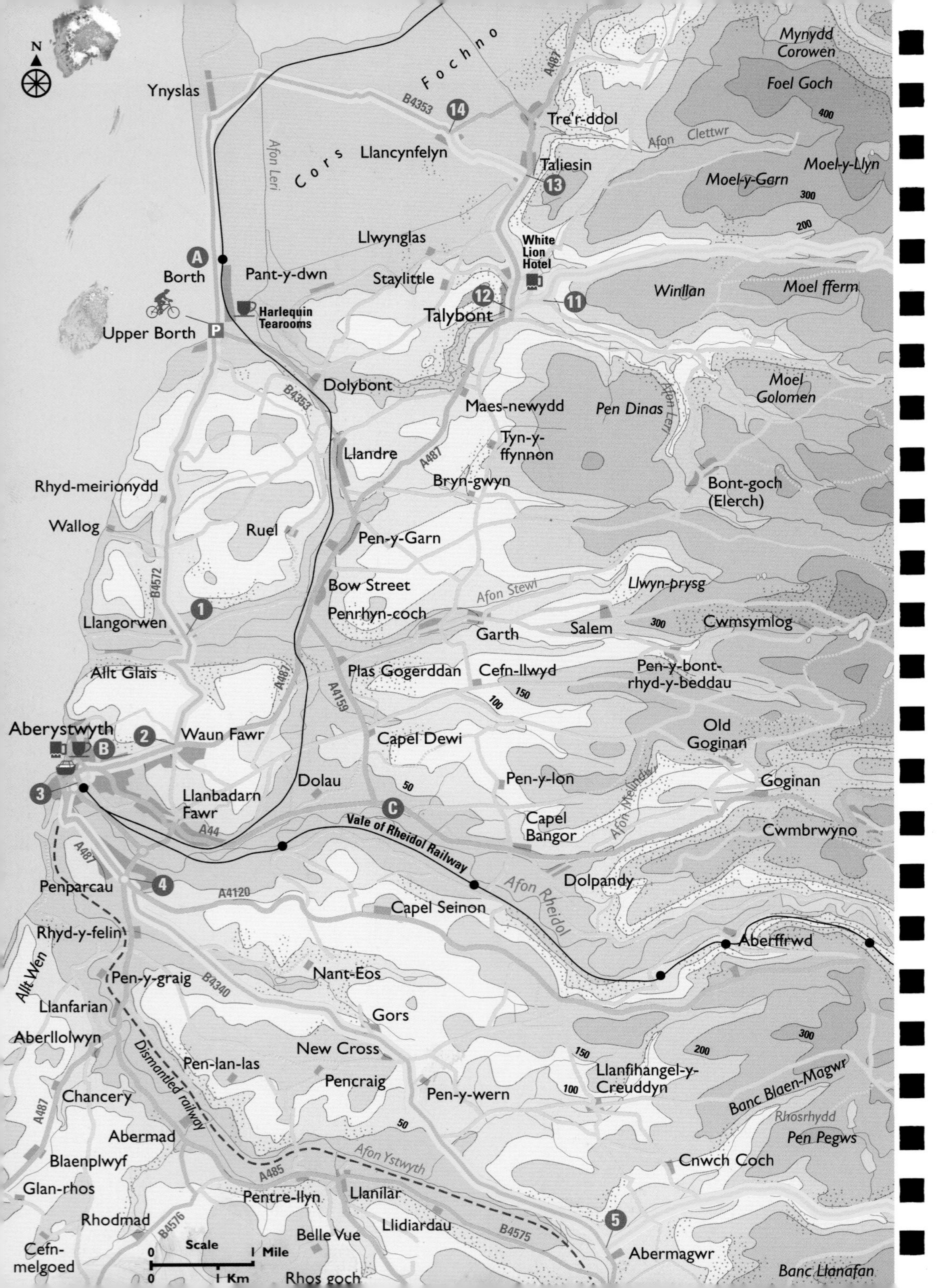

N
Mynydd Corowen
Foel Goch
Ynyslas
Fochno
B4353
14
A487
Tre'r-ddol
400
Afon Clettwr
Cors
Llancynfelyn
Afon Leri
Taliesin
13
Moel-y-Llyn
Moel-y-Garn
300
200
Llwynglas
A
Borth
Pant-y-dwn
Staylittle
White Lion Hotel
12
11
Winllan
Moel fferm
Harlequin Tearooms
Talybont
Upper Borth
P
Dolybont
B4353
Moel Golomen
Maes-newydd
Pen Dinas
Afon Leri
Tyn-y-ffynnon
Llandre
A487
Bryn-gwyn
Bont-goch (Elerch)
Rhyd-meirionydd
Wallog
Ruel
Pen-y-Garn
B4572
Bow Street
Llwyn-prysg
Afon Stewi
1
Penrhyn-coch
Llangorwen
300
Cwmsymlog
Garth
Salem
Allt Glais
A487
Plas Gogerddan
Cefn-llwyd
Pen-y-bont-rhyd-y-beddau
A4159
150
100
Aberystwyth
2
Waun Fawr
Old Goginan
B
Capel Dewi
Dolau
Pen-y-lon
Goginan
3
Llanbadarn Fawr
50
C
Capel Bangor
Cwmbrwyno
A44
Vale of Rheidol Railway
A487
Dolpandy
Penparcau
4
A4120
Afon Rheidol
Capel Seinon
Rhyd-y-felin
Aberffrwd
Allt Wen
Pen-y-graig
Nant-Eos
B4340
Llanfarian
Gors
300
Aberllolwyn
New Cross
200
150
Llanfihangel-y-Creuddyn
Pen-lan-las
Dismantled railway
Pencraig
Pen-y-wern
100
Banc Blaen-Magwr
Chancery
A487
Rhosrhydd
50
Pen Pegws
Abermad
Afon Ystwyth
Blaenplwyf
Cnwch Coch
A485
Glan-rhos
Pentre-llyn
Llanilar
Rhodmad
Llidiardau
5
B4576
B4575
Belle Vue
Scale
0
1 Mile
Cefn-melgoed
0
1 Km
Abermagwr
Rhos goch
Banc Llanafan

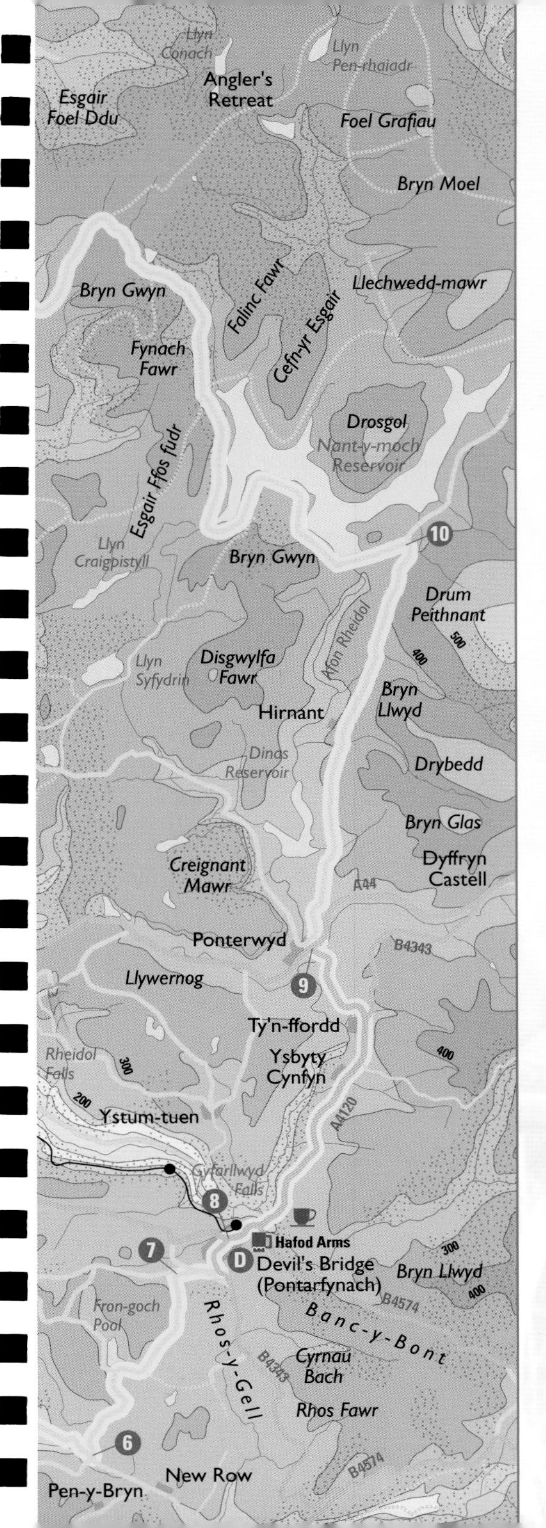

Route description

To start from Aberystwyth railway station, exit railway station and join route at direction 3.

To start from Borth railway station, exit station and head south into Borth.

From Borth car park, TR and take first TL by lifeboat station, no SP. Climb steeply out of Borth then descend towards Llangorwen – excellent views.

1 Enter Llangorwen and SO at XR, no SP (5.5km/3 miles). Continue for climb through woodland.

2 TR at XR onto A487, no SP (8km/5 miles). Enter Aberystwyth and descend. Keep L into one-way system, SP Station (pass station on L).

3 SO at roundabout (second exit), SP Cardigan. To visit town centre, TR by bridge, SP Town Centre, and follow one-way system to rejoin route.

Otherwise, keep L over bridge.

4 TR at roundabout (third exit), SP Devil's Bridge A4120. Take first TR, SP Devil's Bridge, and immediately TR, SP Trawsgoed B4340. Continue on B4340 through New Cross to Abermagwr.

5 TL in Abermagwr, SP Cnwch Coch. (22.5km/14 miles). Gradually climb up through the Nant valley, passing abandoned mine workings.

6 TL at XR, SP Trisant. Climb to Fron-goch Pool and TR by Fron-goch Pool (30.5km/ 19 miles). Climb and descend.

7 TR at TJ, no SP. Then TL at TJ, SP Devil's Bridge B4343.

8 TR at TJ, SP Waterfalls A4120. Pass Vale of Rheidol railway station on LHS. Continue past Hafod Arms Hotel on RHS and cross the Devil's Bridge. Access to waterfalls and tearooms on RHS. Continue along A4120.

---

9 TR at TJ, SP Llangurig A44 (39.5km/24.5 miles). Take first TL, SP Nant-y-moch. Continue on this road, passing Dinas reservoir (look out for Red Kites here). As you approach Nant-y-moch reservoir, there is an information board on LHS.

---

10 TL and follow road around reservoir. BEWARE of cattle grids. Follow road through forest and bear L, no SP, for excellent sea views and long descent. BEWARE of loose stones on descent.

---

11 TR at TJ, SP Talybont (62.5km/39 miles) and continue into Talybont.

---

12 TR at TJ onto A487, no SP. Pass hotel on RHS. Continue along A487 into Taliesin.

13 Take second TL in Taliesin, by Telegraph office. ***66km (41 miles)***

---

14 TL at TJ, SP Borth B4353. Continue through Ynyslas, along seafront to Borth and the end of the ride. ***75.5km (47 miles)***

If you started from Aberystwyth railway station, continue through Borth and follow directions back into Aberystwyth.

Food and drink

Plenty of choice in Aberystwyth. There is a hotel and tearoom in Devil's Bridge. It may be difficult to obtain refreshments along the route out of the summer season.

Harlequin Tearooms, Borth
Snacks and light meals.

White Lion Hotel, Talybont
Bar meals available.

Route 20

WELSHPOOL, LLANYMYNECH AND MELVERLEY

Route information

Distance 83.5km (52 miles)

Grade Moderate

Terrain Mostly quiet country lanes. Care is needed on the short stretches of A road.

Time to allow 4–5 hours.

Getting there by car Welshpool is 27km (17 miles) west of Shrewsbury at the junction of the A483 and A458. There is car parking by the Tourist Information Centre (TIC).

Getting there by train There is a mainline station at Welshpool. Telephone (08457) 484950 or visit www. nationalrail.co.uk for travel information. Leave the station and head towards the town centre and TIC.

A circular route through the Welsh/English borderlands, taking in Welshpool, Llanymynech, and the hamlet of Melverley, and finishing along the foot of Long Mountain. The start of the route is fairly hilly so low gears will be required. The stretch between Llanymynech and Long Mountain is mostly flat with some gentle climbs. The final section of the route is undulating, offering lovely views towards Criggion and Welshpool.

Steam train

Places of interest along the route

A Welshpool

Welshpool is a small market town with many half-timbered buildings, characteristic of the Upper Severn valley. The town sits by the **Montgomery Canal**. Visitors can take a narrow boat trip or hire a self-drive boat. Trips operate April to October, daily. Charge. Telephone for details of times on (01938) 553271. The **Old Station**, designed in the style of a French chateau, contains a selection of gift shops and a café. Open all year, Monday–Saturday 0900–1745, Sunday 1100–1700. Admission free. Telephone (01938) 665522. The **Welshpool and Llanfair Railway** runs steam hauled trains through the picturesque countryside between Welshpool and Llanfair Caereinion. Special events held throughout the year. Trains run April to October and December. Telephone (01938) 810441 for details. Just south of the town is medieval **Powis Castle**, originally built as a fortress by the Welsh princes. The castle is surrounded by a magnificent garden. National Trust property. Tearoom. Castle open 1300–1700, garden open 1100–1800: March to June, September and October, Wednesday–Sunday; July and August, Tuesday–Sunday and Bank Holidays. Telephone (01938) 557018.

B Nesscliffe Hill Country Park, near Shrewsbury

Administered by Shropshire County Council. Telephone (01691) 623323 for information.

Welshpool

Ⓒ Melverley

On the border of Shropshire and Powys, the rivers Severn and Vyrnwy meet in the village and the area is known for good fishing and walking. The village church, **St Peter's**, is one of the oldest surviving timber-framed churches in the country. **Melverley Craft Centre** sells a large variety of locally made crafts. Open Easter–October and during half term holidays, Friday–Sunday 1000–1700. Telephone (01691) 682455 for more information.

Food and drink

There is plenty of choice in Welshpool. Llanymynech has a café, two pubs and a fish and chip shop. Baschurch also has a fish and chip shop and several pubs.

Tontine Inn, Melverley

A popular pub serving real ale and meals.

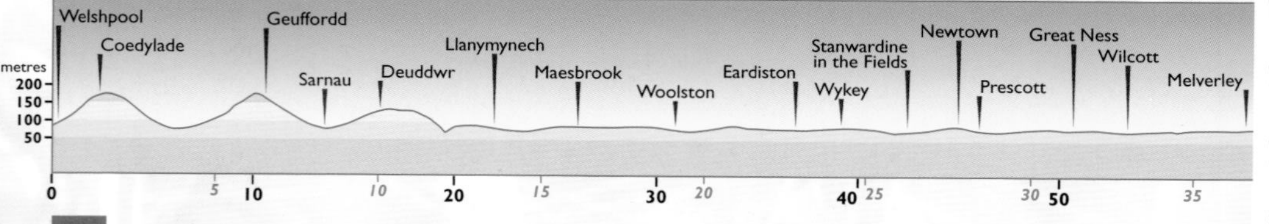

Route description 

Start in the TIC car park and TR onto A458. Pass churchyard and immediately TL – select low gears for a steady climb.

1 Arrive brow of hill. TR, SP Brynfa/Coedylade/Trelydan.

2 At Coedylade, TR, SP Trelydan/Guilsfield. Continue to Folly Farm.

3 TL at TJ by Folly Farm (Folly Lane), no SP (5.5km/3 miles). Continue towards Guilsfield.

4 TR by red brick bungalows, no SP.

6km (3.5 miles)

5 TR at TJ onto B4392, no SP. Immediately TL, SP Geuffordd for climb past nature reserve.

6 TR at TJ, no SP (9.5km/5.5 miles), and follow scenic lane along ridge to Sarnau.

7 Bear left by white Congregational chapel (dated 1829).

8 TR, SP Deytheur.

9 TR at telephone box. ***14.5km (9 miles)***

10 TL, SP Bryn Mawr. Follow lane as it bends to left, descends steeply to stream, climbs and descends to TJ with B4393.

11 TL, no SP (17.5km/11 miles). TR over bridge, SP Llanymynech, and follow B4398 into Llanymynech.

12 In Llanymynech, SO at XR into Station Road (café on RHS). Continue along B4398 past Black Horse pub on LHS and through Maesbrook.

13 Take next TL, SP The Wood.

24km (15 miles)

14 SO at XR with B4396, SP West Felton/Oswestry. Continue to next XR.

15 TL at XR, SP West Felton/Oswestry. Continue into Woolston.

16 On bend in Woolston, TR, SP West Felton/Sandford.

17 In West Felton, TR opposite church (into no through road). Cross A5 via footbridge (Fox Lane) and continue along Fox Lane.

18 SO at XR, SP Tedsmore/Eardiston/Wykey (31km/19 miles). Continue through Eardiston and Wykey.

19 TL (after bend SP Stanwardine). Continue over river through Stanwardine Park.

20 TR at TJ, no SP (38.5km/24 miles). Follow lane to junction with B4397.

21 TL, SP Myddle/Shrewsbury. Continue into Baschurch.

22 TR at XR onto B5067, SP Shrewsbury/Bomere Heath, and continue along this road.

23 TR into Milford Road, SP Little Ness/Great Ness/Nesscliffe. Follow lane through Little Ness. At LH bend, follow SP Great Ness/Nesscliffe.

24 At Great Ness, on LH bend, follow SP Nesscliffe/Shrewsbury. ***46.5km (29 miles)***

Crewgreen
Wollaston
Coedway
Frochas
Buttington
Welshpool
feet
655
490
330
165
60 70 80 kilometres
40 45 50 miles

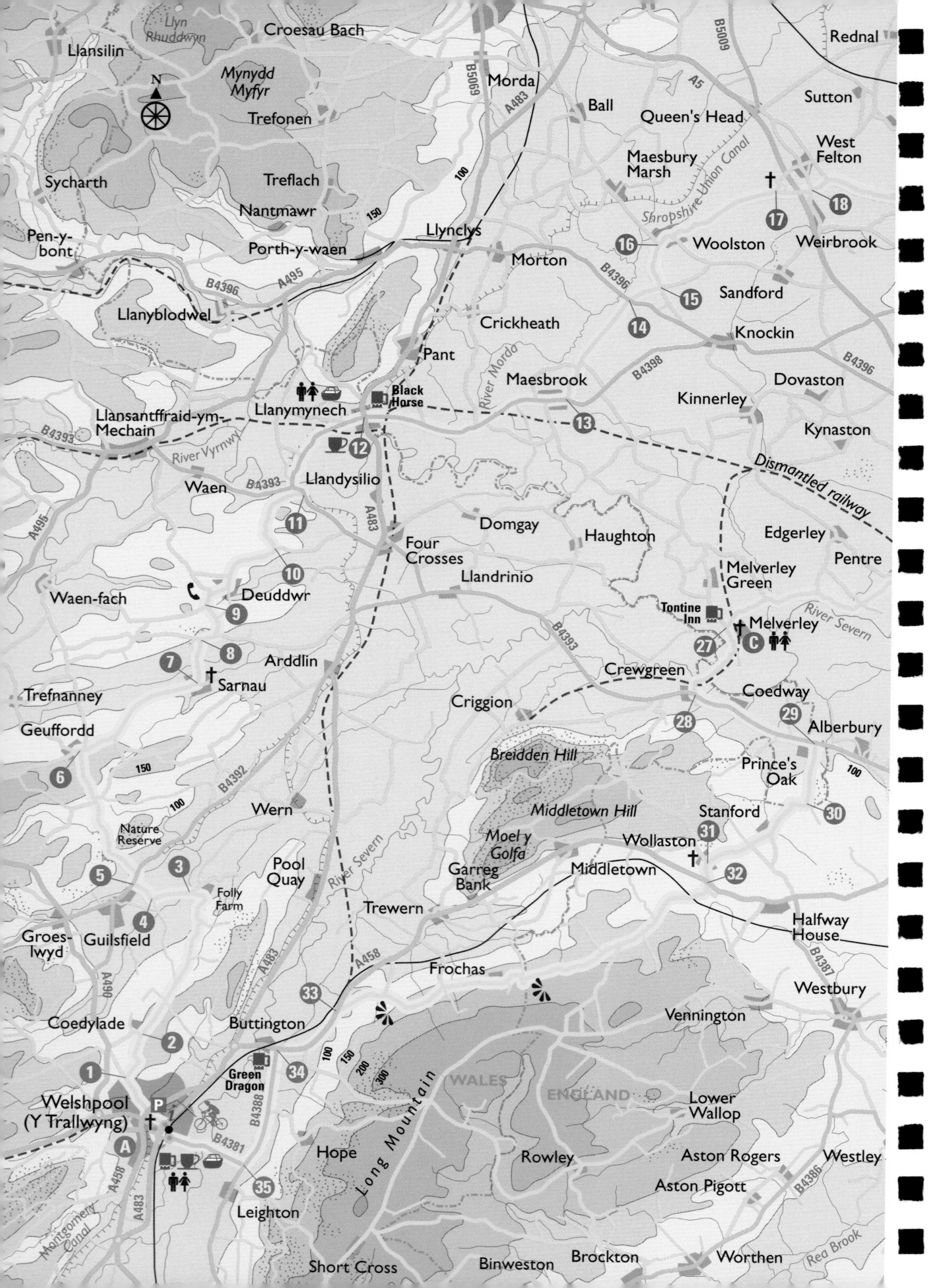

Croesau Bach
Llyn Rhuddwyn
Llansilin
Mynydd Myfyr
Trefonen
Sycharth
Treflach
Nantmawr
Pen-y-bont
Porth-y-waen
Llynclys
Morda
Ball
Queen's Head
Rednal
Sutton
West Felton
Maesbury Marsh
Shropshire Union Canal
Woolston
Weirbrook
Morton
Sandford
Crickheath
Knockin
Llanyblodwel
Pant
Maesbrook
River Morda
Dovaston
Kinnerley
Kynaston
Llanymynech
Black Horse
Llansantffraid-ym-Mechain
River Vyrnwy
Dismantled railway
Llandysilio
Waen
Domgay
Haughton
Edgerley
Pentre
Four Crosses
Llandrinio
Melverley Green
Waen-fach
Deuddwr
Tontine Inn
Melverley
River Severn
Arddlin
Sarnau
Crewgreen
Coedway
Trefnanney
Criggion
Alberbury
Geufforddd
Breidden Hill
Prince's Oak
Middletown Hill
Stanford
Wern
Nature Reserve
Moel y Golfa
Wollaston
Pool Quay
River Severn
Garreg Bank
Middletown
Folly Farm
Trewern
Halfway House
Groes-lwyd
Guilsfield
Frochas
Westbury
Coedylade
Buttington
Vennington
Green Dragon
WALES
ENGLAND
Welshpool (Y Trallwyng)
Lower Wallop
Long Mountain
Hope
Rowley
Aston Rogers
Westley
Aston Pigott
Leighton
Montgomery Canal
Short Cross
Binweston
Brockton
Worthen
Rea Brook
B5009
B5069
A5
A483
A495
B4396
B4398
B4393
A458
B4392
A490
B4388
B4381
B4387
B4386

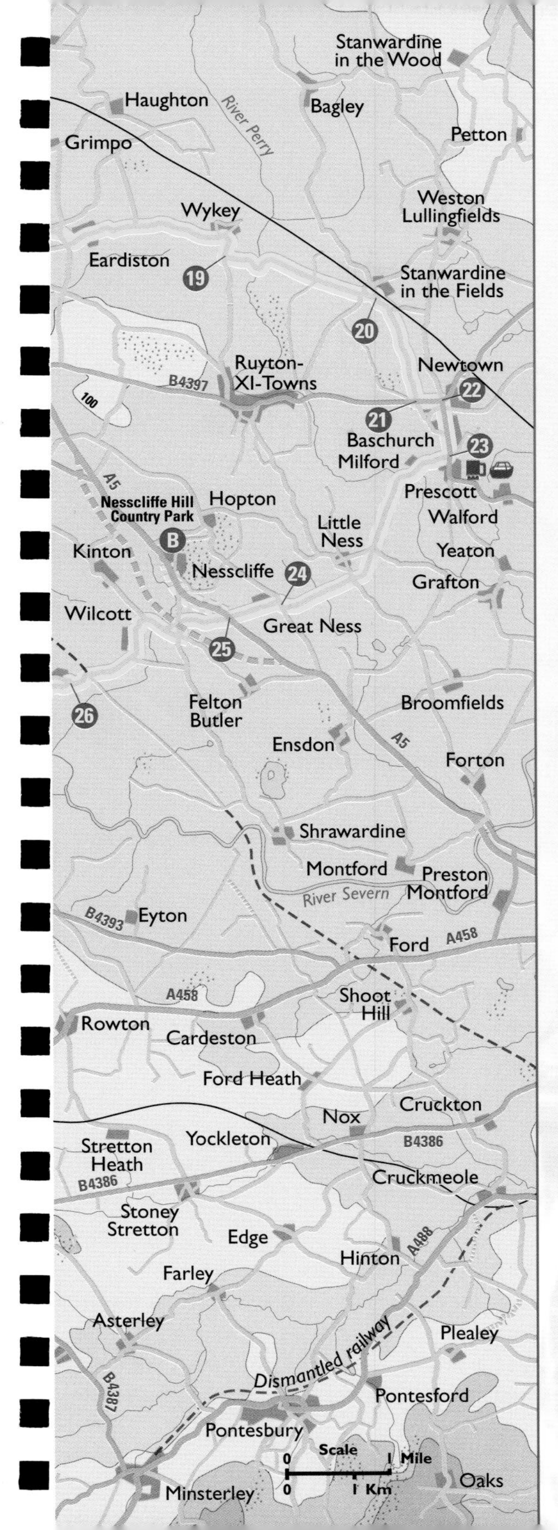

25 To visit Nesscliffe Hill Country Park, TR at XR onto A5 (CARE) and follow A5 for 1km (0.6 mile).

Otherwise, to continue route, SO at XR with A5, SP Wilcott/Pentre/Melverley. Continue along this lane, passing MOD training camp on RHS.

26 At Pentre, TL, SP Melverley/Welshpool (49.5km/31 miles). Continue into Melverley, following SP Welshpool.

27 In Melverley, TL at TJ (opposite caravan site), SP Crew Green/Welshpool (Melverley Craft Centre on LHS). ***57km (35.5 miles)***

28 Arrive TJ with B4393 and TL, SP Shrewsbury.

29 Arrive Prince's Oak. TR, SP Halfway House (61km/38 miles). Continue along this lane.

30 TR, SP Wollaston, and continue into Wollaston.

31 TL at TJ opposite church.

67km (41.5 miles)

32 SO at XR with A458, SP Winnington. Continue along this quiet undulating lane to skirt the foot of Long Mountain, through Frochas. Enjoy the views towards Criggion and the hills of Welshpool beyond.

33 Arrive A458 and TL at TJ, no SP.

34 TL opposite Green Dragon pub, SP Leighton/Forden/B4388. ***77km (48 miles)***

35 TR onto B4381, SP Welshpool. Following SP Town Centre, TL at next two roundabouts. Arrive traffic lights, TR onto A458 and immediately TR (CARE) into the TIC car park to finish the route. ***83.5km (52 miles)***

Route 21

SHREWSBURY AND THE SHROPSHIRE HILLS

Route information

Distance 84km (52 miles)

Grade Strenuous

Terrain Mostly quiet lanes apart from approximately 12km (7.5 miles) of A road on the way out of and back into Shrewsbury. There is a very short stretch along the busy A49 where great care is required. Most of the hills are on quiet roads but some tight, blind bends and poor surfaces need restraint on the descents. The initial climb leads to the top of the Stiperstones which can be cold and exposed in poor weather.

Time to allow 5–8 hours.

Getting there by car Shrewsbury is well served by main road access from all of the Midlands and central Wales. This route starts at the large Abbey Foregate car park (pay and display) opposite Shrewsbury Abbey.

Getting there by train There are regular services to Shrewsbury from Birmingham, Manchester, Chester, and all parts of Wales. The station is approximately 1km (0.6 mile) from the start of the route, via the town centre. Telephone (08457) 484950 or visit www.nationalrail.co.uk for travel information.

A scenic route with some strenuous sections. After a few gentle miles through the lanes south of Shrewsbury there is a steady, steep climb high onto the Stiperstones Ridge. There are many visual reminders of the area's lead mining heritage as you pass by. A steep descent leads once more into narrow, hedged lanes below the Long Mynd before returning to Shrewsbury. Further climbs lead up onto, and over, Wenlock Edge through small, isolated villages and hamlets, along single track roads. After a descent into Acton Burnell, the last few miles are gently undulating.

Places of interest along the route

A Shrewsbury

Evidence of the town was first recorded in 901. Today Shrewsbury is a busy county town, located in a loop of the River Severn. The town centre contains many attractive timber-framed buildings, including Tudor, Jacobean and Georgian buildings, and there is lots for the visitor to see. See Route 10 for more information.

B Coleham Pumping Station, Coleham

Two magnificent steam beam engines housed in a pumping house dating from 1901. Open April to September, every fourth Sunday. Small charge. Telephone (01743) 361196 for more information.

C Snailbeach Mine, Snailbeach

Evidence of mining in this area can be traced back as far as the Roman occupation and the lead mines of Shropshire were once the most productive in Europe. Mining at Snailbeach continued until the mid 1950s. An archaeological survey has identified 20 buildings on the site and a self-guided trail describes the main features and their history. Free access at all reasonable times. Further on along the route other mining relics can be seen, including The Bog, formerly the site of a hamlet and thriving mine, and Nipstone Rock, the site of open mine workings and a good viewpoint.

D Stiperstones Ridge

The ridge and the surrounding district was an important mining area, particularly during the 19th century. Today the Stiperstones are a nature reserve and cycling on the paths is strictly forbidden. Apart from that, the paths soon become extremely rocky making walking difficult and cycling impossible. If you decide to explore on foot, leave your bike secure.

Shrewsbury and the River Severn

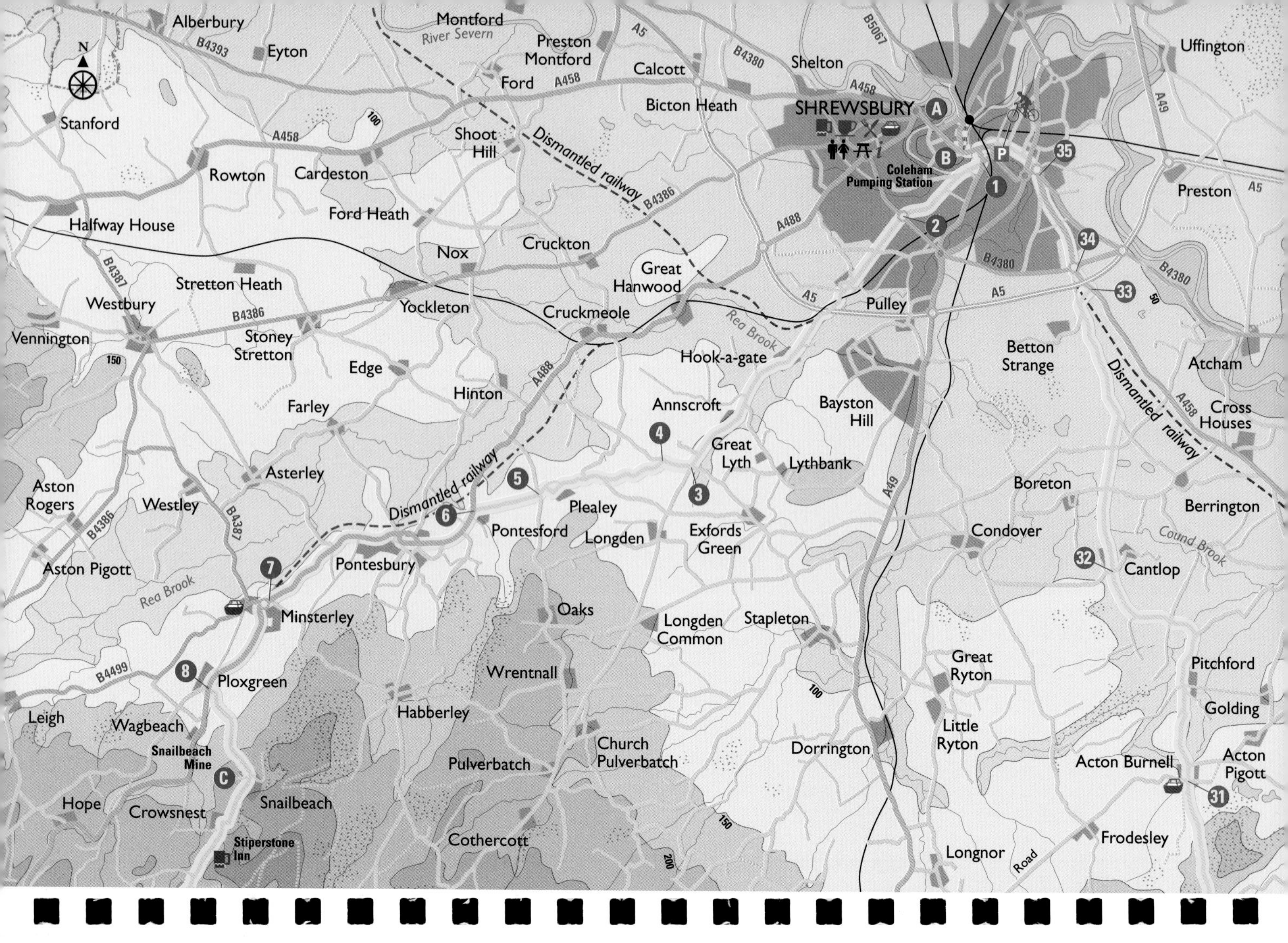
N
Alberbury
Eyton
B4393
Stanford
Montford
River Severn
Preston
Montford
Ford
A458
Calcott
A5
B4380
Shelton
B5067
A458
Bicton Heath
SHREWSBURY
Coleham
Pumping Station
Uffington
A49
Preston
A5
A458
100
Shoot
Hill
Dismantled railway
B4386
Rowton
Cardeston
Ford Heath
Halfway House
Nox
Cruckton
A488
Great
Hanwood
B4380
B4380
A5
A5
Pulley
50
B4387
Stretton Heath
Westbury
B4386
Yockleton
Cruckmeole
Rea Brook
Vennington
150
Stoney
Stretton
Edge
Hook-a-gate
Betton
Strange
Atcham
Hinton
A488
Farley
Annscroft
Bayston
Hill
Dismantled railway
A458
Cross
Houses
Great
Lyth
Lythbank
Asterley
Aston
Rogers
Westley
Dismantled railway
Plealey
A49
Boreton
Berrington
B4386
B4387
Pontesford
Longden
Exfords
Green
Condover
Cound Brook
Cantlop
Aston Pigott
Pontesbury
Rea Brook
Minsterley
Oaks
Longden
Common
Stapleton
B4499
Ploxgreen
Wrentnall
Great
Ryton
Pitchford
100
Habberley
Golding
Leigh
Wagbeach
Little
Ryton
Snailbeach
Mine
Church
Pulverbatch
Dorrington
Acton Burnell
Acton
Pigott
Pulverbatch
Hope
Crowsnest
Snailbeach
150
Stiperstone
Inn
Cothercott
200
Longnor
Road
Frodesley

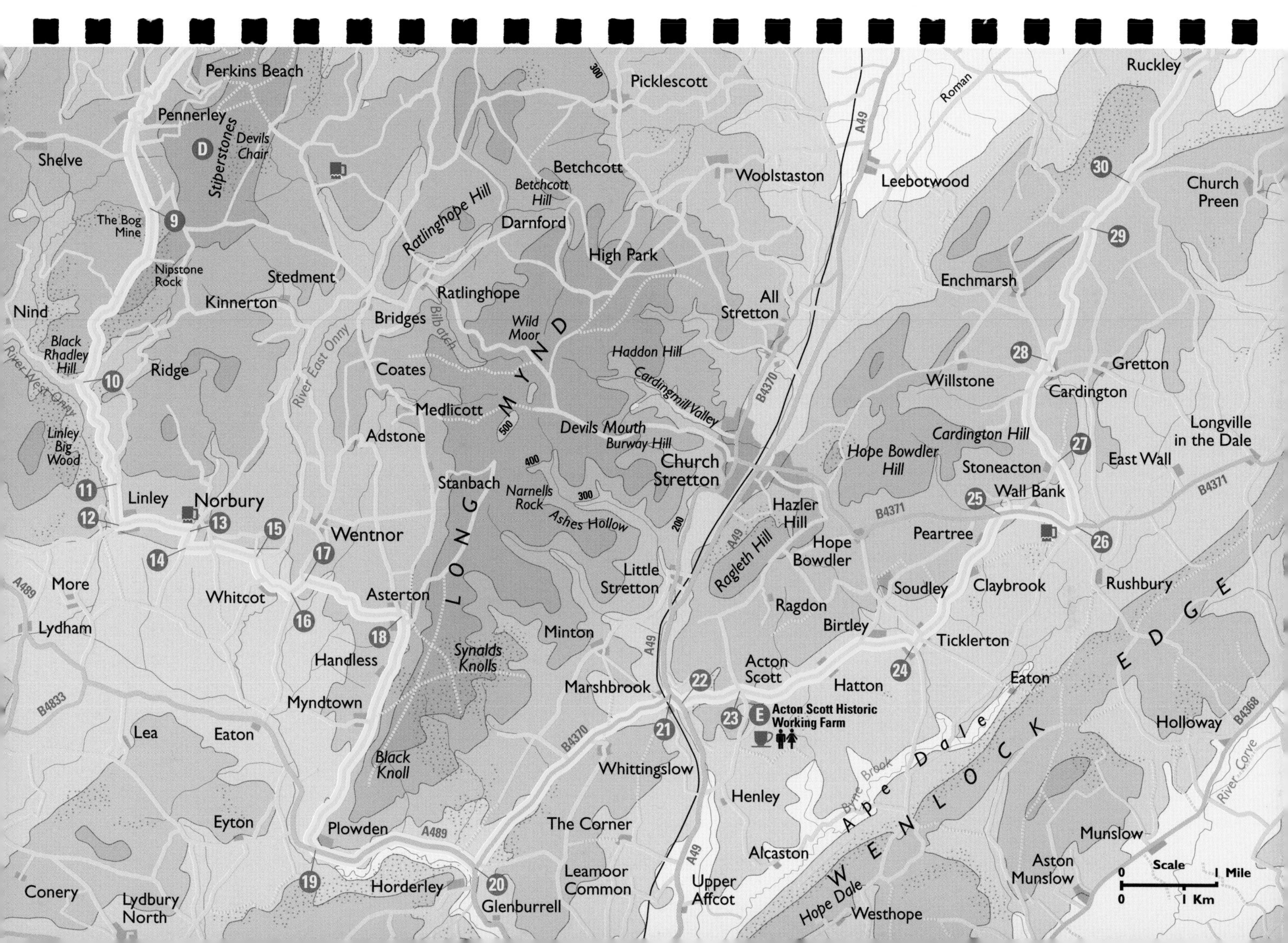

Perkins Beach
Picklescott
Ruckley
Roman
A49
Pennerley
Stiperstones
Devils Chair
D
Shelve
Betchcott
Woolstaston
Leebotwood
30
Church Preen
Betchcott Hill
Ratlinghope Hill
Darnford
The Bog Mine
9
29
High Park
Nipstone Rock
Stedment
Enchmarsh
Kinnerton
Ratlinghope
All Stretton
Nind
Bridges
Bilbatch
Wild Moor
Black Rhadley Hill
Haddon Hill
28
Gretton
River West Onny
Coates
Willstone
10
Ridge
River East Onny
Cardingmill Valley
B4370
Cardington
Medlicott
LONG MYND
Longville in the Dale
Devils Mouth
Cardington Hill
Linley Big Wood
500
Hope Bowdler Hill
Adstone
Burway Hill
27
Church Stretton
East Wall
400
Stoneacton
Stanbach
Narnells Rock
11
Linley
Norbury
Wall Bank
25
300
B4371
Ashes Hollow
Hazler Hill
12
13
15
Wentnor
200
Peartree
26
Hope Bowdler
Ragleth Hill
17
14
Little Stretton
Soudley
Claybrook
Rushbury
More
A489
Whitcot
Asterton
Ragdon
16
Birtley
Lydham
Minton
Ticklerton
18
Synalds Knolls
Handless
Acton Scott
22
24
Eaton
Marshbrook
Hatton
Myndtown
B4833
WENLOCK EDGE
23
E
Acton Scott Historic Working Farm
Lea
Eaton
21
Holloway
B4368
B4370
Ape Dale
Black Knoll
Whittingslow
Byne Brook
Henley
River Corve
Eyton
Plowden
The Corner
A489
Munslow
Alcaston
Leamoor Common
Aston Munslow
19
20
Upper Affcot
Scale
0
1 Mile
1 Km
Conery
Horderley
Glenburrell
Hope Dale
Westhope
Lydbury North

E Acton Scott Historic Working Farm, Acton Scott

A living museum where visitors can experience daily life on an upland farm. Lots of animals and crafts. Café. Open April to October, Tuesday–Sunday and Bank Holidays 1000–1700. Charge. Telephone (01694) 781306; www.actonscottmuseum.co.uk

Route description

If starting from Shrewsbury station, TL at exit traffic lights into Castle Street. Continue on one-way street. Follow LH bend, down steep hill (Wyle Cop). Cross river and arrive at large roundabout. Stay in L lane and SO at roundabout, towards Shrewsbury Abbey. TR into car park when opposite abbey.

From Abbey Foregate car park, TL and join one-way system. Take second exit, SP Belle Vue.

1 TR, SP Longden Coleham. Pass Coleham Pumping Station immediately on RHS, and continue to roundabout.

2 SO at roundabout, SP Longden (7.5km/5 miles). Continue via bridge over A5 dual carriageway.

3 TR at XR, SP Plealey/Pontesbury.

4 TL into Rantipole Lane, SP Plealey/Pontesbury. Continue into Plealey village.

5 SO at XR, SP Pontesbury/Minsterley.

6 TL at TJ onto A488, SP Pontesbury. Pass through Pontesbury (road splits into narrow one-way system before rejoining at far end of village.) Continue on this road until arrive at roundabout in Minsterley. ***16km (10 miles)***

7 Take first exit at roundabout, SP Bishop's Castle A488. NB: there are two convenience stores close to second exit.

8 TL into narrow road, SP Snailbeach/Stiperstones, and begin to climb, passing Snailbeach Mine (25km/15.5 miles). Eventually, road will level off:

9 TR on sharp L bend, SP Linley More (do **NOT** TR onto gravel farm track). Immediately pass the Bog Mine and after approximately 1km (0.6 mile), Nipstone Rock.

10 Take LHF, SP Linley, onto very rough surfaced road – CARE required.

11 TR at TJ, SP Linley.

12 TL at TJ, SP Norbury (32.5km/20 miles). Continue into Norbury.

13 TR at TJ, no SP (to visit pub, TL shortly).

14 TL at TJ onto wider road, SP Pulverbatch/Shrewsbury.

15 As you enter LH bend, TR, SP Asterton/Craven Arms.

16 Arrive TJ at Criftin (grass triangle here). TL, SP Wentnor.

17 TR, SP Asterton. Continue into Asterton.

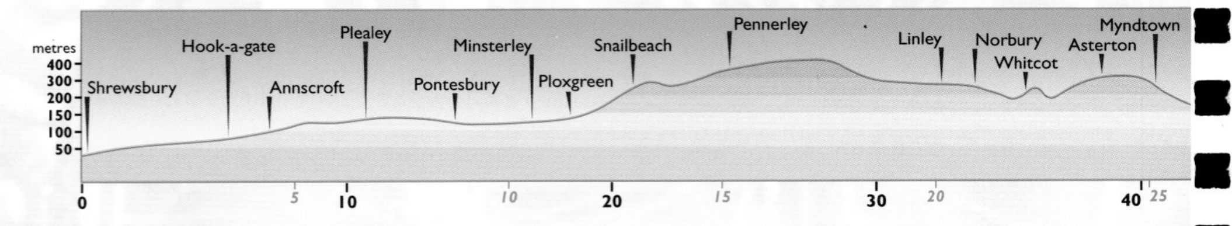

18 TR at TJ, SP Plowden/Craven Arms (42km/26 miles). Continue to TJ with A489.

19 TL at TJ onto A489, SP Craven Arms.

20 TL, SP B4370 (A49) Church Stretton/ Shrewsbury (49.5km/31 miles). Continue to junction with A49.

21 TR (CARE required) at TJ, SP A49 Leominster.

22 TL, SP Acton Scott/Ticklerton. Climb steeply.

23 SO at XR, SP Ticklerton/Much Wenlock (55km/34 miles). Immediately pass main entrance to Acton Scott Working Farm Museum.

24 TL, SP Wall/Much Wenlock. Continue to TJ with B4371.

25 TR at TJ onto B4371, SP Much Wenlock/ Bridgnorth (pub on RHS).

26 TL, no SP, opposite Rushbury Village Hall on RHS. Then climb steeply on narrow road.

27 TR at TJ, SP Cardington. Continue into Cardington.

28 TL at TJ, no SP, and immediately TR, SP Chatwall/Acton Burnell. ***65km (40.5 miles)***

29 TR, SP Ruckley/Acton Burnell.

30 TL on RH bend, SP Ruckley/Acton Burnell. Enter Acton Burnell.

31 For convenience store, TL at XR for short distance. Otherwise, SO at XR, SP Pitchford/Shrewsbury (75km/46.5 miles). Continue into Cantlop.

32 SO at XR. Continue to TJ with A458.

80.5km (50 miles)

33 TL at TJ onto A458, SP Shrewsbury. Continue over A5.

34 Take second exit at roundabout, SP Shrewsbury.

35 At next roundabout, take second exit, SP Shirehall/The Abbey/Football Ground. TL opposite Shrewsbury Abbey into car park to finish the route. ***84km (52 miles)***

To return to railway station, retrace route until reach top of Wyle Cop hill. TR here and walk against flow of traffic to station or cycle around town centre one-way system.

Food and drink

There are plenty of cafés and pubs in Shrewsbury, including a café directly opposite the exit from the car park at the start of the route. There are only occasional convenience stores and pubs along the route, so cyclists should carry sufficient food and drink to sustain them during the ride.

Stiperstones Inn, near Snailbeach
Bar and restaurant meals.

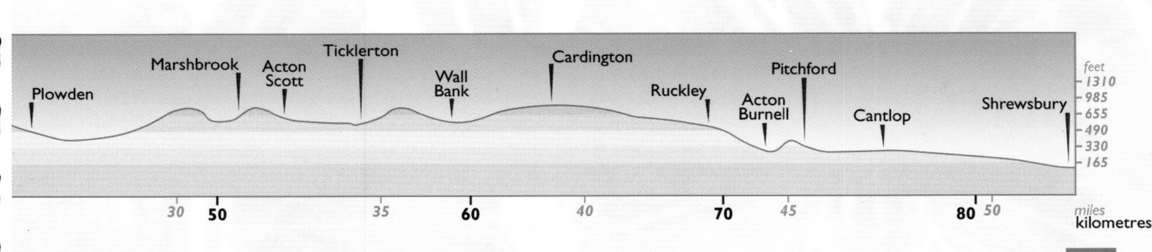

Route **22**

WELSHPOOL, MONTGOMERY AND BISHOP'S CASTLE

Route information

Distance 85.5km (53 miles)

Grade Strenuous

Terrain Undulating country lanes with steady climbs and occasional steeper sections. There is a steep descent from Long Mountain to Leighton.

Time to allow 5–8 hours.

Getting there by car Welshpool is 27km (17 miles) west of Shrewsbury at the junction of the A483 and A458. There is car parking by the Tourist Information Centre (TIC).

Getting there by train There is a mainline station at Welshpool. Telephone (08457) 484950 or visit www.nationalrail.co.uk for travel information.

A route crisscrossing the Welsh/English border, starting from Welshpool and heading south to circuit the Clun Forest, through the Clun valley. From here the route turns north to Bishop's Castle, on to cross Long Mountain, and then returns to Welshpool. An optional short cut bypasses Bishop's Castle and saves 4.5km (3 miles).

Route description

To start from Welshpool station, leave station and head away from Welshpool towards Leighton on B4381. Continue from direction 2.

Otherwise, leave TIC car park and TL onto A458. Immediately TL at traffic lights (XR) onto B4381, SP Leighton.

1 TR at roundabout, SP Leighton. TR at next roundabout, SP Leighton. Continue along B4381.

2 TR at TJ, SP Leighton. Continue on B4388 through Leighton, past Leighton Hall on LHS, to TJ with A490.

3 TL at TJ (opposite Cock Hotel) onto A490 for short distance, SP Church Stoke/Chirbury/ Montgomery. TR back onto B4388 towards Montgomery – you will see the church spire and a craggy hill as you approach the town.

4 TL at TJ, SP Bishop's Castle/Chirbury. Climb up into town (15km/9.5 miles). TR into square for refreshments and follow SP Montgomery Castle/Toilets. Follow sharp LH bend into Kerry Street.

5 On RH bend, follow SP Llandyssil Mountain Road for steep climb.

6 SO at XR, SP Llandyssil/Abermule.

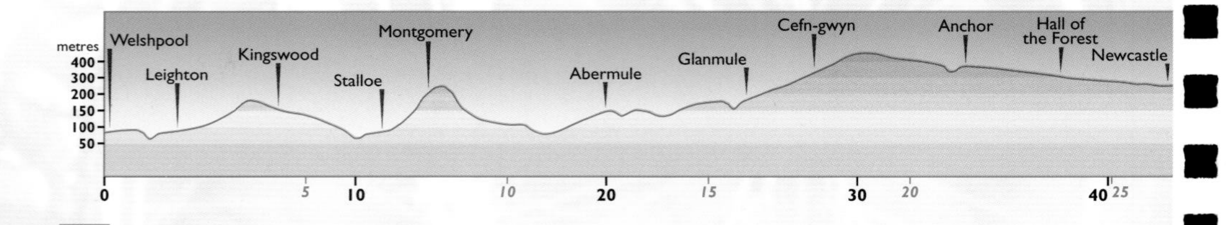

7 SO at XR, SP Abermule.

8 TL at TJ onto B4386, no SP but opposite footpath across railway. Follow B4386 over railway to roundabout where TL into Abermule, SP Newtown/Welshpool/Clun.

9 TL opposite Abermule Hotel, SP Clun/Kerry (22.5km/14 miles). Follow B4368 alongside river and gradually climb up to A489.

10 TR at TJ, SP Kerry/Newtown/Clun. Immediately TL, SP Clun B4368. Continue for steady climb, with a steep section through trees, as you wind your way up to top of hill, with great views on hairpin bend (32.5km/ 20 miles). Climb gently past Anchor Inn for more views and descend into Newcastle.

42km (26 miles)

11 On sharp RH bend, SO across junction into Church Road, no SP.

12 TL up sharp hill, no SP but at junction is Quarry House with picture of bird of prey on wall (43km/27 miles). Descend to TJ.

13 TR at TJ, no SP. Immediately TL, no SP. Continue along this lane, soon passing SP Three Gates/Cefn Einion.

14 Arrive Three Gates XR (farm buildings here). SO, SP Cefn Einion/Shadwell.

15 SO at XR, SP Cefn Einion, down hill and cross river.

16 SO at XR by post box, no SP (48km/ 30 miles). Soon TL, SP Mainstone. TR at XR, no SP. Follow lane for steady climb then steep descent to TJ.

17 TR at TJ, no SP.

18 Arrive staggered junction with grass triangle in middle of road. TR, SP Bishop's Castle. To bypass Bishop's Castle, immediately TL, no SP, onto steep lane descending to B4385.

a TL onto B4385. Soon TR into lane. Continue past Owlbury Hall and TL onto A489. Soon TR into lane, no SP, and rejoin route at direction 22.

Otherwise, continue downhill into Bishop's Castle.

19 TL to climb out of Bishop's Castle on B4385 towards Church Stoke.

20 TR, SP Church Stoke. Continue to junction with A489. ***56.5km (35 miles)***

21 TL onto A489, SP Church Stoke/ Newtown, for approximately 1km (0.6 mile).

22 TR, no SP (57km/35.5 miles). Climb lane to XR.

23 SO at XR into Hyssington.

24 TR at TJ, no SP (59km/36.5 miles). Continue along this road.

25 TL, no SP but on straight, level section of road. Continue for approximately 1.5km (1 mile) and:

26 TL at TJ, no SP (64km/40 miles). Follow road through sharp RH bend by Severn Trent Water site and sharp LH bend (track to Mitchell's Fold Stone Circle SO). Descend steeply, passing Old Miners Arms pub on RHS.

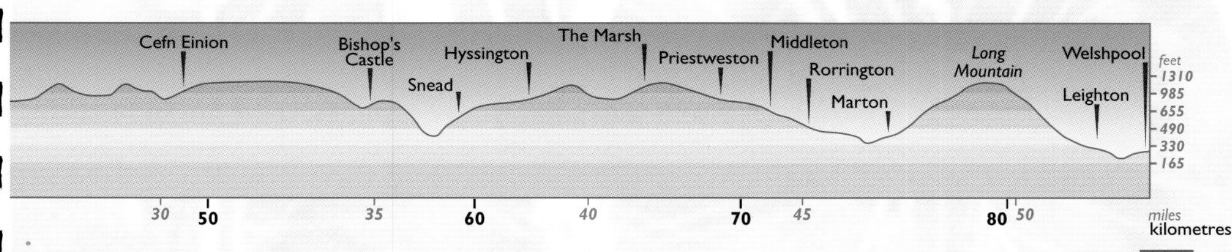

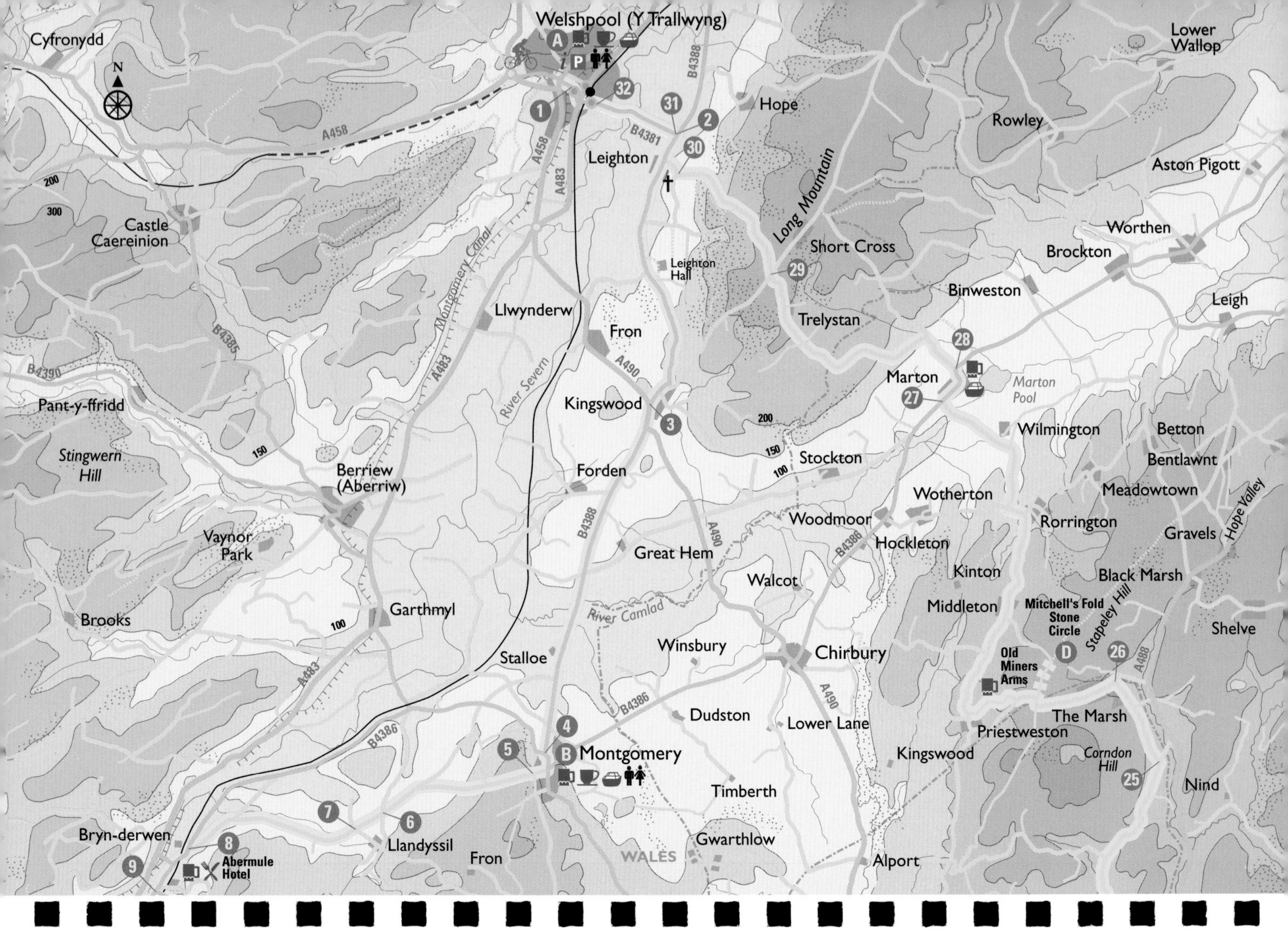

Welshpool (Y Trallwyng)
Cyfronydd
N
Lower Wallop
Hope
Rowley
Aston Pigott
Leighton
Long Mountain
Castle Caereinion
Worthen
Short Cross
Brockton
Leighton Hall
Binweston
Leigh
Llwynderw
Fron
Trelystan
Montgomery Canal
Marton
Marton Pool
Pant-y-ffridd
River Severn
Kingswood
Stingwern Hill
Wilmington
Betton
Stockton
Bentlawnt
Forden
Berriew (Aberriw)
Wotherton
Meadowtown
Woodmoor
Rorrington
Vaynor Park
Hockleton
Gravels
Hope Valley
Great Hem
Kinton
Black Marsh
Walcot
Garthmyl
Middleton
Mitchell's Fold Stone Circle
Stapeley Hill
River Camlad
Brooks
Shelve
Winsbury
Chirbury
Old Miners Arms
Stalloe
Dudston
Lower Lane
The Marsh
Priestweston
Montgomery
Kingswood
Corndon Hill
Nind
Timberth
Llandyssil
Bryn-derwen
Gwarthlow
Fron
Alport
WALES
Abermule Hotel
A458
A483
A490
A488
B4388
B4381
B4385
B4390
B4386
100
150
200
300
A
B
D
P
1
2
3
4
5
6
7
8
9
25
26
27
28
29
30
31
32

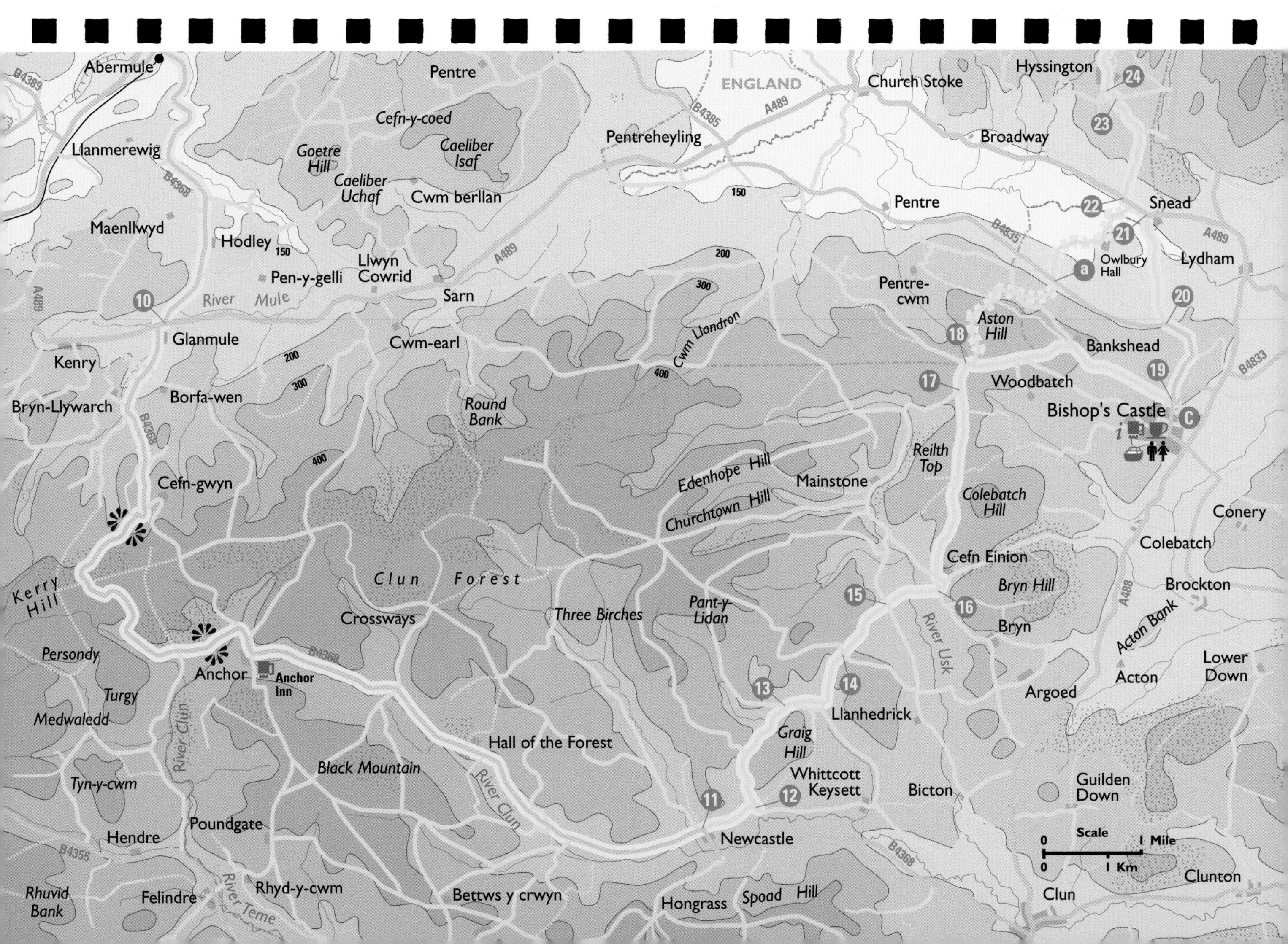
Abermule
Pentre
ENGLAND
Church Stoke
Hyssington
Cefn-y-coed
Caeliber Isaf
Goetre Hill
Caeliber Uchaf
Cwm berllan
Llanmerewig
Pentreheyling
Broadway
Pentre
Snead
Maenllwyd
Hodley
Llwyn Cowrid
Pen-y-gelli
Sarn
River Mule
Owlbury Hall
Lydham
Glanmule
Cwm-earl
Pentre-cwm
Aston Hill
Bankshead
Kenry
Cwm Llandron
Woodbatch
Borfa-wen
Bryn-Llywarch
Round Bank
Bishop's Castle
Reilth Top
Edenhope Hill
Mainstone
Cefn-gwyn
Colebatch Hill
Churchtown Hill
Conery
Colebatch
Cefn Einion
Clun Forest
Bryn Hill
Brockton
Kerry Hill
Crossways
Three Birches
Pant-y-Lidan
River Usk
Bryn
Acton Bank
Persondy
Anchor
Anchor Inn
Lower Down
Acton
Argoed
Turgy
Medwaledd
Llanhedrick
Graig Hill
Hall of the Forest
Black Mountain
River Clun
Tyn-y-cwm
Whittcott Keysett
Bicton
Guilden Down
Poundgate
Hendre
Newcastle
Scale
0
1 Mile
0
1 Km
Clunton
Rhuvid Bank
Felindre
Rhyd-y-cwm
River Teme
Bettws y crwyn
Hongrass
Spoad Hill
Clun
A489
B4389
B4368
B4385
B4835
B4833
A488
B4355
150
200
300
400
10
11
12
13
14
15
16
17
18
19
20
21
22
23
24
a
C

Follow road as it bends R, SP Marton/ Chirbury, and descend into Marton. ***73km (45.5 miles)***

27 TR, SP Worthen/Brockton. Continue on B4386, around sharp LH bend then RH bend.

28 TL, SP Marton Hill/Trelystan. Climb.

29 Arrive XR at top and SO, SP Leighton/ Welshpool. Descend steeply to Leighton. After sharp RH bend by church:

30 TR at TJ, no SP. ***81km (50.5 miles)***

31 TL onto B4381, SP Welshpool.

32 TL at roundabout, SP Town Centre. TL at next roundabout, SP Town Centre. TR at traffic lights onto A458 and immediately TR into TIC car park and the end of the route.

85.5km (53 miles)

Places of interest along the route

Ⓐ Welshpool

Welshpool is a small market town with many half-timbered buildings, characteristic of the Upper Severn valley. See route 20 for more information.

Ⓑ Montgomery

The town grew up around a narrow crossing of the River Severn, now approximately 3km (2 miles) from the modern town. In the surrounding area there are the remains of several Iron Age hill forts, a Roman fort, one Welsh and two Norman castles, including **Montgomery Castle**. This castle was constructed in 1223 by Henry III. Today it is administered by Cadw and the large-scale excavation is well described. There are wonderful views. The castle is on private land. Free access daily, summer 0900–2100; winter 1000–1600. Contact Cadw for more information on 029 2082 6185; www.cadw.wales.gov.uk. The award-winning **Old Bell Museum**, Arthur Street, describes local history and includes scale models of Norman and medieval castles. Open April to September, Saturday and Bank Holidays 1030–1700, Wednesday–Friday and Sunday 1330–1700. Telephone (01686) 668313.

Ⓒ Bishop's Castle

A small market town (market day is Friday), with several antique shops. See Route 5 for more information.

Ⓓ Mitchell's Fold Stone Circle, near Priestweston

A mysterious circle of stones erected circa 2000–1200 BC. The circle was possibly used as a centre for ceremonial and ritual activities, and for trade in locally produced axes. Free access at all reasonable times.

Food and drink

Plenty of choice in Welshpool, Montgomery and Bishop's Castle. There are convenience stores and a pub in Marton.

Abermule Hotel, Abermule
Bar and restaurant meals.

Anchor Inn, Anchor
Bar meals available.

Route

23

LLANIDLOES AND LLANDRINDOD

Route information

Distance 96.5km (60 miles)

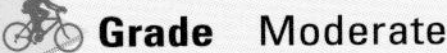

Grade Moderate

Terrain Mostly quiet B roads and country lanes. There are a couple of short sections of route on A roads. The first part of the route is hilly.

Time to allow 7–8 hours.

Getting there by car Llanidloes is 17.5km (11 miles) south west of Newtown on the A470. Park in The Gro free car park in the centre of the town.

Getting there by train The nearest railway station is at Llandrindod Wells, on the route. Telephone (08457) 484950 or visit www.nationalrail.co.uk for travel information.

The route starts in Llanidloes (see route 17 for more information). From here it heads south through Llandrindod Wells as far as Newbridge on Wye. Here the route turns north to Rhayader, and follows the River Wye before heading back to Llanidloes. Two alternative options are given within the route.

Places of interest along the route

A Abbeycwmhir Church and Abbey, Abbeycwmhir

St Mary's Church was built in 1866 to replace an earlier church founded in 1680. The ruined Cistercian abbey was originally constructed during the 12th century on the foundations of a previous building. Many local buildings, including the church in Llanidloes, are believed to have been built using stone from the ruined abbey building. The ruins are on private land, but there is free access at all reasonable times.

B Llandrindod Wells

The site of spa waters well-known to the Romans, the town developed with the arrival of the railway in the mid 19th century. See Route 2 for more information.

C Elan Valley Visitor Centre, Elan village

The Elan Valley estate comprises 112 square km (70 square miles). The visitor centre contains an exhibition showing the local and natural history of the area. See route 4 for more information.

D Rhayader

A small town on the River Wye. See Route 4 for more details.

Route description

To start from Llandrindod Wells station, TL from station. TR onto A483 and join route by direction 9 and the Cycle Museum.

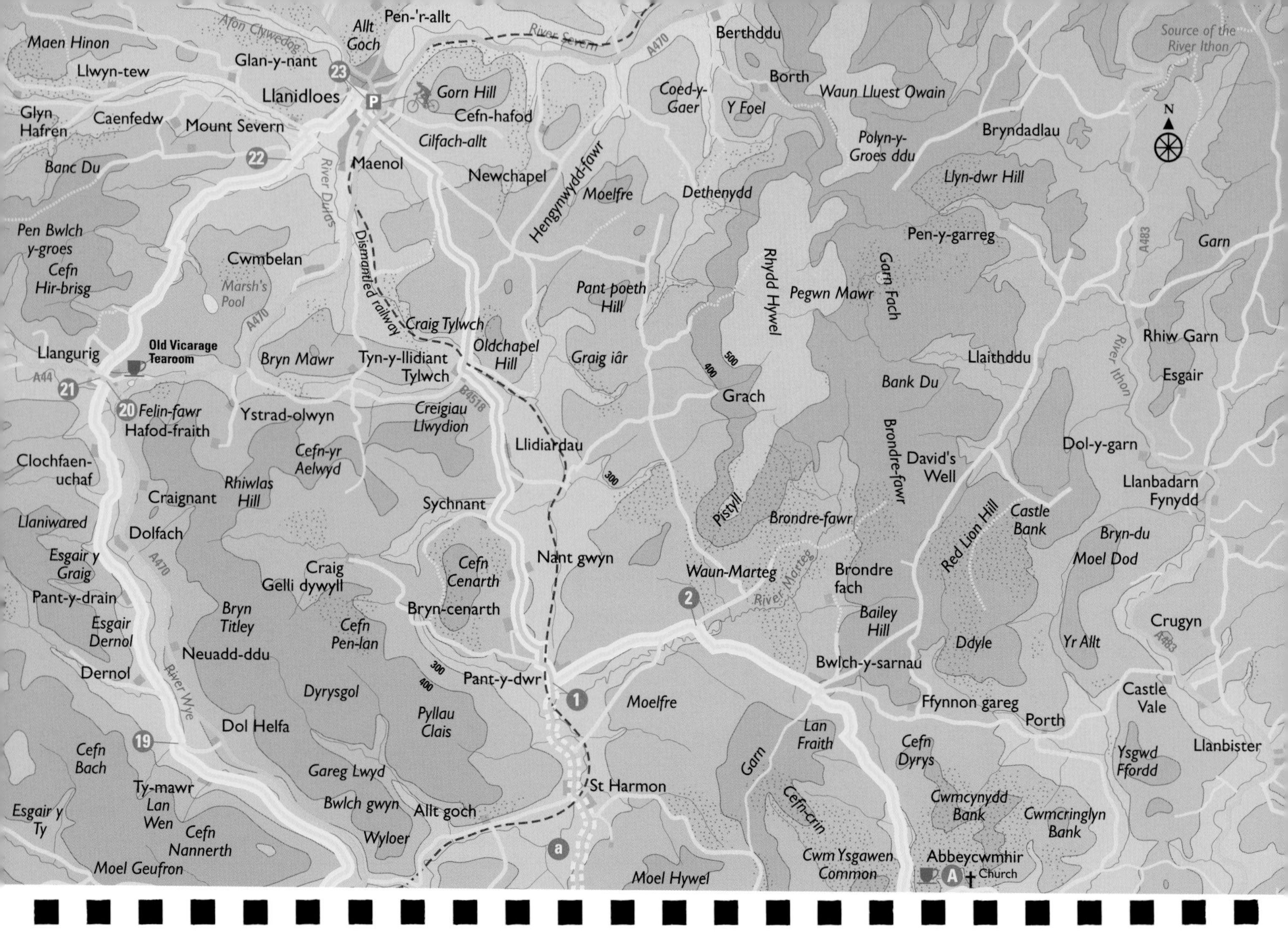

Maen Hinon
Afon Clywedog
Allt Goch
Pen-'r-allt
River Severn
A470
Berthddu
Source of the River Ithon
Glan-y-nant
Llwyn-tew
23
Llanidloes
P
Gorn Hill
Cefn-hafod
Coed-y-Gaer
Borth
Y Foel
Waun Lluest Owain
N
Glyn Hafren
Caenfedw
Mount Severn
Cilfach-allt
Polyn-y-Groes ddu
Bryndadlau
22
Banc Du
River Dulas
Maenol
Newchapel
Hengynwydd-fawr
Moelfre
Dethenydd
Llyn-dwr Hill
Pen Bwlch y-groes
Cefn Hir-brisg
Cwmbelan
Marsh's Pool
A470
Dismantled railway
Pen-y-garreg
A483
Garn
Pant poeth Hill
Rhydd Hywel
Pegwn Mawr
Garn Fach
Craig Tylwch
Llangurig
Old Vicarage Tearoom
Bryn Mawr
Tyn-y-llidiant Tylwch
Oldchapel Hill
Graig iâr
500
400
River Ithon
Rhiw Garn
Llaithddu
Esgair
A44
21
20
Felin-fawr
Hafod-fraith
Ystrad-olwyn
Creigiau Llwydion
B4518
Grach
Bank Du
Llidiardau
Brondre-fawr
Dol-y-garn
Clochfaen-uchaf
Cefn-yr Aelwyd
300
David's Well
Llanbadarn Fynydd
Craignant
Rhiwlas Hill
Sychnant
Pistyll
Brondre-fawr
Castle Bank
Red Lion Hill
Llaniwared
Dolfach
Bryn-du
Esgair y Graig
A470
Nant gwyn
Moel Dod
Craig
Gelli dywyll
Cefn Cenarth
Waun-Marteg
Brondre fach
Pant-y-drain
Bryn Titley
Bryn-cenarth
2
River Marteg
Bailey Hill
Crugyn
Esgair Dernol
Cefn Pen-lan
Ddyle
Yr Allt
A483
Neuadd-ddu
Dernol
River Wye
300
400
Bwlch-y-sarnau
Pant-y-dwr
Dyrysgol
1
Moelfre
Ffynnon gareg
Castle Vale
Porth
Dol Helfa
Pyllau Clais
Lan Fraith
19
Cefn Bach
Cefn Dyrys
Llanbister
Garn
Ysgwd Ffordd
Gareg Lwyd
Ty-mawr
St Harmon
Cefn-crin
Cwmcynydd Bank
Cwmcringlyn Bank
Esgair y Ty
Lan Wen
Bwlch gwyn
Allt goch
Cefn Nannerth
Wyloer
a
Cwm Ysgawen Common
Abbeycwmhir
A
Church
Moel Geufron
Moel Hywel

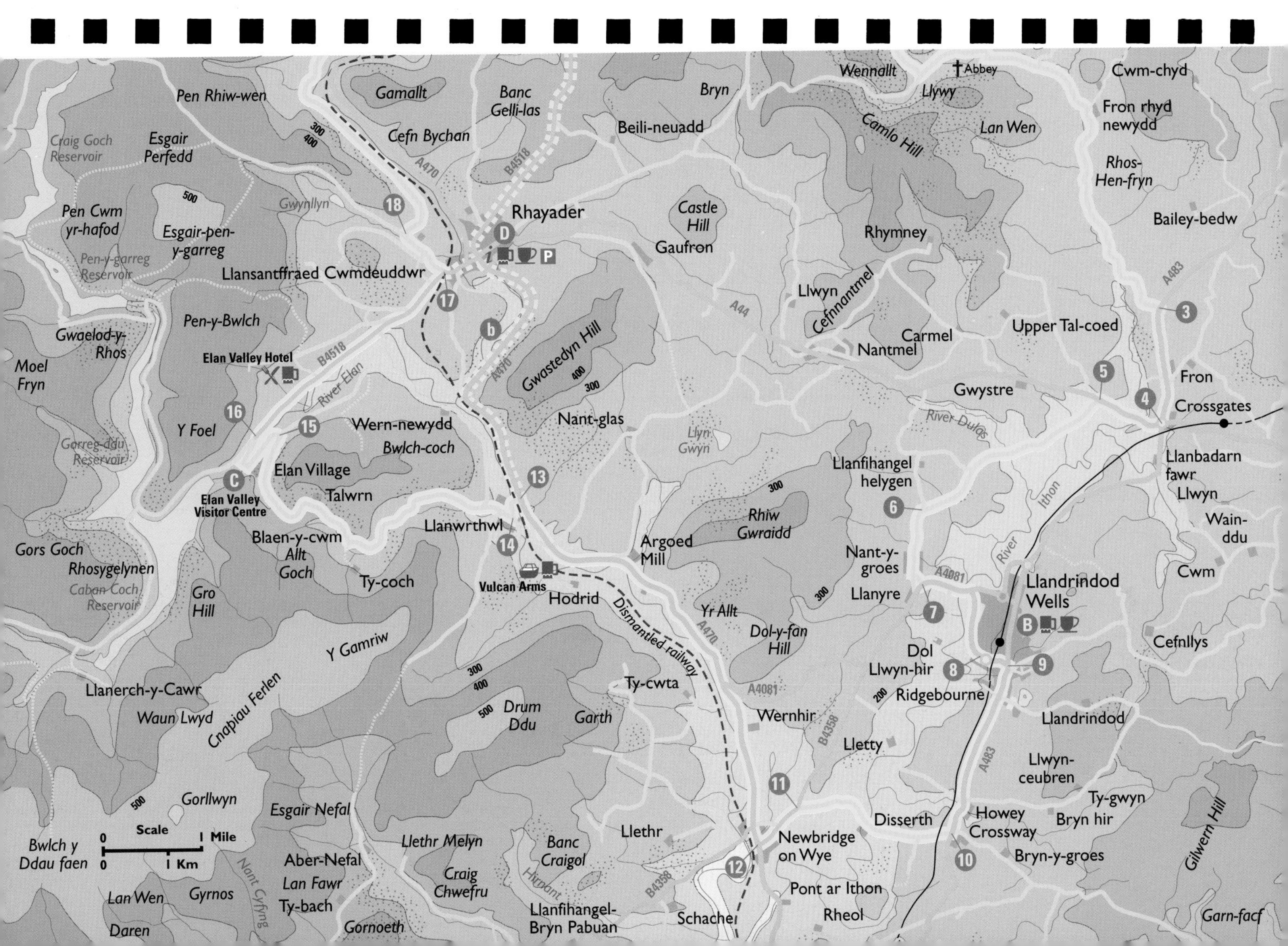

Pen Rhiw-wen
Gamallt
Banc Gelli-las
Bryn
Beili-neuadd
Wennallt
Abbey
Llywy
Camlo Hill
Lan Wen
Cwm-chyd
Fron rhyd newydd
Rhos-Hen-fryn
Bailey-bedw
Craig Goch Reservoir
Esgair Perfedd
Cefn Bychan
Pen Cwm yr-hafod
Esgair-pen-y-garreg
Gwynllyn
Rhayader
Castle Hill
Gaufron
Rhymney
Pen-y-garreg Reservoir
Llansantffraed Cwmdeuddwr
Llwyn
Cefnnantmel
A44
A470
A483
B4518
Upper Tal-coed
Pen-y-Bwlch
Gwaelod-y-Rhos
Moel Fryn
Elan Valley Hotel
River Elan
Gwastedyn Hill
Carmel
Nantmel
Gwystre
Fron
Crossgates
Y Foel
Wern-newydd
Bwlch-coch
Nant-glas
Llyn Gwyn
River Dulas
Garreg-ddu Reservoir
Elan Village
Talwrn
Elan Valley Visitor Centre
Llanfihangel helygen
Llanbadarn fawr
Llwyn
Wain-ddu
Ithon
River
Llanwrthwl
Blaen-y-cwm
Allt Goch
Gors Goch
Rhosygelynen
Caban Coch Reservoir
Gro Hill
Ty-coch
Vulcan Arms
Hodrid
Argoed Mill
Rhiw Gwraidd
Nant-y-groes
Llanyre
A4081
Cwm
Llandrindod Wells
Dismantled railway
Yr Allt
Dol-y-fan Hill
Dol
Llwyn-hir
Ridgebourne
Cefnllys
Y Gamriw
Llanerch-y-Cawr
Waun Lwyd
Cnapiau Ferlen
Drum Ddu
Garth
Ty-cwta
Wernhir
B4358
Lletty
Llandrindod
Llwyn-ceubren
Ty-gwyn
Bryn hir
Gorllwyn
Esgair Nefal
Llethr Melyn
Banc Craigol
Llethr
Disserth
Howey Crossway
Bryn-y-groes
Gilwern Hill
Newbridge on Wye
Scale
0
1 Mile
1 Km
Bwlch y Ddau faen
Nant Cyfyng
Aber-Nefal
Lan Fawr
Ty-bach
Lan Wen
Gyrnos
Daren
Craig Chwefru
Hirnant
Llanfihangel-Bryn Pabuan
Gornoeth
Schachel
Pont ar Ithon
Rheol
Garn-facf

To start from Llanidloes, TR out of Gro car park. TL, SP Tylwch B4518. Staying on this road, cross River Dulas at Tylwch, pass through Nant gwyn and continue into Pant-y-dwr.

1 To take optional short cut **a**, continue on B4518 to Rhayader. TL at TJ onto A470. TR at XR (by clock tower) and rejoin route at direction 17 where TR, SP Aberystwyth Mountain Road.

Otherwise, to follow main route, TL in Pant-y-dwr, SP Bwlch-y-sarnau. ***12km (7.5 miles)***

---

2 Take RHF, SP Bwlch-y-sarnau. Continue through Bwlch-y-sarnau and Abbeycwmhir to junction with A483. ***22.5km (14 miles)***

---

3 TR at TJ onto A483, no SP.

---

4 Take third exit at roundabout, SP Rhayader. ***32km (20 miles)***

---

5 TL, SP Llanyre.

---

6 TL at TJ, SP Llandrindod. Continue into Llanyre.

---

7 TL at TJ onto A4081, no SP (38.5km/ 24 miles). Descend and cross River Ithon for climb into Llandrindod.

---

8 SO at roundabout (second exit). Rock Park and Spa immediately on R.

---

9 TR at TJ onto A483, no SP.

To visit lake, TL immediately before National Cycle Museum (on LHS). TR, SP Lake.

To return to Llandrindod station, retrace route from here.

Otherwise, to follow main route, continue on A483 through Howey.

10 TR at XR, SP Newbridge.

---

11 TL at TJ, SP Newbridge (47.5km/ 29.5 miles). Continue into Newbridge.

---

12 TR at TJ, SP Rhayader A470. Stay on A470, past Vulcan Arms pub and Spar shop on LHS.

---

13 To follow easier but busier route, bypassing Elan Valley Visitor Centre, continue on A470 to Rhayader. TL at XR by clock tower to rejoin route at direction 17.

Otherwise, to follow main route, TL, SP Llanwrthwl, and cross River Wye.

---

14 Arrive Llanwrthwl where route joins Wye Valley Walk (information board on L by church). Cycle through village. TL at TJ onto gated road, SP Elan Village (57.5km/35.5 miles). Descend to cattle grid.

---

15 Keep L, no SP (64km/40 miles). Pass through Elan village, cross River Elan and pass Elan Valley Visitor Centre on L.

---

16 TR at TJ, no SP (65km/40.5 miles). Pass Elan Valley Hotel on LHS. Continue towards Rhayader.

---

17 TR to visit Rhayader.

Otherwise, to continue route, TL, SP Aberystwyth Mountain Road (Cycle Route 8).

---

18 TR, SP Cycle Route 8 (71.5km/44.5 miles). Follow this scenic gated road alongside River Wye.

---

19 TL at TJ, no SP (81km/50.5 miles). Continue into Llangurig.

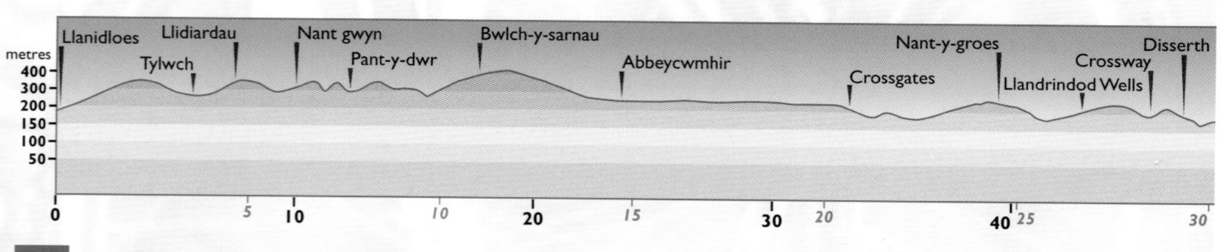

Elan Valley

20 To visit Old Vicarage Tearoom, TR at TJ. Then take first TL, SP Tearooms.

Otherwise, TL at TJ onto A44.

87.5km (54.5 miles)

21 Immediately TR, SP Cycle Route 8, and climb. Ignore all turnings until:

22 TR at TJ, SP Llanidloes Cycle Route 8. Continue into Llanidloes.

23 TR and cross River Dulas. TR by chapel into one-way street, to finish the ride at the car park. ***96.5km (60 miles)***

Food and drink

There are numerous pubs and cafés in Llanidloes, Llandrindod Wells and Rhayader. Tea and biscuits can be purchased at St Mary's Church, Abbeycwmhir.

Vulcan Arms, Newbridge
Bar meals available.

Old Vicarage Tearoom, Llangurig
Tearooms and B&B.

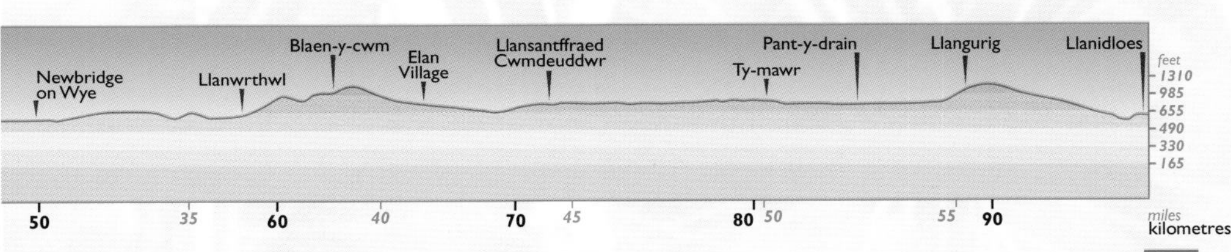

Route **24**

RHAYADER AND THE CWMYSTWYTH MOUNTAIN ROAD

Route information

Distance 103km (64 miles)

Grade Strenuous

Terrain Mostly mountain roads with steep climbs.

Time to allow 7–8 hours.

Getting there by car Rhayader is 18km (11 miles) north of Builth Wells, at the junction of the A470 and A44. Park in the free car park off the A470.

Getting there by train The nearest railway station is at Llandrindod on the Heart of Wales line, approximately 19km (12 miles) from Rhayader along main roads. Telephone (08457) 484950 or visit www.nationalrail.co.uk for travel information.

A challenging but scenic route over steeply climbing mountain roads, through the wild moorland country to the west of Rhayader. The Abergwesyn and the Cwmystwyth moutains roads are used, as well as the 1 in 4 Devil's Staircase. The hard climbs are rewarded by spectacular views and often the sight of a buzzard or kite soaring overhead. Cyclists should carry food and drink with them, together with suitable clothing – refreshments stops are limited and the weather can change rapidly. Check the weather forecast before setting out. This route is not recommended during the winter months, as the roads can be quickly blocked by snow.

Places of interest along the route

Rhayader

A small town on the River Wye. See route 4 for more information.

Route description

To start from Llandrindod Station, leave station and head out of town on A4081. TR to Newbridge on Wye. TR onto A470. Start route at direction 2, where TL, SP Beula.

To start from Rhayader, TR out of car park and immediately TL. TL at TJ onto A470.

1 SO at clock tower, SP Builth Wells A470. Continue into Newbridge on Wye.

2 If returning to Llandrindod Wells, TL in Newbridge and retrace route to station.

Otherwise, to continue main route, TR, SP Beula B4358 (13.5km/8.5 miles). Pass Red Lion pub on RHS (the oldest pub in Powys). Descend into Beula.

3 TR at TJ, SP Llandovery A48 (shop on RHS). Take first TR, SP Abergwesyn (29km/ 18 miles). Continue into Abergwesyn.

4 TR, SP Tregaron. Climb the Devil's Staircase. Continue, ignoring all turnings: Climb and descend to Tregaron.

5 TR at TJ, no SP but Tregaron Hotel on LHS, Spar shop on RHS. ***60km (37.5 miles)***

Abergwesyn Pass

6 TR at XR, SP Pontrhydfendigaid. Continue through Pontrhydfendigaid.

7 TR, SP Pont-rhyd-y-groes/Devils Bridge (69.5km/43 miles). Continue through Ysbyty Ystwyth and Pont-rhyd-y-groes. Cross River Yystwyth and climb.

8 TR, SP Cwmystwyth B4574.

78.5km (49 miles)

9 TR at TJ, no SP, and climb through Cwmystwyth. Pass abandoned mine and buildings (82km/51miles). Continue descent towards Rhayader.

10 TL at TJ, SP Cycle Route 25 (101km/ 63 miles). TL at XR in centre of Rhayader, SP Aberystwyth, and return to the car park to finish the ride. ***103km (64 miles)***

Food and drink

There are plenty of pubs and cafés in Rhayader.

Red Lion, Llanafan-fawr
Bar meals available.

Talbot Hotel, Tregaron
Restaurant and bar meals served.

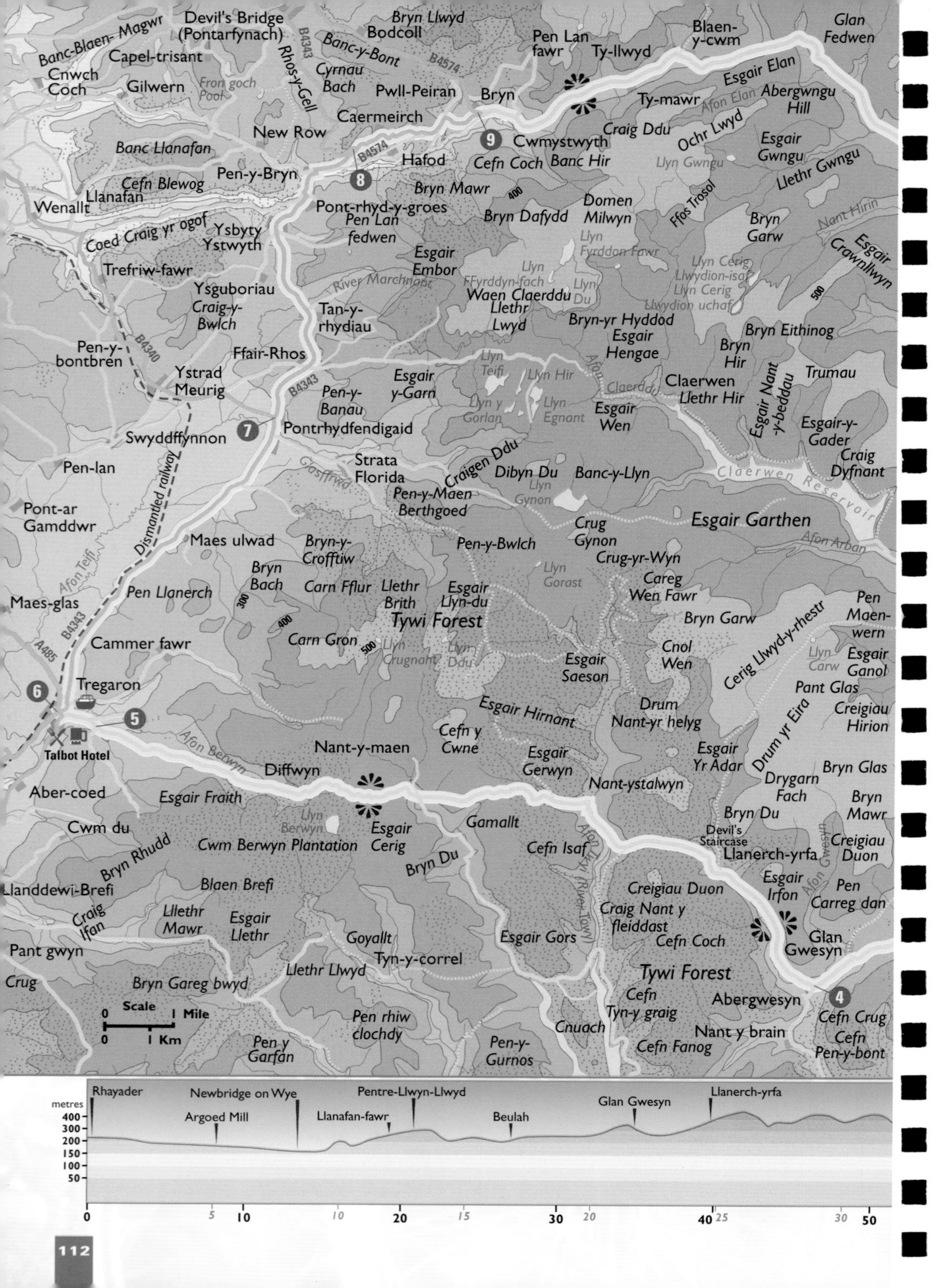

Devil's Bridge (Pontarfynach)
Bryn Llwyd
Bodcoll
Banc-Blaen- Magwr
Capel-trisant
Cnwch Coch
Gilwern
Fron goch Pool
B4343
Rhos-y-Gell
Banc-y-Bont
B4574
Cyrnau Bach
Pwll-Peiran
Caermeirch
New Row
Pen Lan fawr
Ty-llwyd
Blaen-y-cwm
Glan Fedwen
Bryn
Esgair Elan
Ty-mawr
Afon Elan
Abergwngu Hill
Craig Ddu
Ochr Lwyd
Esgair Gwngu
Cwmystwyth
Banc Hir
Cefn Coch
Llyn Gwngu
Llethr Gwngu
Banc Llanafan
B4574
Hafod
Pen-y-Bryn
Cefn Blewog
Llanafan
Wenallt
Bryn Mawr
400
Pont-rhyd-y-groes
Pen Lan fedwen
Bryn Dafydd
Domen Milwyn
Ffos Trosol
Bryn Garw
Nant Hirin
Esgair Crawnllwyn
Coed Craig yr ogof
Ysbyty Ystwyth
Trefriw-fawr
Esgair Embor
Llyn Fyrddon Fawr
Llyn FFyrddyn-fach
Llyn Du
Llyn Cerig Llwydion-isaf
Llyn Cerig Llwydion uchaf
River Marchnant
Ysguboriau
Craig-y-Bwlch
Tan-y-rhydiau
Waen Claerddu
Llethr Lwyd
Bryn-yr Hyddod
Esgair Hengae
Bryn Eithinog
Bryn Hir
500
Pen-y-bontbren
B4340
Ffair-Rhos
Ystrad Meurig
B4343
Pen-y-Banau
Esgair y-Garn
Llyn Teifi
Llyn Hir
Afon Claerddu
Claerwen
Llethr Hir
Esgair Nant -y-beddau
Trumau
Llyn y Gorlan
Llyn Egnant
Esgair Wen
Esgair-y-Gader
Swyddffynnon
Pontrhydfendigaid
Craig Dyfnant
Pen-lan
Dismantled railway
Strata Florida
Gasffrwd
Craigen Ddu
Dibyn Du
Banc-y-Llyn
Claerwen Reservoir
Llyn Gynon
Pen-y-Maen
Berthgoed
Pont-ar Gamddwr
Esgair Garthen
Crug Gynon
Afon Arban
Maes ulwad
Bryn-y-Crofftiw
Pen-y-Bwlch
Crug-yr-Wyn
Afon Teifi
Bryn Bach
Llyn Gorast
Careg Wen Fawr
Pen Llanerch
Carn Fflur
Llethr Brith
Esgair Llyn-du
Maes-glas
300
Tywi Forest
Bryn Garw
Pen Maen-wern
B4343
400
A485
Cammer fawr
Carn Gron
500
Llyn Crugnant
Llyn Ddu
Esgair Saeson
Cnol Wen
Cerig Llwyd-y-rhestr
Llyn Carw
Esgair Ganol
Tregaron
Pant Glas
Esgair Hirnant
Drum Nant-yr helyg
Creigiau Hirion
Drum yr Eira
Cefn y Cwne
Talbot Hotel
Afon Berwyn
Nant-y-maen
Esgair Gerwyn
Esgair Yr Adar
Diffwyn
Nant-ystalwyn
Bryn Glas
Drygarn Fach
Aber-coed
Esgair Fraith
Bryn Mawr
Llyn Berwyn
Esgair Cerig
Gamallt
Bryn Du
Cwm du
Devil's Staircase
Cwm Berwyn Plantation
Afon Tywi
Cefn Isaf
Creigiau Duon
Bryn Rhudd
Bryn Du
Llanerch-yrfa
Afon Gwesyn
Esgair Irfon
Blaen Brefi
Pen Carreg dan
Llanddewi-Brefi
Creigiau Duon
Craig Ifan
Lllethr Mawr
Esgair Llethr
Craig Nant y fleiddast
River Tywi
Goyallt
Esgair Gors
Cefn Coch
Glan Gwesyn
Pant gwyn
Tyn-y-correl
Tywi Forest
Crug
Llethr Llwyd
Bryn Gareg bwyd
Cefn Tyn-y graig
Abergwesyn
Cefn Crug
Scale
0 1 Mile
0 1 Km
Pen rhiw clochdy
Pen y Garfan
Cnuach
Pen-y-Gurnos
Nant y brain
Cefn Fanog
Cefn Pen-y-bont
metres
400
300
200
150
100
50
Rhayader
Newbridge on Wye
Argoed Mill
Pentre-Llwyn-Llwyd
Llanafan-fawr
Beulah
Glan Gwesyn
Llanerch-yrfa
0
5
10
10
20
15
30
20
40
25
30
50

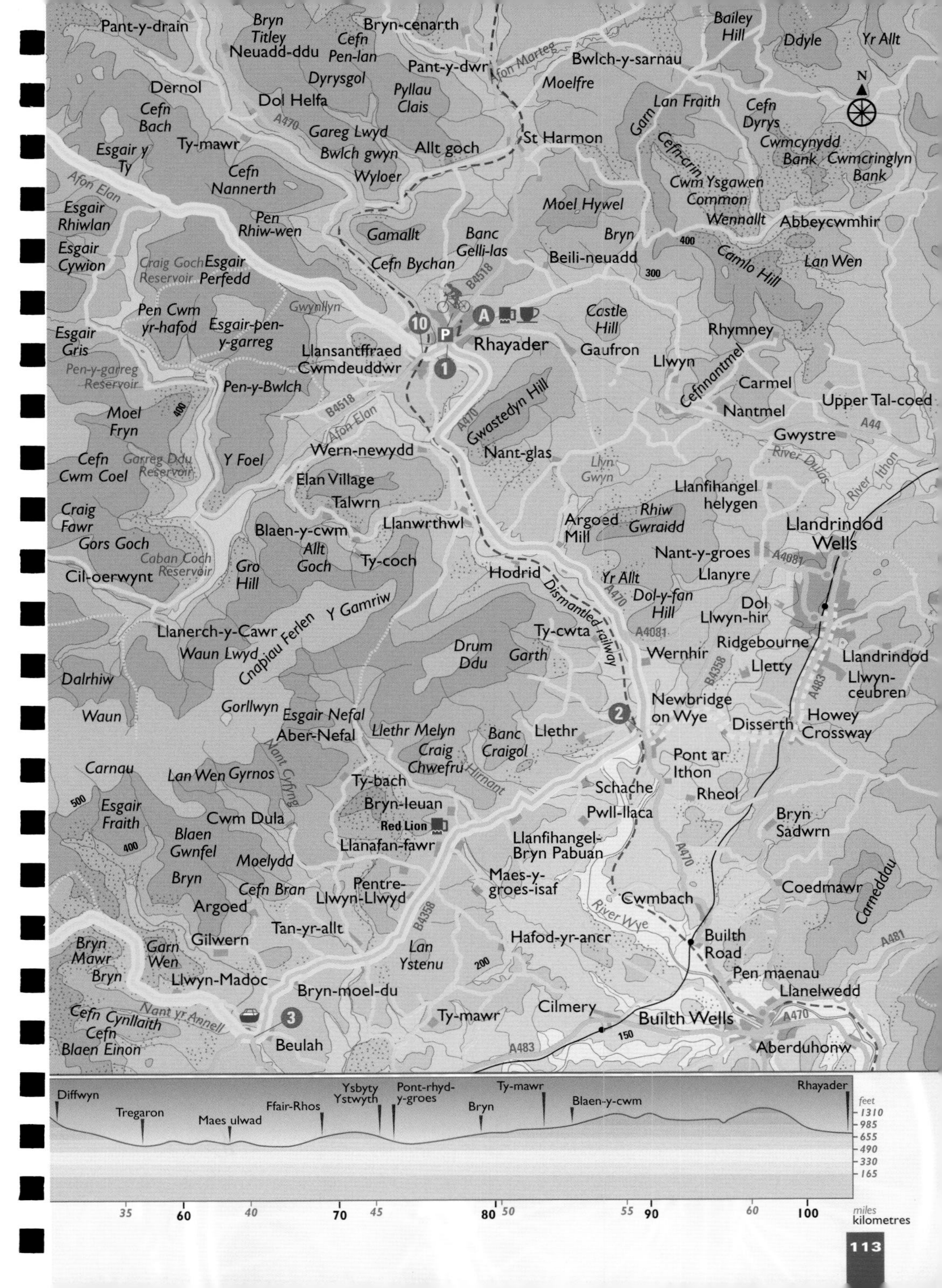
Pant-y-drain
Bryn Titley
Neuadd-ddu
Cefn Pen-lan
Bryn-cenarth
Pant-y-dwr
Afon Marteg
Bailey Hill
Ddyle
Yr Allt
Bwlch-y-sarnau
N
Dernol
Dyrysgol
Pyllau Clais
Moelfre
Dol Helfa
Cefn Bach
A470
Lan Fraith
Cefn Dyrys
Garn
Ty-mawr
Gareg Lwyd
St Harmon
Esgair y Ty
Bwlch gwyn
Allt goch
Cefn-crin
Cwmcynydd Bank
Cwmcringlyn Bank
Cefn Nannerth
Wyloer
Cwm Ysgawen Common
Afon Elan
Moel Hywel
Esgair Rhiwlan
Pen Rhiw-wen
Wennallt
Abbeycwmhir
Gamallt
Banc Gelli-las
Bryn
400
Esgair Cywion
Craig Goch Reservoir
Esgair Perfedd
Cefn Bychan
Beili-neuadd
Camlo Hill
Lan Wen
300
B4518
Gwynllyn
Pen Cwm yr-hafod
Esgair-pen-y-garreg
Castle Hill
Rhymney
Esgair Gris
10
A
P
Rhayader
Gaufron
Llansantffraed Cwmdeuddwr
Llwyn
Cefnnantmel
Pen-y-garreg Reservoir
1
Carmel
Pen-y-Bwlch
Moel Fryn
400
B4518
Afon Elan
A470
Gwastedyn Hill
Nantmel
Upper Tal-coed
A44
Gwystre
Cefn Cwm Coel
Garreg Ddu Reservoir
Y Foel
Wern-newydd
Nant-glas
River Dulas
River Ithon
Llyn Gwyn
Elan Village
Llanfihangel helygen
Craig Fawr
Talwrn
Rhiw Gwraidd
Argoed Mill
Llandrindod Wells
Gors Goch
Llanwrthwl
Blaen-y-cwm
Allt Goch
Nant-y-groes
A4081
Caban Coch Reservoir
Gro Hill
Ty-coch
Cil-oerwynt
Hodrid
Yr Allt
Llanyre
A470
Dol-y-fan Hill
Dismantled railway
Y Gamriw
Dol Llwyn-hir
Llanerch-y-Cawr
Cnapiau Ferlen
Ty-cwta
A4081
Ridgebourne
Waun Lwyd
Drum Ddu
Garth
Wernhir
Llandrindod
Lletty
Dalrhiw
B4358
Llwyn-ceubren
A483
Newbridge on Wye
Waun
Gorllwyn
Esgair Nefal
2
Howey
Disserth
Crossway
Aber-Nefal
Llethr Melyn
Banc Craigol
Llethr
Craig Chwefru
Nant Cyfryng
Pont ar Ithon
Carnau
Lan Wen
Gyrnos
Hirnant
Schache
Ty-bach
500
Esgair Fraith
Rheol
Bryn-leuan
Pwll-llaca
Cwm Dula
Bryn Sadwrn
Red Lion
Blaen Gwnfel
400
Llanafan-fawr
Llanfihangel-Bryn Pabuan
A470
Moelydd
Bryn
Maes-y-groes-isaf
Coedmawr
Carneddau
Cefn Bran
Pentre-Llwyn-Llwyd
Argoed
Cwmbach
River Wye
B4358
Tan-yr-allt
Hafod-yr-ancr
Builth Road
A481
Bryn Mawr
Garn Wen
Gilwern
Lan Ystenu
Bryn
200
Pen maenau
Llwyn-Madoc
Bryn-moel-du
Llanelwedd
Nant yr Annell
Cefn Cynllaith
3
Cilmery
Cefn
Ty-mawr
Builth Wells
A470
Blaen Einon
Beulah
A483
150
Aberduhonw
Diffwyn
Tregaron
Maes ulwad
Ffair-Rhos
Ysbyty Ystwyth
Pont-rhyd-y-groes
Bryn
Ty-mawr
Blaen-y-cwm
Rhayader
feet
1310
985
655
490
330
165
35
60
40
70
45
80
50
55
90
60
100
miles
kilometres

Route **25**

THE WELSH MARCHES – A GRANDE RANDONNÉE

Route information

Distance 103km (64 miles)

Grade Moderate

Terrain Mostly country lanes, with some stretches of B road. There is a short section of off-road through the Downton Estate at Ludlow.

Time to allow 6–8 hours.

Getting there by car Leominster is 19km (12 miles) north of Hereford on the A49 and A44. There are several free car parks in the town, including one by the Tourist Information Centre (TIC), the start of the route.

Getting there by train There is a frequent rail service to Leominster. Telephone (08457) 484950 or visit www.nationalrail.co.uk for travel information.

A attractive grande randonnée through the borderlands of Wales and England. From Leominster the route heads north to Ludlow before turning west through Leintwardine to Brampton Bryan. Here the route turns south, through Lingen to Staunton on Arrow and down to Kington and Eardisley. On eastwards, through Pembridge and Eardisland, and back to Leominster. An optional shortcut reduces the total distance to 68km (42 miles).

Places of interest along the route

A Leominster

A small market town on the River Lugg in the heart of the Marches, the borderlands between Wales and England. See route 13 for more information.

B Ludlow

A small town on the hill about the River Teme, well-known for its festival held each June. See route 6 for more information.

C Kington

A market town on the River Arrow, close to the Welsh/English border. The town is dominated by a tall clock tower commemorating Queen Victoria's Golden Jubilee in 1887. The Norman church was originally built circa 1200. **Kington Museum** describes the local history. Tearoom. Open April to September, Monday–Saturday 1030–1600, Sunday 1430–1700. Charge. Telephone (01544) 231486.

D Pembridge

A picturesque village, formerly a medieval borough, with many old half-timbered buildings and a visitor centre. The castle remains date from the 17th century. Contact Leominster TIC for more information or visit www.mediaeval-pembridge.com.

E Eardisland

Another picturesque village on the River Arrow. The **Dovecote Heritage Centre** is Georgian and was restored in 1999. There are various exhibitions including the AA, local archaeology and dovecotes. Open daily all year. Admission free. The Norman **church of St Mary the Virgin**

Leominster Priory Church

holds changing exhibitions. Open daily all year. Admission free. **Burton Court** has a 14th-century Great Hall, a collection of European and Oriental costumes and a children's working model fairground. Also pick your own fruit in season. Open spring Bank Holiday to September, Wednesday–Sunday and Bank Holiday Monday 1430–1800. Charge. Telephone (01544) 388231. Leominster TIC can be contacted for more details on the above, telephone (01568) 615546.

Route description

From TIC, go R past Woolworths. Take third exit at roundabout into High Street. SO and bear L onto B4361, SP Richards Castle.

1 TR at TJ, SP Tenbury Wells/Richards Castle. ***7.5km (4.5 miles)***

2 TL at TJ, SP Ludlow (15.5km/9.5 miles). Continue into Ludlow.

3 SO at Ludford Bridge traffic lights, up Lower Broad Street to the square and Ludlow Castle. Go L around castle, descend to river, cross bridge and TR onto No Through Road, SP Priors Halton. Follow bridleway through private estate into Bromfield. ***22.5km (14 miles)***

4 TL at TJ onto A49. Immediately TL onto A4113, SP Knighton/Leintwardine.

5 TL on RH bend, SP Downton Estate (25.5km/16 miles). Continue and pass Downton Castle.

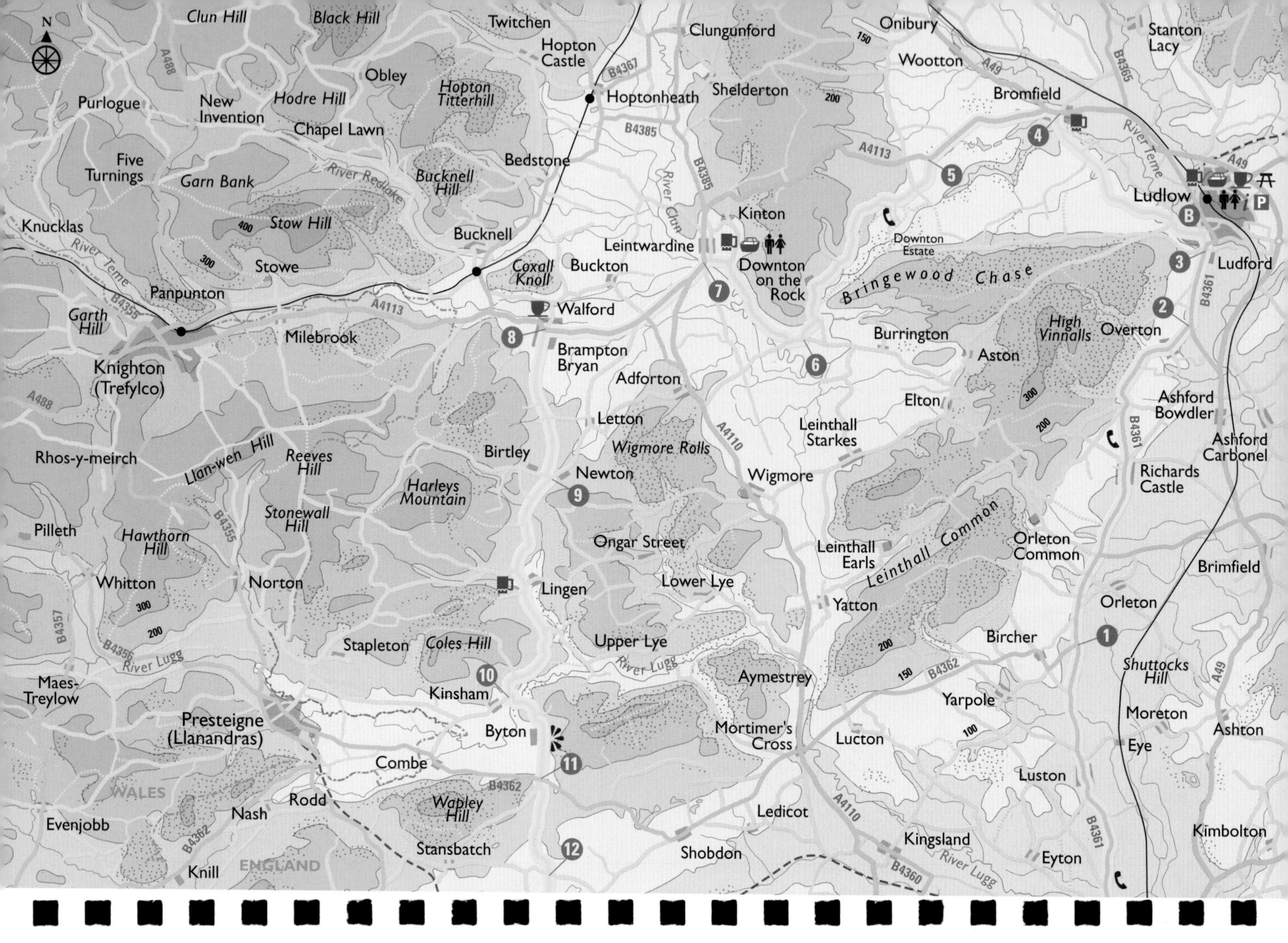

N
Clun Hill
Black Hill
Twitchen
Clungunford
Onibury
Stanton Lacy
Hopton Castle
B4367
Wootton
A49
B4365
150
Obley
Hopton Titterhill
Hoptonheath
Shelderton
200
Bromfield
Purlogue
New Invention
Hodre Hill
Chapel Lawn
B4385
A4113
River Teme
A488
Five Turnings
Garn Bank
River Redlake
Bucknell Hill
Bedstone
B4385
River Clun
Kinton
Ludlow
A49
Knucklas
400
Stow Hill
Bucknell
Leintwardine
Downton Estate
Downton on the Rock
Ludford
River Teme
300
Stowe
Coxall Knoll
Buckton
Bringewood Chase
B4361
Panpunton
B4355
A4113
Walford
Garth Hill
Milebrook
Brampton Bryan
Burrington
High Vinnalls
Overton
Knighton (Trefylco)
Adforton
Aston
A488
Letton
Elton
300
Ashford Bowdler
Leinthall Starkes
200
B4361
Ashford Carbonel
Rhos-y-meirch
Llan-wen Hill
Reeves Hill
Birtley
Wigmore Rolls
A4110
Wigmore
Richards Castle
Newton
Harleys Mountain
Stonewall Hill
B4355
Leinthall Common
Orleton Common
Pilleth
Hawthorn Hill
Ongar Street
Leinthall Earls
Brimfield
Whitton
Norton
Lingen
Lower Lye
Yatton
Orleton
300
B4357
200
Upper Lye
Bircher
200
Stapleton
Coles Hill
B4356
River Lugg
River Lugg
Aymestrey
150
B4362
Shuttocks Hill
A49
Maes-Treylow
Kinsham
Yarpole
Presteigne (Llanandras)
Byton
Mortimer's Cross
Lucton
100
Moreton
Ashton
Eye
Combe
WALES
B4362
Luston
Rodd
Nash
Wapley Hill
Ledicot
A4110
Evenjobb
B4362
Kimbolton
Stansbatch
Kingsland
B4361
Shobdon
Eyton
Knill
ENGLAND
B4360
River Lugg

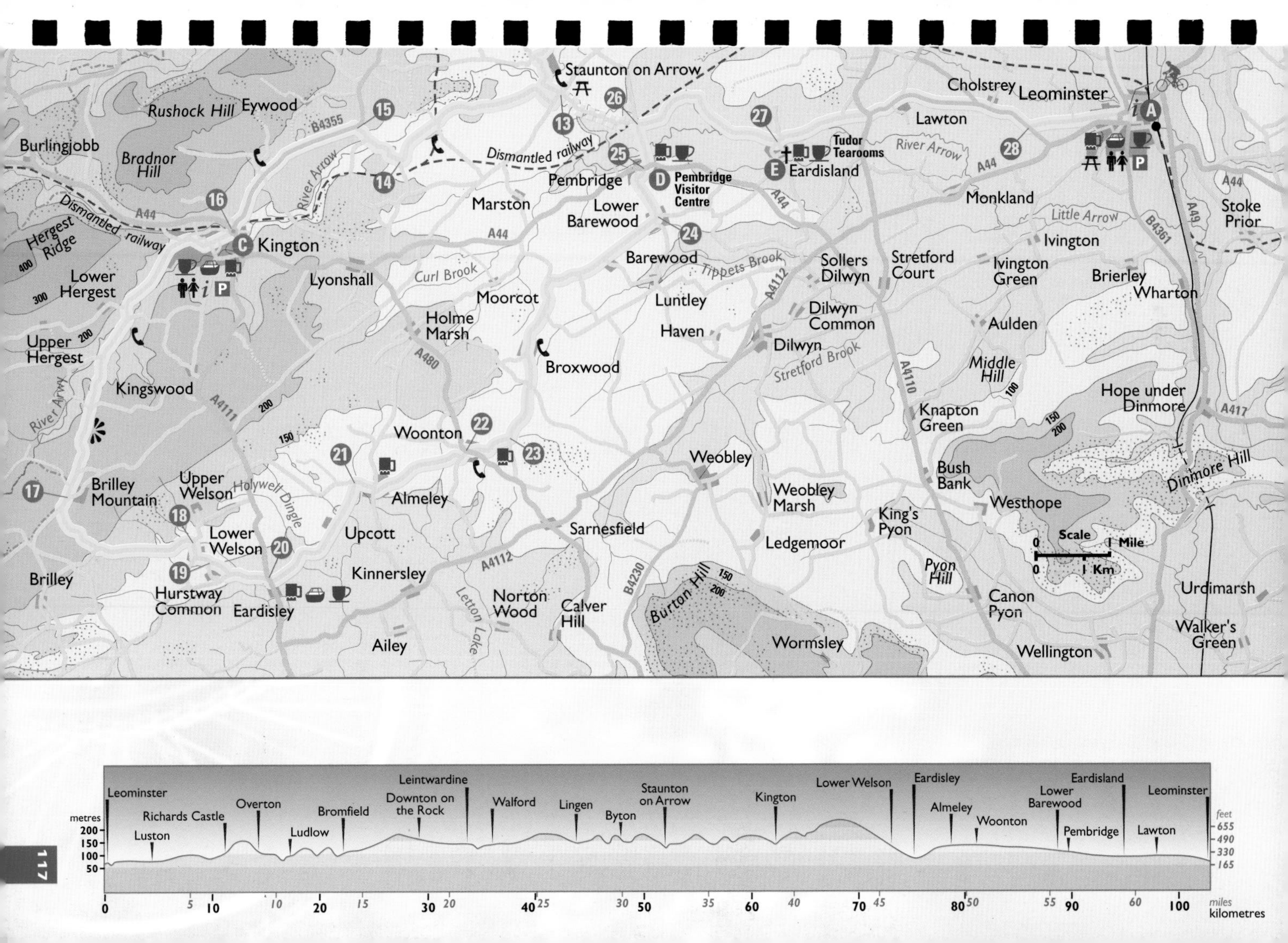

Staunton on Arrow
Cholstrey
Leominster
Rushock Hill
Eywood
B4355
Burlingjobb
Bradnor Hill
Dismantled railway
Lawton
River Arrow
Tudor Tearooms
Eardisland
Pembridge
Pembridge Visitor Centre
Marston
Lower Barewood
Monkland
A44
A49
B4361
Stoke Prior
Little Arrow
Hergest Ridge
Kington
Ivington
Lower Hergest
Lyonshall
Curl Brook
Barewood
Tippets Brook
Sollers Dilwyn
Stretford Court
Ivington Green
Brierley
Wharton
Moorcot
Luntley
A4112
Dilwyn Common
Holme Marsh
Haven
Aulden
Upper Hergest
A480
Dilwyn
Stretford Brook
Broxwood
Middle Hill
Kingswood
A4110
Hope under Dinmore
River Arrow
A4111
A417
Knapton Green
Woonton
Weobley
Bush Bank
Dinmore Hill
Brilley Mountain
Upper Welson
Holywell Dingle
Almeley
Weobley Marsh
Westhope
Upcott
Sarnesfield
King's Pyon
Scale
0
1 Mile
1 Km
Lower Welson
Ledgemoor
Brilley
Kinnersley
Burton Hill
B4230
Pyon Hill
Urdimarsh
Hurstway Common
Eardisley
Letton Lake
Norton Wood
Calver Hill
Canon Pyon
Walker's Green
Ailey
Wormsley
Wellington
Leominster
Richards Castle
Luston
Overton
Ludlow
Bromfield
Leintwardine
Downton on the Rock
Walford
Lingen
Byton
Staunton on Arrow
Kington
Lower Welson
Eardisley
Almeley
Woonton
Lower Barewood
Eardisland
Pembridge
Leominster
Lawton
metres
200
150
100
50
feet
655
490
330
165
0
5
10
10
20
15
30
20
40
25
30
50
35
60
40
70
45
80
50
55
90
60
100
miles
kilometres

6 TR, no SP (30.5km/19 miles). TR at TJ, no SP. Continue into Leintwardine.

7 TL at TJ over river in Leintwardine, no SP. Soon TR onto A4113, SP Knighton. Continue into Brampton Bryan.

8 TL, SP Lingen. ***38.5km (24 miles)***

9 TR at TJ, SP Lingen/Presteigne. Continue through Lingen and Kinsham.

10 TL at foot of hill, no SP (sharp turn is hidden). ***47.5km (29.5 miles)***

11 SO at XR, SP Pembridge/Staunton on Arrow.

12 SO at XR, SP Staunton on Arrow/ Lyonshall/Kington. TL at TJ and continue into Staunton on Arrow as far as XR.

13 To follow alternative route, SO, SP Eardisland. Rejoin route at direction 26, where SO towards Eardisland.

Otherwise, to follow main route, TR at XR, SP Lyonshall/Kington. Soon TR, no SP.

14 TR at TJ, no SP. ***59.5km (37 miles)***

15 TL at TJ onto B4355, SP Kington. Continue into Kington.

16 Take third exit at roundabout, SP Kington Town Centre. Cycle through town centre, uphill and TL, SP Hergest/ Huntington/ Brilley. ***65km (40.5 miles)***

17 Climb. Pass turning for National Trust and TL, no SP. TL at TJ, no SP.

72.5km (45miles)

18 TR at TJ, no SP (74.5km/46.5 miles). TL at foot of hill, no SP.

Food and drink

There is lots of choice in Leominster, Ludlow and Kington.

Tudor Tearooms, Eardisland
Located behind the church.

Pembridge Visitor Centre
Snacks and drinks available.

19 TL at TJ, no SP (75.5km/47 miles). Continue into Eardisley.

20 TR onto A4111 and immediately TL, SP Almeley.

21 TR at TJ, SP Almeley. TR at TJ and immediately TL, SP Hereford/Leominster.

80.5km (50 miles)

22 TR at TJ, SP Woonton/Hereford/ Leominster. Soon TL, SP Meer/Broxwood.

23 TL at TJ, no SP.

24 TL at XR, SP Pembridge.

90km (56 miles)

25 TR at TJ on A44. Soon TL, SP Preston/ Shobdon.

26 TR at XR, no SP except Unsuitable for Long Vehicles. Continue into Eardisland.

27 TL in Eardisland, no SP (96km/59.5 miles). Pass Leominster town SPs and:

28 TL into Grinhall Lane, no SP. TL into Green Lane (cycling permitted here) and continue to finish the ride at the Tourist Information Centre. ***103km (64 miles)***

CTC
(Cyclists' Touring Club)

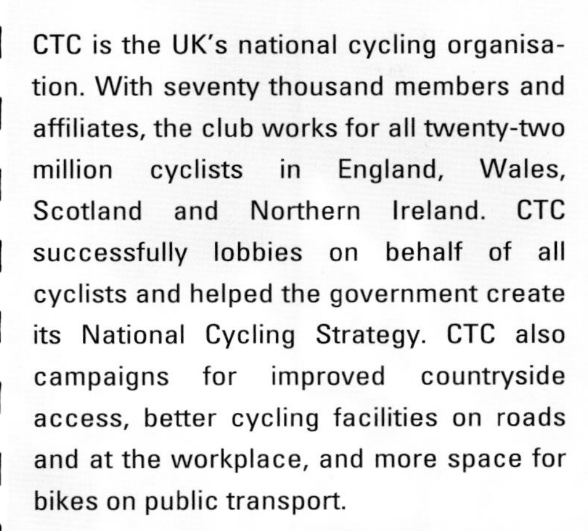

CTC is the UK's national cycling organisation. With seventy thousand members and affiliates, the club works for all twenty-two million cyclists in England, Wales, Scotland and Northern Ireland. CTC successfully lobbies on behalf of all cyclists and helped the government create its National Cycling Strategy. CTC also campaigns for improved countryside access, better cycling facilities on roads and at the workplace, and more space for bikes on public transport.

CTC provides essential services and invaluable advice for novice and experienced cyclists of all ages and abilities. It has 64 District Associations with 204 local groups plus hundreds of local campaigners in its Right to Ride network. New members and volunteers are always welcomed!

Cyclecover Insurance Services

CTC membership includes free third party insurance and legal aid. CTC also offers several cycling-specific insurance policies. Cyclecover Rescue is a unique twenty-four hour rescue scheme for cyclists stranded by breakdown (excluding punctures), accident, vandalism or theft. CTC offers annual travel insurance and single trip cover. Mountain biking, touring, repatriation of bike, luggage and accessory cover are all included. Comprehensive cycle insurance is offered to members and non-members alike, at very competitive premiums.

CycleSafe

Local authorities are being urged to sign up to four CycleSafe objectives, the aims of which are to improve safety for cyclists. That means reducing risks on roads, consideration for cyclists in new road layouts, adequate investment in cycling facilities and in cycling promotion. CTC has offered all authorities advice on engineering measures, education and examples of successful schemes elsewhere. In York, Britain's most cycling-friendly city, the implementation of a comfortable cycling environment has increased cycling by sixteen per cent and led to a ten per cent drop in cycling casualties in the last 20 years.

Technical and Touring Advice

CTC offers advice on buying a bike and other cycling equipment, maintenance and repair. CTC's events department has information on hundreds of routes both in the UK and abroad and experienced leaders run holidays to scores of destinations throughout the world. These tours are suitable for all cyclists ranging from families with young children to experienced distance riders.

CTC Magazine

Cycle Touring and Campaigning is CTC's bi-monthly magazine which is free to members. Articles cover campaign news, tours, technical advice, event reports and equipment tests.

CTC Help Desk

Staff on the Help Desk answer queries on all things cycling, from contacts at your local group to the best route across the continent. The Help Desk can advise on travelling by train or bus with your bike, bike security and parking facilities in public places and on how to make the workplace more friendly to cyclists.

CTC Membership

Membership costs from just £10 per year. Whether you are a roadster, prefer the quiet of canal paths and the countryside, commute by bike or just enjoy a day out with the children, CTC is the essential accessory for you!

For more information contact the CTC Help Desk:

CTC, 69 Meadrow, Godalming, Surrey GU7 3HS
Telephone 0870 873 0060
Email cycling@ctc.org.uk
Website www.ctc.org.uk

Cyclecover Travel Insurance
For a quote or instant cover:
Telephone 0870 873 0068
Visit www.cyclecover.co.uk

Cyclecover Rescue
Telephone free on 0800 212810.

Cyclecover Cycle Insurance
Telephone free on 0800 169 5798.

CycleSafe
Visit www.cyclesafe.org.uk

CTC Cymru

CTC Cymru (Wales) is the regional body which represents the CTC in Wales. It is active at local and national level, with a network of local groups across the country, and organises several events including the Welsh Festival of Cycling.

Contact CTC Cymru via the CTC Help Desk (details above).